LITTLE BIT KNOW SOMETHING

LITTLE BIT KNOW SOMETHING

Stories in a Language
of Anthropology

BY ROBIN RIDINGTON

UNIVERSITY OF IOWA PRESS
IOWA CITY

University of Iowa Press, Iowa City 52242
Copyright © 1990 by the University of Iowa
All rights reserved
Printed in the United States of America
First edition, 1990

Printed on acid-free paper

LIBRARY OF CONGRESS
CATALOGING-IN-PUBLICATION DATA
Ridington, Robin.
Little bit know something: stories in a language
of anthropology/by Robin Ridington.—1st ed.
    p. cm.
Includes bibliographical references.
ISBN 0-87745-268-7 (alk. paper),
ISBN 0-87745-286-5 (pbk., alk. paper)
1. Tsattine Indians—Religion and mythology.
2. Tsattine Indians—Philosophy. 3. Oral
tradition—British Columbia. I. Title.
E99.T77R523 1990   89-48164
299'.782—dc20   CIP

For Jumbie

CONTENTS

FOREWORD

I dedicate this book to Augustine Jumbie, one of the many Dunne-za elders who first taught me a little bit about what it means to "know something." He is still alive on this world as I put these stories together. Jumbie remembers what I looked like when the horse I was riding stepped on a hornet's nest in a tangle of mountain blowdown. He still laughs when he sees me. I have many other teachers to thank. Johnny Chipesia was a magical presence in my life. In his later years, kids called him Little Green Man for his sense of the fantastic. His nickname was Wuscide, "Storyteller." The name became Johnny Bullshit in English.

One of Johnny's stories that was not bullshit gave me an insight into Jumbie's character. Once, the two of them were trapping in territory that was more than a hundred miles from their winter cabins. Wolverine, who is boss for the furs, was giving to them richly. They took his gifts from traps that seemed never to be empty. They had no time to hunt. They kept only enough drymeat and bannock to provision themselves on a quick run back along the well-broken toboggan trail home. At the last possible moment, Wuscide and Jumbie began their return. They expected to run their richly laden toboggan late into the night for several days in succession.

Then the snow came, and with it a fierce wind. Snow filled the air and drifted in their trail. What had once been a slick and easy passage home could now be negotiated only by breaking trail with snow-shoes, step by tiresome step. At night, they burrowed like voles beneath the snow. Their meager food supplies ran out. They struggled on, weak and without nourishment. One morning, Johnny felt he could not go on. He did not have energy even to crawl from beneath the bed of snow. Then he heard Jumbie moving about. The older man had made a fire and was boiling Labrador tea. Johnny managed to find some slight interest in life. He opened one eye. He could see Jumbie's feet making tracks in the fresh snow. Then, he looked again in astonishment. Jumbie was not wearing moccasins. His feet were bare. Johnny managed to whisper a question. Jumbie replied, "Wolverine gave me his feet."

I camped with Jumbie and his wife, Saweh; Johnny and Julie Chipesia; and Sam and Jean St. Pierre in the summers of 1964 through 1969. Sam and Jean took me and my former wife, Tonia Mills, into the life of their camp. They fed us and taught us about learning in an Indian way. Jean is another of the elders who is still a part of my life. Last summer, I visited her at the home of her granddaughter, Katie St. Pierre. As we listened to tapes I had recorded of Sam's singing, Jean was busy making something. I did not really notice what it was until Katie told me, "Grandma has something for you." I took her gift. It was a fish hook made of a beaver bone, moosehide, and sinew. Thank you, Jean. These stories are yours, too.

Dunne-za stories continue to be told by elders at Doig River. I thank Charlie Dominic, John Davis, Albert Askoty, and Alice Moccasin for the stories they told me. I will never forget hearing John Davis speak truly and from his knowledge to Judge George Addy in a federal court in Vancouver or the lunch I had with Albert Askoty in the sky-world of a restaurant atop the Sears Tower, when both these elders were in Vancouver to testify in a court case which the Indians had brought against the government.

Each story I learned from the Dunne-za contains something of every other. Each person I knew gave me something of the whole that was each one's knowledge. I am grateful for the gift that each one gave me. Among the elders who are no longer alive, I especially remember Sam St. Pierre, Granny Jumbie, Johnny Chipesia, Louis Wolf, Charlie Yahey, Anachuan, Japasa, Amma, Anno Davis, Thomas Hunter, Antoine Hunter, Zolie Field, Nancy Wokeley, Alex Moose, Aku, Jack Acko, Eskama, Nachi, Dan Wolf, Murray Attachie, Alice Attachie, Billy Makadahay, Chikenizhia, and Pete Wolf.

I remember many more younger people who were unable to stay in this world as long as I have. Among these are Dick Attachie, Sally St. Pierre, Billy St. Pierre, Mary St. Pierre, Emma St. Pierre, Willy

Olla, George Olla, Patrick Chipesia, Helen Wolf, Bella Bigfoot, Mackenzie Ben, Tar Davis, Deda, Pat Davis, and Tommy Dominic.

To my many friends among the Dunne-za with whom I continue the story, I also say, "Maci cho." The stories in this book came to life as I shared them with people from my own world. I would like to thank Antonia Mills for her contribution to the fieldwork that informed many of these stories. I thank my children, Aballi, Amber, and Juniper, for being part of the stories, and my wife, Jillian, for sharing the stories with me as they emerged into writing. We share a tender thanks for the teaching of Howard Broomfield, "Soundman." Thanks to my parents, Bill and Edie Ridington, for their ongoing support, and to Annette McFadyen Clark for her devotion to the Urgent Ethnology Program of the Canadian Ethnology Service. Thanks also to Tim Buckley for his sensitive and intelligent reading of the manuscript. I thank Lindy-Lou Flynn for suffering the "manuscript madness" that went into putting these stories together.

Note: Augustine Jumbie died on Sunday, July 30, 1989. He will always be a part of my dreaming.

Robin Ridington and his son, Aballi, Doig River Reserve, 1968

INTRODUCTION

This book is a collection of academic papers I wrote between 1968 and 1989 about a northern hunting people, the Athapaskan Dunne-za or Beaver Indians of northeastern British Columbia. The Dunne-za translate their name as "real people." Although I wrote the papers in a form acceptable to academic journals in my field of anthropology, I tried to avoid writing in "anthropologese," the jargon in which members of my profession sometimes talk to one another. Rather than use a style that mostly reflects the experience of scholars within academic anthropology, I searched for a language of translation that would do justice to the Indian style of teaching through which I gained my knowledge of their culture and their experience. That language, I discovered, is one of storytelling.

Like other Native peoples, the Dunne-za experience their lives as stories. While writing for academic journals, I tried also to give voice to Dunne-za experience. I tried to tell Indian stories in a language of anthropology, but within a storytelling style like that of my Indian teachers. I tried to use my own language to tell stories about the storied lives of people who are native to this land. The stories in this book are about Dunne-za knowledge and power as I have come to understand them. My purpose in writing them was to communicate what I was learning from my own experiences of an Indian way of life. I bring these stories together now so that the reader may understand something of the Indian reality.

I first met the Dunne-za in 1959. They were the first Native people I had encountered anywhere. I used the story of that meeting to introduce the Indian world in a "narrative ethnography," *Trail to Heaven*. That book and this one are complementary. *Trail to Heaven* blends Indian voices with my own into a continuous narrative. *Little Bit Know Something* also gives voice to the Dunne-za, but it blends my voice with that of academic anthropology. In *Trail to Heaven*, I chose to make anthropological interpretation integral to the narrative rather than highlight it separately. *Little Bit Know Something* reverses that order. In it, I ask anthropological questions directly. The book's multiple narratives are integral to the anthropologist's world in the way that anthropology was integral to the Dunne-za world in *Trail to Heaven*.

To the Dunne-za, as to scholars within the traditions of Western phenomenology, how a person knows something is as important as what he or she knows. The stories reflect how I came to learn from my Indian teachers. They also reflect what I have learned from teachers in my own world. They explore various possibilities, within a language of anthropology, for translating highly contextualized Dunne-za discourse. In exploring these possibilities, I have consciously sought to expand the range of anthropological discourse. I looked for an academic language that could do justice to Dunne-za narrative style. I sought out a language that retained some flavor of the contextuality of Dunne-za discourse. I wrote in a language that I hoped would translate between Dunne-za reality and the reality of academic anthropologists with whom I am in communication. I wrote particularly for students, to whom anthropology is a point of entry into the thoughtworld of other cultures.

The Dunne-za are northern hunters. Their knowledge of animals and of the land reflects an intelligence that goes back to the earliest human traditions. Their knowledge of the human condition also circles back to times and conditions many of us have long forgotten. I am immensely privileged to be among the outsiders with whom Dunne-za elders shared their knowledge. I am privileged to have experienced something of the world that hunting people brought from ancient times to the present. I am bound by that privilege to give voice to their knowledge with my own individual intelligence and with that of the culture into which I was born. I speak in the pages that follow of an empowering "cultural intelligence" that evolved as we humans perfected the arts of living with one another and with the nonhuman persons of a country that is itself alive. I trust that the stories I tell of Dunne-za life reflect that intelligence.

The Dunne-za say that a person who speaks from the authority of his or her own experience "little bit know something." Knowledge, the elders say, empowers a person to live in this world with intelligence and understanding. They recognize that knowledge is a distinctively human attribute. They recognize knowledge as a form of power. Since the time of their culture hero, Saya, Dunne-za men and women have sent their children into the bush to gain power from the animals and natural forces of their country. From these experiences, children have grown into adults who "little bit know something."

Every person is expected to "know something." What a person knows is a small but complete whole, not a small and incomplete part of the whole. A person knows a "little bit" about the world in its entirety rather than a little part of all possible knowledge. Dunne-za knowledge is highly contextualized within experience rather than instrumental to purposes removed from experience. Every life is a microcosm of life in the universe at large. Every person "knows something" from experience. Every human being is a little bit like Saya, the first person to go on a vision quest, the first person to follow the trails of animals, the first person to "little bit know something."

A person with power reveals what he or she knows through the ongoing story of his or her life. A person with power does not disclose knowledge without a purpose. He or she may use power to heal relatives who are ill. He or she may use it to feed people. A person who "knows something" may even be obliged to use power in defense against an attack. These purposes define the times and places in which power may be revealed. They define knowledge and power in relation to experience. I believe the elders who disclosed their knowledge to me did so to feed me. I pass on this information to you in the same spirit.

The thoughtworld of anthropology is different from that of the Dunne-za. For the Dunne-za, knowledge and power come to a person through direct experience of the world. They come through dreaming and through the instructions of a mythic reality that becomes biographical in the searing transformative experience of the vision quest. For anthropologists, knowledge and power come from books, from institutions, and perhaps only finally from the experience of fieldwork. Anthropological discourse assumes that its own written texts, and their institutionally situated authors, have a privileged authority. As a producer of such texts from within an institutional setting, I have been concerned and even apprehensive about their possible impact on a readership with whom I have no direct contact.

A relief from this apprehension, I believe, lies in the feedback between my texts and those of the Dunne-za. I have attempted to present Dunne-za texts from a variety of anthropological perspectives, assuring that the implicit authority of my voice as author of anthropological texts will be moderated by information about how they are contextualized within Dunne-za discourse. Where possible, I have used recorded actuality as the source of written textuality. I have tried to place Dunne-za texts within their experiential context, using my own authorial voice as a storyteller rather than as an institutionally empowered anthropological authority.

I suggest that you read these "stories in a language of anthropology" as a braiding of many texts and voices. Each story looks at Dunne-za reality from a particular point of view. The stories overlap intentionally because Dunne-za reality is itself a coherent totality, not a set of isolated and unrelated pieces. Although I wrote each story to make a particular statement about the Dunne-za thought-world, each paper reflects the totality of Dunne-za experience and cannot be limited to stating only a part of it. I have organized the papers thematically rather than in the order in which I wrote them. As you may imagine, my own perceptions and use of language have changed over the twenty years these papers span. Rather than attempt to clean up and alter my previous writings in the light of hindsight, I have merely edited the papers to remove obvious redundancy. Thus, the earlier papers use the pronoun "he" to mean "he or she," where later ones are gender-specific or gender-neutral as required.

Because I wrote each paper to stand by itself, some of them repeat the same ethnographic information in the service of different perspectives. Some of the stories are historical in their point of view. Some describe the experiences of particular individuals. Others take a broader comparative perspective, placing Dunne-za reality within the context of hunting people generally. All the stories are implicitly comparative in that the reader must bring to them his or her own knowledge and experience. You, the reader, must authorize your own meaningful reading of these texts. Their authority cannot come down to you from me as author or even directly to you from the Dunne-za; rather, they must come across to you from within the authority of your own experience.

In the reality of Indian experience, each story contains every other. They circle one another like the seasons. They circle like the hunter and his game. They circle like the dreams that connect a child's visionary experience in the bush with those of an old person. Indian stories make sense in the circles they create in the mind of a person who reads or hears them. Listen to these stories for the circles they create within your own experience. Listen to them as teachings. Listen to them and dream into them. In the dreaming they will become your own.

STORIES IN A LANGUAGE

A Dreamer's drawing of his dream of heaven, in the possession of Augustine Jumbie

Indian stories do not begin "once upon a time." They are always beginning and always ending. Like the sun in its journey that ceaselessly defines the days and seasons of our experience, Indian stories move in a constantly transforming pattern of circles within circles. Beginning and end are only points in a person's experience of the stories' circles. The four papers in this section begin to tell the interconnected stories that make up this book. They blend my story with those of the Dunne-za. They tell about my first fieldwork experience and about Dunne-za vision quest experiences.

"Fox and Chickadee" introduces both narratives. It first appeared in a collection of essays on the problem of writing the history of Indian-white relations from an Indian perspective. The editor of that collection, Calvin Martin, asked Native and non-Native writers and scholars to reflect upon the ways they have devised for dealing with the problem of Indian history in their own work. Writing the essay for the volume was an exciting challenge. I wrote the paper within a few days of receiving Martin's request.

Thinking about the problem of writing Indian history gave me a chance to examine how I came to learn *from* the Dunne-za rather than merely *about* them. There is an enormous difference between the two ways of learning. Academic learning generally views information as objective and therefore removed from the learner's experience. Indian learning is contextualized within experience, so that a distinction between separate objective and subjective realities becomes meaningless. "Fox and Chickadee" describes how my understanding of Dunne-za culture came to be informed by Indian systems of explanation. It gives voice to my thoughts about the languages of myth and history.

"Telling Secrets: Stories of the Vision Quest" and "A True Story" are renditions of stories the Dunne-za told me about their vision quest experiences. One appeared in the *Canadian Journal of Native Studies*. The other was in *Anthropology and Humanism Quarterly*, the journal of the Society for Humanistic Anthropology. I am grateful for the forum both these journals have given me and other scholars interested in exploring alternative languages for writing anthropology. Both of these papers give voice to the vision quest narratives through which the Dunne-za inform one another about their experiences of Indian myth and Indian history. I have attempted in the

3

two papers to pass on both the stories and my understanding of how they relate to Dunne-za culture and experience.

"Eye on the Wheel" might be described as a maverick piece. It is the earliest of the four stories in this section. The story is imagistic rather than realistic, although it is informed by realities from Dunne-za culture and our own. It appeared in an obscure but interesting journal called *Io*, edited by Richard Grossinger. The story is a combined narrative. I blend a story Augustine Jumbie told me about a Dreamer who, like himself, knew Wolverine with the story of a whiteman, Neil Armstrong, setting foot on the moon. The image of tracks leading from one world to another creates a resonance between the two stories and between the two cultures. In both stories, visionaries interpret tracks in relation to important passages. In both stories, people find their way from one world to another. In both stories they discover visionary places like those where children go on their vision quests. Visionary places are special. You cannot go there and you cannot go away from there.

FOX AND CHICKADEE

I grew up in Maryland, Pennsylvania, and New Jersey. Until I left this eastern enclave I had no opportunity to make contact with "real live Indians." I never experienced a natural landform or a climax community of plants and animals. Everywhere, the land and its life were transformed by farming and industry. History was written in the stones that settlers sweated and skidded from forest floors and heaped at the boundaries of their property lines. History was a resource to be mined from lodes of artifacts and documents. History was dead and gone from the breath of experience. It was about a past that would not return to life. Beyond history lay myth and legend. Beyond history lay the land as it was before being shaped to our purposes. Beyond history lay the world of Indians, to me as yet a dreamworld.

My first contact with the Indian world began in 1959, when I spent a summer with friends who were homesteading land north of the Peace River in British Columbia, Canada. The land on which they built their cabin was in traditional hunting and trapping territory of Athapaskan-speaking Beaver Indians. According to the government of Canada, the land my friends had chosen belonged to the Crown. According to the Indians, Native people belonged to the land because they knew it in ways the government could not even imagine.

As I came to know the Indians, I began to widen my own ways of thinking. I saw a connection between people and environment that could not be represented by legal documents alone. When I returned to school in the East, I studied anthropology. In 1964, I began the anthropological rite of passage known as fieldwork. I wanted to understand the cultural psychology of people who lived by hunting. I headed back to the Peace River country.

In August 1964, I had been doing fieldwork with the Beaver Indians of the Prophet River Reserve for about six weeks. I was camped with a small band of about two dozen people just off the Alaska Highway between Fort St. John and Fort Nelson, British Columbia. A large oil-drilling camp run by the Majestic Construction Company was less than two miles from our fires, but the distance between us could also have been measured in thousands of years. Our camp was an irregular cluster of wall tents, a tepee, and a brush-sided double lean-to set on either side of a seismic oil exploration line which had been cut through the brush by huge D-8 "Cats." The Indians called these tractors "kettles walking" in their language. The Indians were there to make drymeat. I was there to administer projective tests and collect data for a Ph.D. dissertation.

In my research proposal I had said I would use the test results to examine the hypothesis that low accumulation hunting economies are associated with high levels of a personality variable called Need for Achievement, or "N Ach," as it was referred to in psychologese. The Indians were doing very well in their hunting, but my testing was not going well at all. The Indians were reluctant to take the tests. When they did take pity on my desperate need to accumulate "data," their responses were minimal. Preliminary analysis indicated they were severely withdrawn, if not virtually autistic, but they did not act that way outside the test situation. My questions, on the other hand, clearly revealed my own high level of performance anxiety. In order to elicit responses from them, I generally had to ask questions that were longer and more revealing than their answers. From time to time they suggested that they knew "Indian stories" that were much more interesting than the ones I wanted them to make up in response to the set of standardized pictures I had brought with me. For a long time I rejected their suggestions. These stories were not the scientific data I required.

One day a tiny, frail old man was led into our camp by his grandson. I had met him before, first in the Fort Nelson hospital and later at the reserve, where people lived during the winter. He had been in and out of the hospital for several months, suffering from a series of heart attacks. Despite pressure from white doctors and the local schoolteacher to return to the hospital as the attacks became more frequent and more severe, he wished to be in the bush with his people. He needed moose meat, wind, stars, his language, and his relatives rather than the narrow white bed on which I had seen him perched cross-legged, like a tiny bird. His name was Japasa, "Chickadee."

On the evening of his arrival, the old man suffered another attack. As he struggled and moaned two of his grandchildren and two old men held him while they rubbed his arms and chest. A young daughter also came in to touch him. Outside the tent a circle of people watched in silence. Rainwater, collected as it ran down the trunk of a living spruce tree, was sprinkled on the fire. Gradually he became quiet and passed into a normal sleep. A few people remained to watch over him through the night and to keep a large fire burning.

The next evening, people gathered around the old man's fire after the day's work of hunting and preparing meat and hides. His son told a story about how he and the old man had survived the terrible flu of 1918–19 that had killed many people. Then Japasa began speaking softly, apparently to himself, as if he were looking back into a dream to find the words. His son whispered a simultaneous translation into English for my benefit. It must have been important to him that I share this event. He wanted me to understand enough of what was going on at the time that I could discover its meaning later in my life. This is the essence of Japasa's revelation as related to me by his son. I have told it in my own words from notes I made later that evening.

My dad said that when he was a boy, about nine years old, he went into the bush alone. He was lost from his people. In the night it rained. He was cold and wet from the rain, but in the morning he found himself warm and dry. A pair of silver foxes had come and protected him. After that, the foxes kept him and looked after him. He stayed with them and they protected him. Those foxes had three pups. The male and female foxes brought food for the pups. They brought food for my dad, too. They looked after him as if they were all the same. Those foxes wore clothes like people. My dad said he could understand their language. He said they taught him a song.

At this point in the narrative, the old man sang the boy's song. He sang his medicine song. I did not know then that this song could be heard only when death was near to the singer or to the listener. I did not know he was giving up the power the foxes gave to him in a time out of time, alone in the bush in the 1890s.

My dad said he stayed out in the bush for twenty days. Ever since that time foxes have been his friends. Anytime he wanted to he could set a trap and get foxes. When he lived with the foxes that time he saw rabbits, too. The rabbits were wearing clothes like people. They were packing things on their backs.

The first night out in the bush he was cold and wet from the rain. In the morning when he woke up warm and dry the wind came to him, too. The wind came to him in the form of a person. That person said, "See, you're dry now. I'm your friend." The wind has been his friend ever since. He can call the wind. He can call the rain. He can also make them go away. One time when I was twelve, I was with my dad and some other people when we got trapped by a forest fire. One of our horses got burned and we put the others in a creek. My dad told all the people to look for clouds, even though it hadn't rained for a long time. They found a little black cloud and my dad called it to help us. In just about ten minutes there was thunder and lightning and heavy rain that put out the fire. We were really wet, but we were glad to be saved from the fire.

My dad sang for the rain to come a couple of days ago. He sang for it to come and make him well. That rain came right away. This morning he called the wind and rain. They came and then he told them to go away. He told them he was too old and he didn't need their help anymore. He wanted to tell them he was too old and didn't need them. He said it was time to die. He told them they could leave him now.

After he had been in the bush twenty days he almost forgot about his people. Then he heard a song. It was coming from his people. He remembered them and he went toward the song. Every time he got to where the song had been it moved farther away. Finally, by following that song he was led back to his people.

After Japasa had told the story of his medicines the normal life of a hunting camp resumed. Men continued their hunting. They were very successful. Women were busy making drymeat and scraping hides. The old man stayed near his fire. From time to time we could hear the sound of his voice rising and falling in song like a distant wind. He had no more attacks. On the seventh day after giving away his medicines he remained well throughout the day. In the evening I returned to camp with some older men and boys after riding all day out to where a large moose had been killed. It took four packhorses to bring back the meat. The hunter's wife received it and then distributed meat to the other women of our camp.

Suddenly, it felt as if a wind were sweeping across the camp. It was a wind of alarm, of emotion, of change. I saw people flying toward Japasa's camp as if they were leaves in a wind. Their words were snatched away like cries in a storm. My fatigue and saddle sores from the day's ride vanished as I joined the flow of people. For the first time in my life I heard the rattle of death wrack a human body. People rubbed the old man as they had done before, but it was clear his breath would not return this time. A stillness came over us, then a gentle rain of tears. The tent was rolled back to make a kind of backdrop. The body was turned around to lie open to the sky. A friend and I dressed the old man's body in good clothes he had brought to be buried in. On his feet we placed a new pair of beaded moccasins, made for him by a young woman who had died the year before. The moccasins may have helped him follow her song on what I learned later was called the "trail to heaven." Wearing these new moccasins, the boy who knew foxes would be able to follow a trail of song to another camp.

After Japasa's death the tests seemed less important to me. I cared less about data relevant to the language of personality theory and more about data relevant to understanding the stories the old man had made known to me seven days before I heard his death rattle. In the years that have passed since I heard Japasa give away his songs, I have never again been close enough to death to hear a person sing the songs of his or her medicine. I have, however, listened to a wealth of Indian stories. I have studied them, dreamed them, told them, taught them, and made them my own.

The stories are windows into the thoughtworld of Indian people.

Their time is different from ours. The old man and the boy circle around to touch one another, just as the hunter circles around to touch his game and the sun circles around to touch a different place on the horizon with every passing day. During the year it circles from northern to southern points of rising and setting. It circles like the grouse in their mating dance. It circles like the swans who fly south to a land of flowing water when winter takes the northern forest in its teeth of ice. The sun circles like the mind of a Dreamer whose body lies pressed to earth, head to the east, in anticipation of its return. The sun and the Dreamer's mind shine on one another.

On the evening when Japasa gave up his medicines, he gave me two stories as well. One was about how Indian people from far and wide used to gather in the prairie country near the Peace River to dry saskatoon berries. They came down the rivers in canoes full of drymeat, bear tallow, and berries. They sang and danced and played the hand game, in which teams of men bet against one another in guessing which hand conceals a small stone or bone. The other story was about frogs who gamble, just like people. He said he knew frogs because he once lived with them on the bottom of a lake.

The old man's stories recalled times that we would think of as being very different from one another. One we would call history, the other, myth. Written documents going back as far as the late eighteenth century describe Indians coming together to sing, dance, and gamble in the Peace River prairie country. We can use the traditions of historical scholarship to substantiate that what Japasa described really happened. There is no documentary or scientific evidence to indicate that frogs really sing and dance and gamble beneath the waters of a pond, but the old man said he experienced this, too. Because we lack documentary evidence, we are compelled to class his second story as myth. In our thoughtworld, myth and reality are opposites. Unless we can find some way to understand the reality of mythic thinking, we will remain prisoners of our own language, our own thoughtworld. In this world one story is real, the other, fantasy. In the Indian way of thinking both stories are true because they describe personal experience. Their truths are complementary.

Both of Japasa's stories were true to his experience. When he was a boy, Japasa knew frogs and foxes and wind. He knew their songs. He entered the myths that are told about them. He obtained power by joining his own life force to theirs. He knew them in the bush away from the society of other humans. He knew them in the searing transformation of his vision quest. He became their child, one of their kind. He saw them clothed in a culture like his own. He carried them through to the end of his life, and then he let them go.

Japasa also knew the social power created by his people when they came together in good times. At the time of his death both forms of power were strong all around him. Hunters were making contact with their game. Women passed the meat from camp to camp, making the people strong together. On the morning after he told us the stories of his medicines we saw a moose cross the seismic line within sight of camp. Never before or since have I known game animals to come that close to where hunters are camped. People said the animals were coming around the old man to say good-bye to him. They said they knew from the tracks that foxes came to his camp in the night. For seven days after Japasa let go of his powers the people were all around him. He became like the child he was before his vision quest. He was within the strength of his people when he left on the trail of a different song.

Historical events happen once and are gone forever. Mythic events return like the swans of spring. The events of history are unique and particular to their time and place. They cannot be experienced directly by people of different times and places. I can know about Napoleon, but I cannot be Napoleon if I wish to be regarded as sane. Mythic events are different. They are essential truths, not contingent ones. I can be a frog or a fox and still be a person. I can know them as I know myself. If I am Indian, I can be led toward a place where this knowledge will come naturally. The foxes that came to Japasa before he died were the same as the foxes he knew as a boy. The wind came to him as a person, the foxes wore clothes and spoke in a language he could understand, the frogs gathered to drum and gamble. They gave this boy their songs as guides to the powers he would have as a man. Throughout his life he returned in his dreams to that visionary time-out-of-time. His powers were forces within him as well as forces of nature. His experience was always within nature. Even in times of hardship he did not move against it. At the end of his life people and animals came together around him. When he died he returned to the mythic time, like the swans who fly south in the fall. As long as mythic time remains, we can expect his return.

For northern hunting people, knowledge and power are one. To be in possession of knowledge is more important than to be in possession of an artifact. Their technology depends upon artifice rather than artifact. They live by knowing how to integrate their own activities with those of the sentient beings around them. The most effective technology for nomadic people is one that can be carried around in their minds. Hunting people are able to create a way of life by applying knowledge to local resources. Their dreaming provides access to a wealth of information. Their vision quests and their myths integrate the qualities of autonomy and community that are necessary for successful adaptation to the northern forest environment. The truths of the hunting way of life are essential and unchanging from generation to generation. In spirit, they may very well reflect Paleolithic traditions of our own distant ancestors.

The mythic thinking of northern Native people combines the individual intelligence we all have as members of a common species with a cultural intelligence embedded in the wealth of knowledge they carry around in their minds. Their stories tell them how to make sense of themselves in relation to a natural world of sentient beings. Their dreams and visions give direct access to this wealth of information. Individual intelligence and the intelligence of cultural tradition work together. Both are dedicated to making sense of human life in relation to the life of nature. These hunters act on the basis of knowledge and understanding rather than on orders passed down through a social hierarchy.

Our own traditions strongly stress obedience to duly constituted authority. This authority is frequently intellectual as well as social and political. We are more often taught answers than how to solve questions that come to mind. We are literal-minded in interpreting the meaning of experience in a hunting culture. We misunderstand myth by interpreting it as flawed history. For hunters, it is appropriate to place human life within nature. For historians, human life is inevitably placed within the stream of history. For hunters, dreams and visions validate and explain the past in terms of present experience. For historians, the past is validated by documents rather than by personal experience. When historians attempt to write the history of hunting people, they must find ways of recognizing the validity of personal experience without violating their own scholarly traditions of obtaining valid information about the past. Historians must be wary of dreaming up other cultures, but they can, perhaps, dream into the rich store of information that hunters have given us about themselves. The true history of these people will have to be written in a mythic language. Like the stories of Japasa, it will have to combine stories of people coming together with other people and those that tell of people coming together with animals.

When I heard old man Japasa speak in 1964 about his medicine animals, I knew with absolute certainty that this man was neither lying nor deluding himself. It was I who indulged in self-delusion when I persisted in asking for data in a form that could not accommodate Beaver Indian reality. In his last days on earth, the old man gave me his vision of that reality. I hope that the trust he placed in me has been justified in some small measure by the work I have chosen to do in my life.

The American Indian and the Problem of History, 1987

TELLING SECRETS

Stories of the Vision Quest

We humans have lived in small-scale band-level societies for most of the time since our emergence as a self-reflective species. The channels of communication we now think of as intrinsically human must have evolved to meet the needs of a social order where people living together were well known to one another. In band-level societies today, stories of individual lives are an important part of every person's cultural competence. This intimacy and interdependence of band life is often represented by the language of kinship, but there are other exchanges that connect people to one another even more deeply. These are the lifelong exchanges through which a person's life becomes a story that is part of the cultural competence shared by others.

As in any human society, each person lives both within his or her own subjectivity and within the intersubjective embrace of common understandings, but in bands there are special channels to facilitate a flow of information between subjective experience and intersubjective understanding. Band traditions are sustained orally and through personal contact. Storytelling is more than entertainment. It is a way of communicating important information from one person to another and from one generation to another. Stories are culturally coded interpretations of personal and collective experience. When something important happens to a person it becomes a story shared with others. Each story that is shared contributes to the knowledge others have of an individual. Each individual is a character in the story of a group's life together. Stories are interpretations of experience through which subjective information is organized and communicated intersubjectively. They are a medium particularly adapted to the conditions of life in band-level societies.

Typically, in band-level societies known to us ethnographically, the story of an individual's life comes to be associated in one way or another with traditional mythic stories. In these societies, mythic events are often viewed as being like dreams in their relation to the events of everyday experience. They are recognized as real, authentic, and immediate, but meaningful primarily as interpretations of everyday events. Individual stories, myths, and dreams are all abstractions of ordinary experience. They are all coded media of communication. Storytelling may be used both to communicate one's own personal experience and to recount the archetypal experience of beings from mythic times. These times are often associated with dreaming, and the dream experience may serve as a point of contact between individual experience and cultural archetype. The dreamer comes into contact with mythic tradition, bringing this form of cultural intelligence to bear upon his or her own personal experience. Through dreaming, the collective representations of myth may be related to the events of a person's own life. The use of dreams to mediate between personal and mythic narrative must go back to the time when humans first began to communicate on an interpretive level with one another. As the capacity for reflective thought emerged, dreams must have been recognized as subjective reflections of common understandings.

The Australian aborigines' associations of mythic dreamtime and individual identity have come down to us in what we call totemism. There, the story of a person's life is instructed by his or her identification with a totemic ancestor from the mythic dreamtime. Among many North American band-level hunting societies, associations between personal experience and mythic archetype are established through the vision quest. Dreaming in these societies is an essential link between the events of a person's life and the events of mythic time. Individual visionary experience and dreaming bring a person into relationship with the interpretive symbols of mythic thought. This paper describes how one North American hunting society, the Athapaskan Dunne-za of the Peace River area, tells the stories of its vision quest experiences.

In traditional Dunne-za life, every person experienced a series of childhood vision quests to which he or she referred in later life as a source of power and identity. By the time a person had become an established elder of the band, his or her "medicines," as these powers are called in English, were known to everyone within a circle of related bands. During the course of a lifetime, what had once been intensely personal became a focal point of public information. The circle of a person's life among the Dunne-za was a trail of telling secrets.

The childhood vision quest experience is private and secret. If a child reveals the story that came to life during the dream space alone in the bush, the power may turn against him or her. Only the old people know, through their dreaming, what story may have possessed a child away from camp. Only people whose dreams visualize the trails of animals in the bush can articulate the vision of children when they are away from camp. Only by dreaming back to their own encounters with the medicine animals of mythic times can they see themselves in the visions of children. When the children return to camp from their time alone, they sense a balance has been realized between themselves and the old people. Growing up in camp, they had come to know the medicine stories active in the lives of the old people but had not yet discovered their own connection to the medicines. They had known the taste of every kind of meat and the warmth of fur against their skin, but not the animals themselves, alive and autonomous. They had known the medicines within the old people, but not these same medicines within themselves.

When the children return to camp from the bush, they can look to the old people within themselves. They can look ahead to the circle of their lives, to telling secrets of the vision quest. In the span of life between child and old person, the medicine stories of a child's experience alone in the bush become an old person's stories known by everyone in camp. The stories become real in the theater of their telling. They always remain secrets, but during the course of a lifetime become known to a widening circle of people. By the manner of their telling secrets, Dunne-za children establish themselves as people of knowledge. Thus, the story of an individual's life becomes part of the stories known to all. This diffusion of information balances the vision quest, during which a story known to all becomes part of the child's experience.

In any small-scale society where every life is known to others as a story, transformation of personal experience into culturally recognized knowledge is a powerful medium for bonding people to one another with meaning. The art of telling secrets is an important medium of communication in communities where people know one another from living together interdependently. My own knowledge of Dunne-za medicine stories comes from participating for a time in this interdependence. As I came to know the old people, the stories of their lives became part of my own cultural competence. I learned in much the way a child learns before his or her own vision quest experience. During the course of daily life in camp, I observed that the space around these old people was treated differently from other spaces. Each old person's space was distinctive, just as the life story of each one was distinctive. I learned, as a child would learn, the facts of life about what could or could not be done in the presence of each old person. I learned that one person does not eat red berries, and that it is incorrect to throw eggshells into his fire or take flash pictures in his presence. In another person's camp, the sound of a stretched string may not be heard. Another did not play the drum.

I was told these facts about the lives of old people because it was necessary for me to know how to act properly within their spaces. Direct inquiries about the meaning of these personal taboos were not answered. Receiving replies like, "Old person don't like that kind," I quickly learned that in this culture you must figure things out for yourself in order to claim the knowledge as your own. In responding to me as a child, the Dunne-za showed me how they expect children to learn. Thus, I learned that they come into possession of knowledge only by putting together pieces of information into a meaningful pattern for themselves. Children and anthropologists learn to learn by interpreting the special attributes of old people. Later, as old people, they apply themselves to the more difficult task of interpreting the special attributes of children.

The key to the child's (and my own) learning to interpret the special actions of old people is coded into traditional Dunne-za stories. For each medicine power, a story describes how a giant person-eating animal of old was overcome by the culture hero-transformer. The hero's name was Swan, a high voyager between seasons. After his own vision quest, he became Saya, sun and moon in the sky, another form of high seasonal voyager (Ridington 1978a). The distinctive identity of each giant animal as recounted in traditional stories is a link to the qualities that distinguish the space occupied by old people. Their personal identity and actions bring stories from the realm of long ago and far away into the center of camp life. Red berries, eggshells, and camera flash link to stories about the power of Thunderbird, whose red eyes flash lightning and whose eggs are laid in nests high in the mountains. The sound made by stretched string was used by giant Spider Man to lure his human game to a giant web. Frogs, living like people beneath the lakes, used drums in the gambling games they played with one another. Even a child is able to see the medicine stories in the lives of old people.

Every old person lives both in camp with other people and at the center of the medicine stories revealed to him or her as a child. A person's growth is measured by the pace of his or her revelation of these secrets to the people at large. They must be revealed in such a way that they are discovered by people rather than imposed upon them. A child, fresh from the direct experience of medicine powers in the vision quest, must guard the secrets closely, perhaps even direct them to some quiescent place below everyday consciousness. Later, with maturity, a person may dream back to that visionary moment, recalling it into everyday life. In these dreams, the child's experience becomes an active point of reference in the life of the adult.

Through dreaming, the adult learns that the time has come to construct a medicine bundle containing objects symbolic of the medicine story. The bundle is an outward sign of inner growth. It can only be put together on the authority of a dream that goes back to the child's vision. The bundle is hung above and to the east of a person's sleeping place. The act of producing a medicine bundle indicates that a person has begun to dream back to this visionary moment. The bundle is a physical representation of a story becoming active in a person's life, but it does not give any clues to the identity of the story or its power. Outwardly, it is a plainly wrapped bundle, the contents of which are never revealed directly. The secret must be revealed slowly, if it is to be accepted as true to the person's deepest identity.

A person's relatives must figure out the slowly emerging pattern of his or her medicines in the same way that a child figures out the medicines of old people. The secrets must be told bit by bit, so that they are discovered by others rather than claimed directly. Medicine powers are shown gradually as people become teachers within their bands. The powers are real only as people discover them for themselves. Children first discover the powers of old people from the special quality of the space around them. In the vision quest, they apprehend power through overwhelmingly direct transformative experience. Later, they dream back to that time and begin to release information for the people living closest to them. When a person begins to dream back, the child's vision gradually emerges from his or her subjectivity to touch an inner circle of closest relatives and then outward to more distantly connected people. As a person's household grows, more people have an opportunity to observe the medicine bundle. In times of crisis, it may be used ritually in an attempt to restore well-being. The bundle and the dreaming of its owner become important to the household's sense of self-sufficiency. Success in the food quest attests to an ability to see connections between the trails of people and animals. Dreaming back to the child's vision is associated with dreaming ahead to the point of contact between hunter and game. The present moment is seen to be framed by visions of past and future encounters with medicine power. Knowledge of the future must be balanced by knowledge of the past.

At every stage of the life cycle, medicine powers are secrets that must be discovered in order to be valid. The ability to discover meaningful patterns is as important to the mastery of bush skills as it is to the learning of medicine stories. Mastery of one is taken as indicative of having mastered the other. The ability to figure out meaning in the pattern of animal movements in the bush is the same ability through which the meaning of medicine stories is learned. Only when a person has begun to demonstrate an understanding of subsistence skills will the external tokens of medicine power be accepted. The secrets of a person's deepest subjective experience become part of his or her public identity only when they also contribute to an intelligent identification with the powers of nature through which all of Dunne-za life descends. Both medicine powers and bush skills are learned through a combination of intelligent observation and intense transformative experience. Stories of Saya, the culture hero, and stories of individual medicines are learned as part of the interpretive process through which Dunne-za children become competent and contributing members of their society.

The Dunne-za refer to medicine power as "knowing something."

To know something is to have both experienced and interpreted it. The vision quest is an intensely personal transformative experience which possesses all Dunne-za children. The medicine powers that grow out of this experience are socially validated personal interpretations of traditional stories. This powerful union of personal experience and cultural program is demonstrated most dramatically on the rare but significant occasions when a person's medicine space is willfully and knowingly violated. Because the giant medicine animals were people-eating monsters, a person whose story is deliberately challenged within his or her personal space is said to become "too strong." This person is then compelled, by the logic of the medicine story and the authority of having truly experienced the story in a vision quest, to begin a transformation into the person-eating mythic monster. The resulting anthropophagous being is called Wechuge (Way-chu-gay), and the performance leading up to the completed transformation is highly stylized. In it, the person whose medicine power has been violated reenacts, within camp, the events of the empowering medicine story. A person whose frog power was violated, for instance, began to jump up and down like a frog. (For other examples and a more thorough description of the Wechuge performance, see Ridington 1976a.) Usually, the community supports the person whose power has been violated. Others, whose medicines are well recognized, use their own powers to bring the Wechuge under control before the transformation has become irrevocable.

The Wechuge performance is dramatic in that, energized by the fire of interpersonal conflict, it makes manifest secrets that otherwise are left to inference. Wechuge is a stylized cultural performance. It can only be understood by people within the culture. The child who sees someone he knows performing a medicine story as Wechuge learns both the story's content and its extraordinary power. The clues that ordinarily reveal a person's medicines suffused within the background of camp life emerge to dominate the entire camp during a Wechuge performance. I only know of older people actually having carried off such a performance. It seems that when a younger person's more covert medicines are challenged, the result is more likely to be a private medicine fight (Ridington 1968). Because a younger person's medicines are still largely secret and not an established fact of social identity, defense of a challenge is less likely to result in a public drama.

Dunne-za stories of personal vision quest experiences and traditional Dunne-za myths are private and public versions of the same information. To a young person, the myths are public information, while stories of the vision quest are personal secrets. During the course of a person's life, his or her identity becomes more mythlike until, as an old person, the events of the medicine story encountered as a child become public information. Storytelling is a form of communication of great antiquity. In small-scale band-level societies, stories are an important channel for interpreting and communicating personal experience. They are a bridge between subjectivity and the intersubjective realm of culture. The anthropologist's distinction between myth and narrative obscures the interpretation of these two levels of symbolic communication in band-level societies. In communicating a personal experience to others, the storyteller uses the same system of meaning found in traditional myths. At least among the Dunne-za, personal and cultural communications are systematically related to one another.

Canadian Journal of Native Studies, 1982

A TRUE STORY

A story of personal experience presupposes a world that is common to storyteller and listener. In 1968, I was deeply engaged in the study of a world that had already flown away from immediate sensation into the dreaming of old people among the Dunne-za. One of these old people was Nachi, "Big," a seventy-eight-year-old woman known to whitepeople as Mary Pouce-Coupe. I had set up my tape recorder on her kitchen table in the new pastel plywood house with linoleum tile floors where she lived with her widowed daughter and granddaughter. They were settled then on the Doig River Indian Reserve, but Nachi remembered back to the time even before her people began to use horses and to spend their winters in log cabins.

I had asked her to tell stories into the tape recorder. Her grandchildren told her I wanted to hear about the times when giant animals ate people and the great traveling changer, Saya, circled the world, making it right for the people of old. Nachi spoke from the world of her own memory. She chose to give her grandchildren and the anthropologist a glimpse into the world she knew from personal experience. She left it to us to make the connection between that world and our own. I have attempted to fulfill her expectation. Nachi knew that I was interested in learning about her world. Her story nourished that interest. I trust that my story will nourish your interest in other worlds. Ultimately, it is this interest that we hold in common. A true story brings us together within a common world. Nachi brought me and her grandchildren to the world she knew as a girl. I am bringing you to the world I know as an anthropologist.

22

As an anthropologist, I learned that Dunne-za hunters did not travel the bush at random in search of game. The trails they followed were already known to them through dreams. They did not take the lives of animals; rather, they received the gift of life from animals that were known to them. To be Dunne-za was to be in possession of knowledge. Every child gained knowledge and power from the moments of visionary encounter with the spirits of animals in the bush. Every old person lived at the end of a child's trail. The story of a person's life evolved from the child's visionary moment, just as the story of a hunt reflected the hunter's dreaming. A person did not brag about the power. Nachi gave only clues in the telling of stories. She gave to her audience her own thrill of discovery. Nachi told her grandchildren and the strange whiteman interested in other worlds about her encounter long ago with the spirit of a dreaming bear. She trusted that we would make her story part of our own knowledge. My own story is told in reflection of that trust.

NACHI'S STORY IN HER WORDS

It used to be we had a hard time. We didn't have horses. We had to pack our stuff on our backs. We would hunt beaver from boats. It was hard. There wasn't much to eat. Sometimes we would eat a little. Sometimes someone would get a moose. We would eat a little and then it would be gone. Then we would move around, move from place to place to place until fall time. In July and August we would walk from Moberly Lake to Fort St. John to Dawson Creek, all over the places where the big towns are now, making drymeat. That's how far we went for moose. Sometimes we made a round trip from Doig River to Moberly Lake in ten days. That's what my *songe* [mother's sister, also stepmother] told me.

Some people don't believe that we had to pack all our stuff and drymeat on our backs. When my grandfather [Yeklezi, her father's father] was alive, he used to tell me about how they had to make four trips back to the places they cached the drymeat. In wintertime, too, they had to go back to the cache for the rest of the drymeat. Then they got horses, and they could make them pack the drymeat back. That's how we Dunne-za used to live in wintertime. There wasn't any flour or grub. We ate just straight meat. Today, with potatoes and flour and everything you think one moose is lots. You think it will last a month. In those days, one moose wouldn't last long—not one month. We ate only meat. You old buggers like that [jokingly to her grandchildren], don't laugh at me.

We used to go hunting in Alberta. We would go hunting for moose. There are really good people down there. You were never stuck for food. They would always feed you. They were really good people. They treated you like a baby. There weren't many Indians [Dunne-za] over there. Mostly half-breeds [Dish-inni, meaning Cree Indians]. Lots of girls and boys, but not very many Dunne-za. They were good to us. Today you eat well, but it used to be that we went starving all the time, all the time, all the time. Today if you don't have meat, you can eat bannock. It used to be when we didn't have any meat we didn't have anything to eat. In the fall time, we would bring our drymeat back to Doig River.

It used to be there was lots of meat. There are lots of moose still. Why don't you boys go out and hunt instead of just sitting around? I don't like whiteman's food. I don't like it now. I used to have lots of relations. Now I have none. Some old people have lots of relations still, but not me. Sitama is the only relative I have left. Get some soup for me from next door. Some kind-hearted man gives me money; that's why I get groceries from town. [She is referring to her government old-age pension.] If it wasn't for that kind-hearted whiteman giving the three of us money, we'd all starve. It used to be that the old people packed heavy boats for the whiteman. I guess they are paying us back for that. That's enough. I don't like to talk. I can't tell them anymore how I live. I live too poorly. Some people around here kill meat but they won't give us any.

One time I was camping with two old men, my *aspe* [father's sister or mother's brother's wife], and some other people. We were starving. We moved from place to place. We moved to another place and those two men didn't even go out hunting for moose. So my *aspe* and I decided to hunt for porcupines. We set out, and *aspe* went along the river. I went up along the crest of some mountains. It was late wintertime and there was deep snow. I looked down the slope but I didn't see any porcupines. The days were getting long but already it was getting dark, so I started straight down the mountainside. There was a river at the bottom, and I thought that if I followed it back to camp I might find something. The snow was deep down there and there was lots of brush. I was wearing snowshoes but the snow was too deep for them, too.

I was walking slowly when I saw some sticks broken under a medium-size spruce tree. It looked like something had broken them. I went over there. There were no tracks. I was on top of a bear den, but I didn't know it. I took off my snowshoes and started to look around. There was a small hole where the snow was falling in. I took a stick and poked it. It went inside. I looked inside. There seemed to be something in there but I couldn't see. It was dark. I poked again with a long stick. It felt like there was something in there, but it didn't move. It didn't growl. I was wondering what it could be. I threw lots of sticks and stones in there but nothing moved. Then I noticed a stick by the entrance that had been chewed so I put it in my pack and started back. It was late. I was tired. It was after the middle of the night when I got back. My grandfather was angry. "I thought you got a porcupine or something. I thought you were carrying some kind of meat in your pack. That's why you were late, but you didn't bring anything."

I showed my grandfather the chewed stick. "I found a bear's den, but I don't think he is in there now." My grandfather called to the other people, "Hey, my granddaughter found a bear's den." That same night we all set out to find it in the moonlight. I drank tea, and then I went on with them. We took a dog with us. After we had gone some way he could smell the bear, and he started barking. He wanted to chase after it but we held him. When we came to the hole we took the bear and killed him. It was a big black bear, the kind that is almost like a grizzly, and it was very fat. They started to skin it while I made a fire. We were so hungry we ate the bear's liver and guts. That night we packed the bear meat back, and we ate it. The next day we were feeling better and we moved camp again. A chinook came and it turned nice and warm. Then we got two moose. It was all right then.

NACHI'S STORY IN THE WORDS OF ROBIN RIDINGTON

It used to be we went starving all the time, all the time, all the time. When we didn't have any meat, we didn't have anything to eat.

In fall time, the people hunted moose and made drymeat. During the winter they returned to where they had cached the food. When it was gone, they had to find fresh meat. They coursed along the trails of their dreams to find a point that crossed with an animal's trail. They searched in every direction for some sign that the animals would give them life. At the end of a long cold winter the people of old man Yeklezi could not find enough to eat. They moved from place to place hoping to end their hunger, but their dreaming did not give them a point of contact. Everyone was hungry and everyone did what they could to bring them through the hard times. A young girl and her *aspe* set out from camp wearing snowshoes that left deep, wide tracks in the direction of their hope. Step after step they kicked over the soft snow in silence. Their trails parted. One followed the river through the low country. The other ascended to the height of land and followed its dividing line. The still, cold land passed beneath the two moving clouds of breath, each a woman, each a hungry human being. They traveled different trails because each knew the camp to which they would both return. By hunting individually, they were able to cover twice the territory. Each hunter was prepared to recognize a sign of life should she come upon it in the bright stillness of that late winter day.

Animals are always at home at the end of their trail. The women hoped to come to the place where a porcupine was living. If they were successful in this task, the people would taste food and be able to move and hunt another day. The young girl kept to the high country throughout that long day of late winter. Beneath her horizon a moon, near full, arced unseen toward the upcoming night. She scanned the smoothly whitened slopes below where her feet left their moving marks on the high country's snow. She saw nothing. She saw everything, but her mind could not find a point of focus. She saw no signs of porcupines. She saw no signs of her coming encounter with the Dreamer, but she was prepared to recognize whatever significance lay on the trail ahead. She saw the sun progressing down his perfect path toward the horizon of night. As always, she took her direction from that of the sun in relation to her knowledge of the country. Her mind told her to make a circle back to camp, this time following the line of the river. She did not know that a Dreamer lay waiting for her. Under the frozen river, water was flowing to the ocean she had never seen. Under the deep snow, by the thick willows marking the bank of the river, the Dreamer lay awaiting her discovery. Under the rim of the world, her knowledge and power lay in readiness for this girl at this moment in the turning of time. In the moment of dreaming and vision the person of knowledge will be given a sign.

Weariness and cold and unappeased hunger possessed her. Her hopes fell with the fall of the sun. The circle back to camp was harder than the outward journey. She was alone. Her *aspe* had already returned to the camp of Yeklezi. Down by the river the snow was much deeper than on the high ground. Her snowshoes sank heavily into the drifted powder, dragging feet and body down to numb resignation. Poised between setting sun and rising moon, between the hunger and cold and her weary determination, she could only continue to place one foot after another slowly in the silent valley through the great spruce trees that stood tall and straight by the hidden river. She was looking for tracks. She left a weary trail of tracks behind her in the snow. Only the Dreamer could go beyond his own trail. The connection between person and animal had to take place first in the mind before it could be realized in substance. Inside the darkness of his sleep, he was dreaming of the girl child. Through him, the people of old were sending a song to the girl child. From where the sun shines behind clouds, from where the moon, its nighttime shadow, will shine upon the girl child on the snow by the frozen river, from where one spruce tree, the world pole, a grandmother, is standing, the old people were dreaming of her. The Dreamer left a sign for this child. He broke sticks for her and marked them with his teeth. This was his sign. He had long since left his tracks far behind.

The storyteller recognized his sign in a moment that existed out of time. She accepted the gift as her own. His dreaming song flowed over her and into her. She became the one through whom the life of her people flowed, in that hungry end of winter long ago. She was the one who could give away to the people. She was the one on whom both sun and dreaming moon were shining. She was the one who occupied the Dreamer's sleep. She took up his sign with understanding. She took up her trail at the point where he had left his own tracks behind in the light of another season. She was a young girl. She was to be an old woman of knowledge. In this visionary moment of time out of time, she made the connection. The tracks of a young girl were drawn to this place. Those of an old person made their way back to camp.

The woman took off her snowshoes. Something had broken those sticks. Something had marked them for her with its teeth. She discovered a hole into which snow was falling. She took a stick and poked inside the cold darkness. She knew there might be life within. She could not see. She reached inside to touch his flesh. It was to be the life of her people. The old people could dream ahead of their bodies. This was to be his gift to her. Something was alive inside his darkness, but the girl child did not know what it was. The old woman knew. The people of old knew. In time the girl would grow into her gift. In time she would pass it on to her grandchildren. The Dreamer was waiting for her in silence. He did not move. He did not growl. He reached out to her from the trail he left in the snow of another season. She picked up the stick he had marked for her. She picked up his moment as her own. She turned toward the camp of Yeklezi bearing a sign of recognition.

Step by step, she took up her trail, the seeds of the dreaming within her. Step by step, she returned to the ordinary world of physical need and satisfaction. Past the middle of the night she returned to her grandfather. "Where are your porcupines?" he asked with a voice like winter. "I thought you were carrying meat in your pack. I thought that is why you were late. But you didn't bring anything." Then she showed him the sign. "I have found the place where he left his tracks, but I do not know if he is still there."

Yeklezi showed the people her sign. He led them beneath the moon, back over the trail of the girl to whom the sign had been given. The people were all walking together under the cold moon to receive her gift. They took a dog with them, and he caught the scent of the one within. They came to the place where the Dreamer remained and took the gift. The people ate by their fire at the end of a cold, moon-washed night. A warm wind would be coming. The old people would be dreaming and their trails would be crossing those of the moose once again. As before and always, the sun would move one step every day. Within the fulfillment of time an old woman would tell a true story.

Anthropology and Humanism Quarterly, 1980

EYE ON THE WHEEL

Only when you come to the place
Where you remember what is happening to you
Will the circle of time
Turn around you
Only when the tracks before you are your own
Will you turn with the circle
When your feet enter the tracks
Of every other being
You will see them as your own
And leave them all
Behind you

"Eye on the Wheel" is a myth that begins in the symbols and experience of the Dunne-za and works its way into the context of our own symbols and experience. If there is one thing we know for certain about mythic symbols, it is that they cannot be completely pinned down to any particular time and place. The same symbols, images, messages, relationships turn up in widely separated locations in geography and history. The Phoenix appears as shamanic Dreamer, Quetzalcoatl, Pharaoh, Christ, and the spark of sentience that always passes on from generation to generation to reappear changed in form but the same in essence. The same symbolic patterns return in new foliage, like the seasons, and undergo rapid and regular changes in polarity, like the transformation of night into day. As Joseph Campbell, Heinrich Zimmer, Carl Jung, Mircea Eliade, and others have shown, mythic symbols reflect the same recurring patterns of human experience the world over. To imagine that the message of a culture's myth relates only to the context of a particular cultural experience is to deny the possibility of an understanding flowing from one tradition into another or of the same understanding emerging independently in isolated traditions. There is abundant evidence that the same symbolic patterns emerge from very diverse adaptive conditions. Mythic symbols live, like the Phoenix, as they enter and reenter the lives and times of real people.

Although some elements of a story's message may relate particularly to a concern embedded in a particular time and place, the story would be entirely obscure and untranslatable without some degree of commonality with our own experience. A story can be reduced to its logical structure and examined in this anesthetized state by white-coated technicians, but in order to achieve a transformation from one tradition to another it must regenerate itself with new images and messages appropriate to the experience of our lives here and now. This transformation and regeneration is what has happened to the Dunne-za story told to me by an old medicine person and Dreamer named Jumbie. It is a story about the Dreamer's vision in a time when the People are in danger.

The Dunne-za send their children out into the bush on a vision quest where they encounter a giant animal, a monster they already know from the myths they have been told by the old people. In the vision quest they experience the reality of the mythic times when the giant animals hunted and ate people. In the vision quest they begin a transformation from the innocence and dependency of childhood into the competence and understanding of adulthood. As the child grows older the meaning of his or her visionary experience comes into focus. The growing child learns to use this medicine power to focus his dreaming and to see the larger pattern of which every small step is only a part. Each medicine animal gives powers and understanding appropriate to its nature. For each medicine animal, there is a story telling how the culture hero who travels around the world like the sun changed the person-eating monster into the animal that is seen in the here and now of everyday reality. A person's medicine power gives him or her the vision to see, from among the many paths that may or may not lie ahead, the clearest path of possibility. Dreaming and vision quest are focal points of Dunne-za culture and experience. In our own culture, neither are institutionalized. Our need to see the larger pattern of which our immediate present is only a part is perhaps even more, for us, a matter of life and death. For the Dunne-za, a small band may be overtaken by starvation, but the People as a whole will carry on. We now realize that the whole species must face the possibility of its own extinction.

"Eye on the Wheel" begins as a story about the danger an old Dunne-za Dreamer sees in the emerging pattern of his dreaming. It is both a story of the danger that lies ahead, out of sight of an ordinary vision focused on everyday reality, and a story of the vision quest experience through which the Dreamer grew into his ability to focus his dreamsight, like an eagle, on faraway realities. The story then undergoes a transformation from the context of a time and place removed from our own experience to the one in which we live from day to day, unable to see with a dreamsight focused beyond the events of everyday reality, until a member of our species first leaves the planet Earth to look back upon her from his tracks, 240,000 miles out in space on the surface of the moon. In the alchemy of mythic transformation Neil Armstrong's "giant leap for mankind" becomes a shamanic journey. The two stories of transformative experience merge into one. We come to learn that Dunne-za refers to "our people, our relatives" and that the monster we feared as children is really one of us in ceremonial mask.

STORY TOLD BY JUMBIE

Once upon a time in April, in late winter, when there were monsters, one old medicine person felt *nagata*, the feeling that something bad was going to happen.

AND ROBIN

The medicine person is a dream traveler, able to leave his tracks in sequential time and ascend to where he can look back on them to see a pattern emerging from the extinguished sunshine of a day that has passed or has not yet come to pass. His medicine is a song—a trail of song leading up and out of the middle earth to a more perfect one at the center, beyond the appearance of reality. An old person's trail leads back, step by step, to the experience of a child's vision. Beyond the monster's appearance, a child lies quietly in his own time and space, waiting for the sun to rise and reveal the trail that lies ahead.

The old person has already been over the trail, three days out and three days returning. In either direction, it leads to the time when there were monsters and the monsters were eating the people. *Na-gata* is the Dreamer's premonition.

Monsters are eating people. People are becoming monsters. Long ago there used to be monsters on this world. They were driven down beneath the earth's surface. It has been painted over to hide their resting place, but the Dreamer, looking back on his trail, remembers them. The whitepeople drill down beneath the earth's surface to get oil from their remains. Whitepeople use it to make their cars go. A person's trail ends when he steps into one of their cars. To pick it up again, the Dreamer must go back to confront the monster. The call of his medicine is on the trail behind him. Even when the sunshine has gone, he can follow with his mind the trail of song. His heart drum sets the pace, step by step, from there to then, and the ebb and flood of voices wash over the landscape to give it an appearance of reality. For three days you follow the song's turns, up and inside, to the very center of the emergent pattern. For three days the trail leads you back to the body you left behind. On the seventh day all connections come together and explode in a burst of light. You cannot go there and you cannot go away from there. At the pattern's center, old eyes are reflected in those of the child. Together they are the Dreamer.

He felt like that all the time until the time came when the bull moose were getting really fat. Then he and his people moved up the river that comes out of the mountains. They camped three places along the river, past where it turned into the mountains, and they killed a really fat bull moose. Before, they hadn't got anything and they were hungry. The people who were camped with the old person laughed at him when he said he felt strange. But for six days he felt that way. He couldn't eat because he was afraid. The people just laughed at him. "You won't see any monster," they said, but on the sixth day he said, "Tomorrow the monster will come."

On the seventh day the pattern will come into focus. What had been the uneasy premonition of a dream will materialize in a burst of light, assuming for a time the appearance of reality. The dream tracks before you circle round, like those of a hunter, to come up behind you. Monsters circle round to hunt the people and consume the appearance of their reality. On the seventh day the dream will appear on the trail behind you. For three days the Dreamer follows the trail of his song to the center; for three days he follows its circle back to the place where his body lies waiting. The monster on your trail will come into focus in the place where you made your camp three days before. Only when the people see their fear closing with their reality three days before them will they turn again to see the center. Perhaps it will then be too late. If anyone knows it will be the Dreamer. He has been there and returned. He couldn't eat because he was afraid. The people just laughed at him. Before the child left camp he did not eat because he was afraid. Monsters are eating people. The people are becoming monsters.

The next day he told the people to move up on top of the high mountain with a flat top. The people moved up there, women and children and the rest. The old person stayed down, but then he got really scared and he went up on top of the mountain with the rest of the people, for he had seen something really big where the river turned, where they had camped three days before. That was about thirty miles away. If that thing he saw was little like a moose or a horse he wouldn't have been able to see it from that far away. It was a really big monster and it was following their tracks toward them.

The old person went on top of the mountain and he told the people, "See, you didn't believe me. Look there and see what is coming." The people went with him and they saw that animal. It had already passed the second place where they had camped. It went fast like a wolverine, and it was huge. It had a white back with two great humps on it. It was Nowe Nachi, a giant wolverine. When they saw that, the women all started to cry for their babies, because they knew that the animal was going to eat them all.

They saw the animal get to their third camp. When they had run away they had left the fire burning, they were in such a hurry. The animal went into their camp. He went to that fire but there was nobody there and he kept on going, right up that mountain after the people, right straight up. The people's tracks went either side but he came on up the steep part.

An old person lives in the story of this medicine animal. He wears the mask of its nature as he moves from camp to camp, fire to fire, center to center with the people. By these signs, they come to know the reality of his dreaming. He is the animal of his story wearing the mask of a human being. His story is real in the space around him. The stories are true for all to see as he moves with the sun through his day and at night, following the echo of his song, painting the appearance of another reality from the place where the sun will return in its own time. In dreaming the old person turns from darkness to the light. With every revolution the pattern of changes comes more clearly into focus. In the quiet time the Dreamer is waiting for events to catch up with his vision. The monster will soon be ransacking the camp that was our home and center only three days before now. In the pattern is the Dreamer's premonition.

Nowe Nachi, giant Wolverine, is one of the medicine animals. As an animal, he is unlike all the others in intelligence and ferocity. Only Wolverine understands the nature of traps and snares. While other animals struggle to be free and in their desperate drive for survival take their own lives, Wolverine understands his situation and calmly extricates himself from it. Only Wolverine can go back on his own trail. The others press forward until they are overcome by blackness, but Nowe sees the light behind him. He knows that the way ahead sometimes lies in the opposite direction. He is the one whose back is painted white. He is the master of traps, able to go back from the illusion of his own reflection. While others strangle in the trap of a reality that cannot be, Wolverine deftly pulls back into the world of possibility. He is master of the feedback signal between existence and possibility. He knows to turn away from where the sun was setting to anticipate its return in the East. To follow the trail of light you must turn to meet it where you know it will return. To follow the trail of your own life you must see the pattern, of which each step is only a small part. To turn away from the trap you must know in what direction the path of possibility lies.

When Wolverine breaks into a cache of food the people have stored away, he takes what he needs and pisses on what is left. He does not try to live in a place that is dangerous. He leaves his sign to stop those who would follow in his tracks from taking into themselves the flesh that bears his mark. Monsters are eating people. People are becoming monsters. The Dreamer turns to see a giant wolverine on the trail behind him. Only Wolverine can turn from darkness to the light. Only Wolverine has a white trail painted along the darkness of his body. Only the planet turns, half in darkness, half in light.

When the Human Being became Wolverine, he put on his animal mask and pretended to be the victim of Wolverine Man's trap, a pit of pointed stakes painted over to look like an ordinary trail. Only Nowe, the wolverine, can escape the trap by going back over his own trail. Only Nowe's song goes back from the blackness to the light. Wolverine Man found him, a bloodstained limp bundle at the bottom of the trap. Behind the appearance of darkness there is light. Along the back of his black body there is painted a trail of light, a pit of stakes painted over to look like an ordinary trail. You are going back to Nowe's camp in his game bag, a rabbit-size limp bundle bedraggled with blood. Nowe can only escape the trap by going over his own trail from darkness to light. While others strangle in the trap of a reality that cannot be, Nowe deftly pulls back into the world of possibility. You are the child of the monster you turn to meet on your own trail, closing the gap between then and there and here and now. Monsters are eating people. People are becoming monsters.

Wolverine Man says to his kid, "Look, I got a nice fat dude for dinner." You wink at the kid. "Hey, Dad, your dude just winked at me." "Like hell he did. I got him from the bottom of the pit, bloody as an afterbirth." You wink again to the kid. Then you jump up and chop the old monster down. Your medicine name is Nowe. From that point on, wherever you may go, the humpbacked monster with the streak of light on his back, a pit of stakes painted over to look like an ordinary trail, will be behind you, coming closer in your dreams, until he becomes the focus of your reality. When game becomes hunter, the monster will be behind you. Only Nowe can turn back upon his trail from darkness into light. When the monster is only three camps away from the People, you must begin the journey home to where the People are keeping a fire burning for you.

The People have found a way to use energy that comes from there and then. It is a monster growing on the trail behind them. Two hundred million years ago the sun rose and set, rose and set, over the photosynthetic factories of the Mesozoic. With every turning of the earth from darkness into light, the power flowed into the bodies of plants and in them the power remained, through the long gestation that brought about our birth as people. The pipelines reach back two hundred million years. A person's trail ends when he steps into one of the whiteman's cars. To pick it up again, the Dreamer must go back to confront the monster. The child is born, limp and bloody, from a pit of stakes. People are becoming monsters. You wink at the kid in the mirror. Then you jump up and chop the old monster down.

People are living from energy that overbalances their understanding of it. No one dreamed that the sun of the Mesozoic would return, but now it is only three days' camp from where we are. When the feedback signal between what you have and what you need becomes too far removed from your experience of what is real, you begin eating up parts of your body before you realize what you are doing. Even to have begun as we did was to have gone too far. The Eye on the Wheel is too far from both brain and ocean to bring them both around to a common center. Looking back, the pattern that emerges is clear from the tracks of the embryo, but when we were high on the wave of energy there was only the desire of here and now to rush along with it. Your back was turned when Nowe winked at the kid, but you remembered it as you grew into understanding. Only when the energy is nearly gone is the message finally delivered. In a story the medicine person turned into a child. In time the child grew into a medicine person. The pain of touching fire keeps the child safe from its burning. The feedback is instantaneous. The pain of living high off a Mesozoic credit card will not withdraw the body to the path of possibility in time for all to find their way back along the trail.

The children who grew into the understanding of their age will follow an old person's trail back, step by step, to the experience of a child's vision. The reality of here and now is painted to look like an ordinary trail over a pit of stakes. The People are moving forward together toward darkness. They are animals struggling to be free, and in their desperate drive for survival they are taking their own lives. The medicine person is feeling that something bad is going to happen, but the People cannot yet feel the pain of their loss.

Trap makers are flying through the atmosphere, high on two hundred million–year–old sun power, reading *Time* magazine. They are flying into an unacknowledged pattern at the center beyond the appearance of their reality. The species is flying to the common center where Brain and Ocean are in balance. The child looks back to remember his emergence, limp and bloody from a pit of stakes. Look back. Look back. Cretaceous, Jurassic, Triassic, Permian, Carboniferous. They are a parabolic time mirror, concentrating the energy into a laser beam burning painlessly through the vital organs. The trail leads three days out from the edge of the possible universe and three days back to where the planet body spins in waiting before birth and after death. On the seventh day the monster will return as a child, but no one will believe it. When the People have run as far as they can go they will turn to Nowe. The monster has been eating the People for a long time. He has been taking their tracks into his machines and blasting them far and away from their here and their now. Only the Dreamer can go back to where the tracks rejoin the path of possibility. Only the Dreamer can see by the light of his song when the appearance of reality is darkness.

> The Dreamer took off his clothes and wrapped himself in a pure white moosehide and he went down the mountain to that giant animal. When the old person was pretty close he called out to the animal, "Where the hell do you think you are going?" The animal didn't see him. He looked back to where he was coming from. The old person met the animal and he put his hand on the animal's chest and he said, "Stop!" The animal looked at him and said, "You're the one I am looking for." That old person knew that animal from when he was a child. "Follow me down the river," he said, and the giant animal went back from where he came.

The Dreamer's body rotates on its axis once a day and circles around the Primary once a year. When the tracks before you are your own, you will turn with the circle and leave them all behind you. You are the one I am looking for.

The Dreamer left his body rooted in the Earth and turned to face the monster in his tracks. It was the body of a child whose tracks were pressing on to the place where the trail would have to cross a pit of stakes, painted over to give the appearance of reality. In his hand the child holds a toy plastic spaceship. "One small step for a man, one giant leap for mankind." In two hundred million years the tracks of Neil Armstrong will still be fresh and clear on the lifeless body whose rotation perfectly matches her own revolution. It is 240,000 miles from sea to shining sea. One is the ocean that received the first spark and grew you in embryo; the other is a sea of lifeless tranquillity, able only to reflect the spark but not to receive the seed.

Two hundred million years ago, the tracks of ancient animals led them to extinction, but the energy of their age has jolted us out of our body's familiar orbit into the pattern of an unfamiliar dream. "It involves a technology so complex no one person can understand how to master it all. Twenty thousand contractors; twenty million pages of manuals, instructions and other material printed monthly by the Kennedy Space Center alone." The trail ahead has the appearance of reality. "The rocket and spacecraft encompass more than five million separate parts; the engines, the most powerful in the world, gulp fifteen tons of kerosene and liquid oxygen a second and get five inches to the gallon." The child's toy plastic spaceship is real. The sight of a living planet rising from the rim of her satellite sky mirror is real. The trail to extinction is also real in its possibility.

The species has gotten itself into a high-risk occupation. Neil Armstrong said, "I have been in relatively high-risk businesses all my adult life. Few of the others, however, had the possibility of direct gains in knowledge which this one has. I have confidence in the equipment, the planning, the training. I suspect that on a risk-gain ratio, this project would compare very, very favorably with those to which I've been accustomed in the last 20 years" (Neil Armstrong, *Toronto Globe and Mail*, July 21, 1969). In two hundred million years, the tracks of Neil Armstrong will still be fresh and clear on the reflecting body with no biosphere, 240,000 miles from the nearest moving ocean. What life forms then will swim and swarm inviting spaces? The dinosaurs may know, but they can only say to us, "Fifteen tons of kerosene and liquid oxygen a second, five inches to the gallon, 240,000 miles out from the ocean of birth and two hundred million years into lifeless tranquillity." On a risk-gain ratio, only the Dreamer knows how this project would compare with those to which you have been accustomed in the last two hundred million years.

"The Dreamer wrapped himself in a pure white moosehide and went down the mountain to that giant animal." The dinosaurs did not look ahead to see their own extinction. The child with his toy plastic spaceship cannot see to the extinction of his reality. "Where the hell do you think we are going?" Both Dreamer and child look back along their tracks. The future of the species depends upon the reality to which the child has been accustomed for the last twenty years. The Dreamer can see the child's reality in the embryo's coded memory, but the child cannot see the Dreamer moving from the world of possibility into his reality. The child holds onto the appearance of his reality, a toy plastic spaceship made of Mesozoic hydrocarbons, but the Dreamer has long since let it go. "Stop!" You cannot come to where I am, and you cannot go away from our common time and space. The child holds on while the seed is letting go. The moment of reality is here and now. Put down your *Time* magazine and turn to see the reflection of possibility in a Dream. I am the one you have been looking for. At the end of his trail, the old person, wearing a pure white moosehide, turns to meet the monster. It is a child tightly holding a toy plastic spaceship. Face to Face, Mind to Mind, Planet to Planet, Experience to Experience, Image to Reflection, all connections come together and explode in a burst of light beyond illusion. The message from the Mesozoic is a feedback signal between experience and possibility.

In eons to come, should astronauts from the deeps of space—from other solar systems in other galaxies—pass this way, they may find our spoor, our abandoned gear. A plaque of aluminum affixed to the deserted LM descent stage portrays the two hemispheres of our planet. Upon it are engraved the name of our spaceship, the date of our mission, and a roster of the crew. From these data, the equipment, and even the dimensions of our footprints, intelligent beings will readily deduce what kind of creatures we were and whence we came. We leave a piece of fauna—a falcon feather—and of flora—a four-leaf clover. (David R. Scott, *Apollo 15* commander)

While others strangle in the trap of a reality that cannot be, the Dreamer deftly pulls you back into the world of possibility. He is dreaming of the One Child, cradled in a nest of frankincense and myrrh. You are the child of the monster you turn to meet on your own trail, coming together face to face, experience to experience, to close the gap between then and there and here and now. You are flying back to the nest of life, the blue-green biosphere, flowing along the Dreamer's trail down to the river of water painted over the low places, inclining in a single direction down to an ancient under-standing Ocean of Time and Space.

"Follow me down the river," he said, and the giant animal went back where he came from. Follow the river down to the Ocean Mother, weeping salt tears of joy at your birth and transformation. Follow the Mesozoic hydrocarbons back, inclining in a single direc-tion to a flash of sunshine, on the surface of the ocean of then and there. Follow the tracks of the dinosaurs, down past the darkness of their extinction, to become a toy plastic spaceship landing, with less than twenty seconds of Mesozoic hydrocarbon fuel remaining on the dust-strewn, impact-etched, basalt-filled, three thousand five hun-dred thousand million–years–old, lifeless sea of tranquillity shim-mering into focus out of the ages. The Eagle has landed. "That's one small step for a man, one giant leap for mankind." The last frontier has become a lifeless world able only to reflect the seed but not to nourish it. The Eagle has been given the gift of reflective vision, looking back on his nest of frankincense and myrrh from 240,000 miles away.

In a dream, the child Neil Armstrong could, by holding his breath, hover over the ground (*Toronto Globe and Mail*, July 21, 1969). In two hundred million years, his footprints will continue to walk upon the Sea of Tranquillity, his rotation perfectly matching his own revolution. From the eagle's perspective, intelligent beings will readily deduce what kind of creatures we are and whither we are going. The man must labor step by step from one extremity of his life to another, but the Dreamer within him can hover above the ground by holding his breath, take a giant leap to enter the tracks of every other being, and leave them all behind him. The child is hold-ing on at the same time the seed is letting go.

Follow me up to the flowing river trail inclining in a single direc-tion to an ancient understanding ocean of time and space. Where is the giant animal when he has gone back to where he came from? Intelligent beings will know from the tracks he leaves behind. One of the monster's small steps is a giant leap for mankind. A day is when his body rotates once on its axis. A year is when it circles once around the Primary. A life is when he meets a point of transformation and returns to carry on in different form. Looking back, the pattern that emerges from the dreaming is clear from the tracks of the embryo. Follow them back to the moment of joining and the body is a sphere, touched by a seed on the sea of the Mother. While the child holds onto a toy plastic spaceship, the seed is letting go. The giant animal is a sphere spinning once a day and circling round the Primary once a year. Turn to meet the body's image and see yourself reflected in her living reality. You cannot go there and you cannot go away from there.

The people moved back to their camps. The old person was still wearing his moosehide and he told them he was going out to meet the monster. He said he wouldn't be gone very long, and he went out. Not too far away he met that big animal. He was gone four days and the people began to worry about him. They thought something had happened to him.

You were a child when you first encountered the monster. The camp to which you returned on the seventh day has long since passed into memory, but you have lived on to become the old person who sent you alone to the edge of your child's world. Now you must return to recover the child's remains in the camp of your memory. "Tranquillity base here. The Eagle has landed." When you turn to meet the giant on the trail behind you, it will be a little child. In a dream the child Neil Armstrong is holding onto the breath of a distant earth, hovering above his tracks, wanting more than anything to fly away on a trail of song. In your embryo a tadpole is swimming, gill-breathing the ocean of two hundred million years ago. His breath hisses through the regulator, hisses through his pursed voice strings singing the moment of return, hisses through the transformations of modality and frequency to penetrate the 240,000 miles of emptiness to where we wait in suspended animation before the swimming picture tube images hissing breathlessly before us. "Tranquillity base here; the Seed has landed, the Embryo is letting go. I'm going to step off the LM now. That's one small step for a man, one giant leap for mankind." The child who held his breath for thirty-nine years, eleven months, two weeks, and two days has finally come down to a different world. His breath releases in the words that fly across the emptiness to reach our minds.

The surface is fine and powdery. I can, I can pick it up loosely with my toe. It does adhere in fine layers like powdered charcoal to the sole and sides of my boots. I only go in a small fraction of an inch, maybe an eighth of an inch, but I can see the footprints of my boots and the treads in the fine sandy particles. Beneath the treads I can feel the thin crust of a reality that moves with my tracks through sequential time.

What has passed never goes away, but it will change constantly as we ourselves change. There seems to be no difficulty in moving around. As we suspected, it's even perhaps easier than the simulations at one-sixth g that we performed on the ground. Its meaning is determined by our understanding of its place within a completed circle. If we would be free of the shadows lurking in our tracks we must turn to face them. It's actually no trouble to walk around.

The shadows are the dark reflections of ourselves as we might have been. They are the fear of darkness behind us. To follow the trail of light you must turn to meet it where you know it will return. We're essentially on a very level place here. It's quite dark here in the shadow and a little hard for me to see that I have good footing.

The People's trail begins when a person steps out of the child's toy plastic spaceship and comes together in a burst of light. It has a stark beauty all its own, much like the High Desert of the United States of Concentration and Release. It's different but it's very pretty here. Here Men from the Planet Earth first set foot upon the moon, July 1969, A.D. Here the People turn to illuminate the shadow world behind us. Here the child walks in tracks we laid down before him. Out of the many have come a single destiny, "E Pluribus Unum."[1]

You wink at the child and read the rest of the plaque: "We Came In Peace For All Mankind."

The old person went back to the camp. His old old father was named Tsuketa, "Father of Tsuke." He knew that animal too; he knew it better. The old person, his child, didn't want to follow that animal, but his father told him he should go. "You should go. He will make you a strong medicine person. It's good medicine." So his child went after the monster. The old person–child went out to meet that animal. He stayed with him seven days, and the animal showed him every kind of trick. The monster slept on top of him. On the seventh day the monster told him to go back. He knew that Tsuketa was worrying about his child. He told him, "If you go a little way from here you will meet your father."

A sleeping past covers the appearance of your reality, receding into blackness in every direction. Only the Dreamer can see by the light of his song when the appearance of reality is darkness. Even when the Mesozoic sunshine is gone, you can follow with your mind the trail of song. The spinning planet's heart drum sets the pace, the ebb and flood of seasons stepping one after another over the intervening ocean of time. The language of its resonance and harmonic connection with what you already know from experience leads you on, with the appearance of reality. For three days you follow its feedback signal inside to the very center of the vanishing and reappearing pattern. For three days you will have to follow your own tracks back toward a new beginning. On the seventh day the pattern comes into focus. Breath is released, becomes past, and passes on in waves to dissipate on the shoreless immensity beyond. Waves become song, become pathway, become master of the feedback signal between experience and possibility. If you go a little way from here, you will meet the living shadow of the seed from which you grew, nourished in a blue-green biosphere scented with the gifts of frankincense and myrrh. The seed is dreaming of his child, the species of our embryo two hundred million years ago.

Before you return to join the planet of your birth, seed for the coming generations, listen to the voice of the monster crackling through the earphones of your toy plastic spaceship. Intelligent beings will be able to deduce, even from the dimensions of his footprints, what kind of creature he is and where he came from.

The monster told Tsuke, for that was the old person's name, "I am going to meet your *saze* [sister's child]." Tsuke's *saze* knew the monster, too. He, too, was old but he had known him when he was young. The monster said, "His mouth stinks too much. He doesn't have much power now." He said that the relative would go out hunting but he wouldn't see him, even when he was close. Then Tsuke went back a little way and met his father. "You're still alive," his father said, and Tsuke said, "Yes." They went back to camp together.

Tsuke's *saze* went out hunting the next day. He saw tracks of the great big monster and he started following them. All day he followed those tracks. He saw that they were coming from where his relatives were camped, and he thought that the monster must have eaten all of them. But it soon got dark and still he hadn't seen the monster, so he went back to his camp. He told the people, "All day I followed the tracks of Onli Nachi, but I couldn't catch up with him. Maybe he didn't want me to see him. His tracks were coming from where my relatives camped. Maybe he ate them all." That's how the story goes. That is the end of the story.

Wolverine is seldom seen, even when he is close to you. The child wishes to believe in the reality of every possibility, the old person only in what he has experienced. Look back to when his tracks were last on the surface of another reality. Look back to the feedback signal from the Mesozoic. With less than twenty seconds of fuel remaining, Eagle has landed on the tranquillity of three thousand five hundred thousand million years, without transformation in the appearance of its reality. Eagle has landed at the bottom of the pit of stakes painted over with an image of reality, the trap baited with a rabbit-size limp bundle, bloody as an afterbirth. To bring the Eagle down, the hunter lies in a pit beneath the surface of the earth and covers his body with blood. When the Eagle has landed, the hunter must grasp it with his bare hands and take its life bloodlessly by cutting off its breath. From the old person's story, we know that the child whose tracks lead back to Nowe Nachi must grow up to become Eagle hunter, baiting the trap with an image of his own earth embryo. Take from Eagle his breath of wind, the sound of feathers holding onto air, and letting air pass him by. Take from the highest flier the trackless path of his song. Follow it to where he lives, a nest of frankincense and myrrh, a sweetly scented biosphere.

"There is a certain bird which is called a Phoenix. This is the only one of its kind and lives five hundred years. And when the time of its dissolution draws near, that it must die, it builds itself a nest of frankincense and myrrh, and other spices, into which, when the time is fulfilled, it enters and dies. But as the flesh decays a certain kind of worm is produced which, being nourished by the juices of the dead bird, brings forth feathers" (early Christian Father Clement, *Secret Teachings of the Ages*). A falcon feather and a four-leaf clover. When the child rises as Eagle he is painted with the rainbow colors. Only the Dreamer's vision can know how this project would compare with those to which you have been accustomed in the last two hundred million years. Only the Dreamer remembers the trail before him as a place he has been before. Only the dream traveler leaves his tracks on this world to take up ones on another. Only the Dreamer sees his body 240,000 miles away, supported by a thin crust of reality. Only the Dreamer sees Mesozoic sunshine in his toy plastic spaceship. Only the Dreamer sees the path of possible reentry into a life-sustaining biosphere. The trail of song is coming from the center of where the People are camped. The monster's trail leads to the center of the planet's body. A fire is burning in the center of camp. The people are singing and dancing, the sound of their voices together passing upward with the smoke. When he saw that the monster's trail was coming from where his relatives were camped, he thought that the monster had eaten them all. All day he followed the tracks of the monster but could never catch up, even with his shadow.

Within the dark generation of her dream-shrouded body, the Ovum rotates once a day and circles round the Primary once a year. You are a drop of seed falling home from one dream into another, a drop of clouded earth falling through space, a drop of sentience reflected on the motionless sea of tranquillity. You are person, ape, monkey, lemur, shrew, lizard, salamander, fish, worm, egg growing in a nest of frankincense and myrrh. You are growing feathers, catching your breath, painting the visible spectrum in a circle around your moment in time and space, turning to meet the People on the path of possibility. All energies revolve around a single point of light. All darkness is where the light is unseen. You cannot go there and you cannot go away from there. In the quiet time, the Dreamer is waiting for events to catch up with his vision. His eye is on the wheel.

NOTE

1. Some of the words of this quotation were actually uttered by Neil Armstrong, but they have been adapted for my purpose, and I have added to them words which I feel would have been appropriate for Armstrong to say but which he did not.

Io, 1976

THE WORLD OF THE HUNTERS

Charlie Yahey listening to Dreamers' songs, 1968

As I listened to Dunne-za stories and made them my own, I also directed my thoughts to the world in which hunting people have lived for many thousands of years. The Dunne-za gave me a sense of continuity with that world. What I learned about them gave me insight into the lives of hunting people in other times and places. It also gave me insight into what it means to be human. "Beaver Indian Dreaming and Singing" is one of the first attempts I made to describe the logic of connections that hunters make between thought and substance, the mental and the physical. It appeared in a 1971 special issue of *Anthropologica* in memory of Diamond Jenness.

I wrote "From Hunt Chief to Prophet" sixteen years later for a special issue of *Arctic Anthropology* edited by Sergei Kan. The papers in that volume discuss "Native Cultures and Christianity in Northern North America." My contribution describes how Dunne-za Dreamers, at the time of first contact, redirected their ability to understand communal hunting to address the problems their communities faced at the beginning of the fur-trade era.

The final two papers in this section describe knowledge and personal power as the forms of technology appropriate to the hunting way of life. Both papers use information from the Dunne-za but also go on to place Dunne-za culture in a comparative perspective. "Technology, Worldview, and Adaptive Strategy" appeared in the *Canadian Review of Sociology and Anthropology*. In it, I argue that the world view of hunting people is as much part of their technology as the artifacts of their material culture. Their technology, I suggest, depends upon artifice as much as artifact. In "Knowledge, Power, and the Individual," I survey anthropological writing about other subarctic hunting cultures for evidence that would expand the range of comparison. It grew out of an American Anthropological Association session that Fred Myers and Asen Balikci organized to discuss the contributions of northern ethnography to anthropological theory. The paper appeared in the *American Anthropologist* in 1988.

BEAVER INDIAN DREAMING
AND SINGING

Diamond Jenness must have been a magnificent fieldworker, for the descriptions he gives us of the Indian worlds he visited are rich in the kind of detail only a trusted and sympathetic friend would be told. In his fine ethnography of the Sekani Indians, he gives us fifteen pages of vivid first-person accounts of Sekani religious practice (Jenness 1937). We are told of people who died and returned to become medicine men and of a variety of personal medicines and spirit quests. Because Jenness's account is so detailed, concrete, and true to what he was told, one senses that the northern Athapaskan conceptual world must be more complex than their social institutions, a world of totemic thought set in shamanic cosmic structure. Nonetheless, the descriptive excellence of Jenness's work and a great deal of North American ethnography in the Boasian tradition leave the reader tantalized but curiously unfulfilled because of its inability to find an appropriate conceptual framework with which to translate the meaning of what it describes.

I think it right that a paper in honor of Diamond Jenness should attempt, in terms relevant to our present needs and understandings, to discover and translate the meaning of totemic and shamanic symbolism among the Beaver Indians, close neighbors of the Sekani. Like the Sekani, Beaver men and women have died and brought back songs from heaven as well as, in Jenness's words, "the belief that man and the animal world are linked together in some mysterious way and that animals possess special powers which they may bring to man if he seeks them in the proper manner" (Jenness 1937: 67–68). As Jenness intimates, these two religious forms are manifestations of a single cosmic order, and the underlying link between the two is in dreaming and songs. Elsewhere, I have written of the Beaver "messianic" practice as a form of shamanism (Ridington and Ridington 1970). Now I will concentrate on explaining the underlying media of dreaming and singing that connect Beaver shamanism with the quest for medicine power.

What I know of Beaver thought is incomplete both in detail and adequacy of conceptualization. I will have to ask the reader to take some of my statements on trust, particularly where an interpretation comes from my knowledge of a large body of myth which I cannot reproduce here. The reader's problem in following what the Beavers say directly parallels my problem in following what the Beavers say to me, because in both cases the context that gives an event meaning is an extensive culturally patterned background of experience. For a participant in Beaver culture, the symbols penetrate every level of experience, but the outsider attempting to enter that world of symbolically mediated experience must find shortcuts through abstractions within the context of his own culture's symbolization. A Beaver Indian cannot "tell you the meaning" of the vision quest and its symbols in your terms unless he has a symbolic key to unlock your experience; however, he can tell you about it in the terms through which he conceptualized it, those of his own experience and his culture's symbols. The anthropologist must take on trust that it is meaningful and find experiences and symbols that will bridge the cultural gap. I will try to communicate something I know is meaningful both to the Beavers and to me. My background as an anthropologist attempting to translate Beaver meanings includes my formal education, my experiences in Beaverland, and my experiences teaching Beaver ideas to others. My understanding of Beaver thought depends upon my willingness to take what they tell me seriously and personally (learning *from* them rather than merely *about* them) and my ability to find a symbolic framework that will encompass their experience, my own, and yours as well. There is no qualitative difference between the symbolic transformation involved in bridging the gap between my experience and yours and the transformation involved in bridging the gap between mine and theirs. We are all humans enclosed in the ultimate solitude of our subjectivities, but as humans we all share the common capacity for giving each other experiences through the interaction that symbols make possible.

You and I cannot directly enter each other's experiences, and I cannot recreate within you either my own life history or that of a Beaver Indian, but I can abstract and describe, through a medium common to our cultural understanding of each other, my understanding of the experiences of Beaver life within whose context their dreaming and singing are meaningful. The meaning of their symbols is neither imposed upon nor derived from but is rather inherent in the experiences of their lives. Thus, before I talk of symbolic abstractions, I must give you some idea of the way in which the reality of Beaver life is constructed. I will talk about how Beavers learn about being human. Being a male myself, my account will undoubtedly show a male bias and be more from the perspective of a boy growing up in Beaverland than of a girl. Crossing cultural gaps seems enough of a task at the moment without also crossing sexual ones. My neglect of women in this account does not imply that Beaver culture neglects women.

Human infants live in a world of experience unmediated by symbols, and Beaver infancy is not sufficiently distinct from our own (and no more easily fathomable) to warrant discussion on my part. I shall begin at the stage of life where experience begins to encounter symbol. A Beaver child generally sleeps with his mother and father until he is weaned, on the birth of a new baby. Later, he may sleep with an older brother, uncle, or grandfather until he moves into a camp that some unmarried boys have set up. His sleeping is as important to him, in its own way, as his daytime activity. Every night and day of his life impress upon him, gently and unselfconsciously, the unquestionable and almost unspoken realities of existence. Night comes when the sun sets (*sa na'a*, literally "daytime sun goes under"), each sunrise and sunset moving "one chicken step" toward its winter- or summertime turning point and each day increasing or decreasing in length according to season. While night lasts, the nighttime sun, *hatlege sa*, or "moon," is seen as it follows its own revolutions. It is the shadow of the sun just as "ghosts," about which a child hears much talk, are the shadows of men. The people always sleep toward the sunrise place in anticipation of the sun's return. The experience of sleeping in that way is so much a part of the background and fabric of life that a child can hardly be consciously aware of it, yet, as he will discover at some point in his life, it is as important to him and as unobtrusive as his breathing.

The dwellings in a typical Beaver nomadic camp are a sort of double lean-to with a fire in between the two halves. At times during the winter people may live in circular log tepees, more recently in log cabins. Now they rather confusingly find themselves in prefabricated government-designed pastel plywood boxes set in rows. The double lean-tos are still in use by some of the people some of the time, and I have lived in and around camps like the ones described here. Children do not seem to know that they sleep facing the sunrise place because, I think, they do not yet know what it means. Yet it is obvious to a child as he observes countless camps set up and struck on the family's yearly rounds that the orientation (an appropriate symbol from our own culture that you may have used without knowing what it meant) of a camp is part of the way things are. The living space of the camp and its relation to the cosmic cycles of sun and moon form a constant backdrop for the large and small events of a child's life.

Children can recognize men before they can understand them, for their understanding must ultimately come from within their own experience. A man is unmistakable because of his medicine bundle hanging behind where he sleeps and testifying to his existence even in his physical absence. Children are not told directly about the content or meaning of a medicine bundle, but many people my own age told me that as a child they had fooled around with the bundle of some relative and received a terrible fright because there were things in it that moved; they were alive. The medicine bundle usually hangs from one of the poles of the lean-to above where a man sleeps, and he leaves it there during the day when he is away from camp. Children know, from the very special way it is handled and referred to, that it is somehow connected with the deepest powers of an adult's understanding. In my own experience of Beaver camp life, the medicine bundle seemed a constant presence, and I picked up the quality of respect with which it is treated long before I knew anything about its symbolic meaning. A child feels its power as he might feel the power of a gun from the respect with which adults treat it.

Sometimes a child will find himself precipitated into the powers of the medicine bundle long before he begins to understand it. Nearly every Beaver child has at some time in his life been seriously ill, and in this uncertain and otherworldly state of mind has been touched by someone's medicine bundle. When this happens, the familiar yet mysterious medicine bundle leaps out at him from its place in the background of his everyday experience and touches him with the force of life and death. It is a reminder of the power that exists in the universe and of the understanding that he will seek as his experience grows.

Children learn from experience that the space behind where a man sleeps, behind his medicine bundle, is somehow different from the space in front of a camp. When families camp together no one puts his house between another's house and the sunrise place. There are no trails behind the houses. As a child learns the spaces within which people order their lives, he is also learning the spaces within which experience becomes symbol.

I am told that traditionally men and women, boys and girls, used different places for leaving and entering a house, men to the north and women to the south. The most important difference I observed between men and women in their use of space had to do with a distinction between bush and camp. On the camp side of a house there are trails connecting the houses of a camp together and leading from each to wood, water, and toilet. Everyone is free to walk these trails and it seems natural to follow them rather than strike out across unbroken terrain. On the other side of the house there are no regular trails. Men and children may walk there, but women, particularly women who might be menstruating, may not cross behind where a man sleeps, behind his medicine bundle. This means that for every camp there is a camp area where cooking, hide working, and other domestic activities take place and a bush area that is exclusive to the hunters. The camp is associated with women and family life and the bush with men and the animals they mysteriously go out to hunt and miraculously bring back to be transformed into food by the women.

From an early age children hear stories of giant animals that existed long ago and hunted men. They are told that these animals are still sometimes seen in the bush, that the culture hero, Usakindji, both divided and dispersed them in their present form and drove them to a place beneath the ground. The bush is a place that both surrounds and sustains every camp through the actions of men, and it is also the place where the creatures of the stories actually exist. It is an ultimate reality testified to by the past and surrounding the present, a place of living symbol, a mythic dimension. Ghosts are found in the bush, but they can only go around to the places where people used to camp along the trails of their own past lives. They pass through the bush but are not of it, and they seek the camps that are no longer there.

As children learn the physical layout of the world in which they play, they also begin to observe its immaterial terrain. Certain spaces belong to the activities of women and others to the activities of men. The medicine bundle links a man to the bush realm and the sunrise place, the world where giant animals may still be found and from which the actual animals he eats every day have come. Hardly a day passes without some mention of a dream and its possible relation to past, present, or future events. Nearly every time a hunter brings meat into camp he connects the event to his dreaming, and his dreaming is related to the bush through his medicine bundle. The north and east are associated with men, the south and west with women. This symbolic terrain is laid out in a variety of ways in the stories a child hears.

Singing and dreaming and eating, sunrise and sunset, birth and death, winter and summer, bush and camp, myth and experience build into a totality as a child grows. Dreaming, medicine bundles, and songs are a mystery to children, but not an exclusive one. They know them in their way and as they grow older they grow into knowledge appropriate to their new experiences. Even children under five often find themselves away from the trails of camp and into the bush realm, a symbolically charged transformation, although they may be barely out of earshot of their people. When it is discovered that a child has wandered into the bush, the parents think and dream about what animal might be calling him. As children grow older and begin to learn the stories, they are prepared, told to fast and abstain from drinking water, and sent out early in the morning to spend time alone in the bush. By the time a child is eight or ten he is ready to receive experiences that will change the character of his later life.

I cannot tell you what "really happens" to children in the bush, just as they cannot tell other people their experience directly. I was told that if a child has the right thoughts, if his head is in the right place, a medicine animal will come to him. There is a moment of meeting and transformation when he is "just like drunk" or in a dreamlike state. In this experience he can understand the animal's speech, and the animal speaks to him. It may seem to him that he stays with the animal for days or even weeks. The animal usually tells him when to leave, and when he starts to reenter everyday reality he lurks in the bush outside the people's camp, afraid of the smell of smoke and unable to understand human speech. Eventually the people spot him, bring him in, and give him food and water. An older man puts his medicine coat around him and he sleeps. When he wakes he has returned to the world of men. He can talk to them again, but he cannot reveal anything, because he has not fully understood what happened in the bush.

What actually happens in the bush? I believe that children do live with animals and learn to speak their language. If ethologists can do this, surely Indians, whose way of life brings them onto intimate terms with animals, can attain the same rapport. So much for the physical events that may happen. A more complex question is, What does it mean? I can only begin to answer that question, just as a Beaver child newly returned from the experience can only begin to learn the answers over the rest of his life. However, it is clear that the experience goes far deeper than learning the habits of animals and attaining a rapport useful for hunting in later life. Although it is all these things, it is also and more fundamentally the beginning of a path seeking to understand a person's own humanity. People do not find animals in themselves but rather begin to find themselves in the natures of animals. Each species has its unique and distinctive nature, and people can see in themselves qualities that are most like the qualities of a particular animal species. Animals, besides being themselves, are symbols for men of the varieties of human nature, and a man can learn his combination of qualities through getting close to the qualities of animals. The experience with a medicine animal in the bush is the culmination of childhood and the beginning of adulthood. Children do not find their medicines then, but they do find the path that will lead them to this discovery later on. It is a path of dreaming and singing.

Children no longer seek to live with animals after puberty. For a girl, puberty is marked by an important ceremony on her first menstruation, and for boys, the first kill of every major species of game is the occasion for a giveaway and dance. Their vision quest experiences are not exactly forgotten but are pushed to the background of an exciting, busy adolescence. When a boy-man becomes one of the core adults of a band and has his own children (sometimes not until

he is around thirty, as he is likely to marry an older widow first), the
experience of his preadolescent vision quest and postadolescent maturity come together in a powerful symbolic synthesis. He dreams.
Of course, he has always dreamed and he has known that dreams are
crystallizations of reality, but these first dreams of maturity are special because they show him his medicines with the clarity of wisdom
that adds a new direction to the innocence of childhood and to the
illumination of the vision itself. This clarity and wisdom can only
come when he has entered responsibly into the lives of others and
has learned to see himself in them. He has always in a sense known
his medicines, but now he knows what they mean. The path his life
has taken from the moment of his birth has come full circle, and he
is ready to begin other paths to the completion of other circles. In
the dreams he sees himself as a child living in the bush and knows
that the stories he has both taken for granted and taken literally are
about *him*. When he entered the world of animals as a child, he also
entered the stories. The animals he knows and *is* are the animals of
creation.

The knowledge that comes through dreaming is absolute because
it comes from a level of symbolic association that is deeper than
consciousness. Throughout Beaver life, this link through dreaming
to a level of absolute certainty is given the importance it deserves.
Dreams reveal the often hidden significance of events, and the im-
mediacy of their imagery is accepted as an important gift. In this
respect dreams, for the Beavers, are linked with songs, since songs
are experiences that convey the imagery of a dream into the conscious realm and allow this kind of experience to be communicated.
Both songs and dreams are paths that take one into the realm where
symbol and experience merge. The most important dreams a Beaver
can have are those in which he follows a song, for the thread of a
Beaver's song is the path his mind can take into the deepest realms
of his subjectivity and out to reach the subjectivities of others. It is
frustrating to have to use words to describe what must essentially be
heard and experienced, but you must use your imagination, and perhaps some experience with Indian music, to see how songs become
the medium of this inner journey. As you follow the turns of the
song and learn them, you are learning the inner paths of the mind.
The Beavers translate *songs* into English as *prayer*, because they reach
simultaneously inward and outward.

The Beaver word for medicine is *ma yine*, "his/its song," and the central symbol of a man's medicine dream is a song given to him by his medicine animal. The songs are those sung by the giant animals when they hunted men, and the medicine dream reveals that the childhood experience with the animals was also the mind's journey into its song. The dreams also reveal to a man how to assemble a medicine bundle of objects symbolizing the powers of the mythic animals and instruct him to avoid certain food or situations. By these signs other men know that he "knows something."

A man's medicine bundle hanging above where he sleeps toward the rising sun is a focus for his dreaming, a point at which the paths of thought and song begin and end. Through dreams, he can receive and assimilate the flow of events into a significant order. Let me try to explain my understanding of what is, after all, the innermost subjectivity of people in a culture very different from mine. Hunters nearly always say that a successful hunt has been preceded by a dream. Elsewhere, I interpreted this as an *ex post facto* claim for having caused the outcome (Ridington 1968: 1152–1160). Now I believe it would be more in line with what I know of their dreaming to say the dream grasps the essence of a particular moment rather than causing it in our objective sense of cause and effect. Perhaps it would be better to say that the dream brings an event into being from the multitudinous events of possibility. There are many more possible occurrences than can actually be realized, and in hunting, as in gambling, one seeks to know the dimensions of possibility and to know something of the odds with regard to various classes of possible events. There are many animals in the bush, and any one could be willing to give himself to the people.

When man and animal do meet it is a moment of transformation, like the moment of meeting in the vision quest, when the child enters the animal's world of experience and is devoured by another realm of consciousness. In hunting, the animal enters the man's experience and his meat is eaten by the people. Through their meeting the man can be instrumental in bringing into actuality a transformation that existed before only as a possibility, just as through the meeting of child and animal in the vision quest the child is given a path to the realization of his humanity. The vision quest symbolically transforms the child's meat into spirit, and the hunt transforms the animal's spirit into meat. But the moment of killing is also a moment of creation, for it brings potential into actuality, the manifesting into the manifested. The hunter's dreams come from the sunrise, the place where the new day is created, and come to him through his medicine bundle, the symbols of his entry into the world of animals and myth.

The Beavers symbolize the creative mystery of this transformation by saying that the shadows of animals killed in hunting return to the sky to be born again in the meat of another body. This completes and begins the circle of creation, for the animal's spirit continues its journeys through the people's respectful acceptance of its meat. That is why the Beavers place such a great emphasis on proper care of meat and respect to the remains left at the kill site. The hunter's dream is as much of a shadow waiting to be born as it is of an animal preparing to die. The dream does not cause the meeting between man and animal, but it puts them into the proper sense of under-standing that can make the meeting possible and meaningful. The dream emanates from an unconscious repository of the man's whole lifetime of experience and reaches out to touch a possible moment of creation. At every stage in his life his culture has provided symbols that help him organize and understand his experience, and these symbols are almost literally compacted and bundled together in a little pouch that hangs above his head as he sleeps in anticipation of the sun's return to the earth and an animal's return to the sky. The songs of his medicine are always in his inner ear, for they tell him what it is to be a man.

I have only once heard a Beaver medicine song, *ma yine*, for they stem from the deepest reaches of a person's subjectivity. They are the songs of the medicine animals within the man, and they well up and reach out only when he, or one close to him, is in some way close to death, either in a fight or grave illness or great need to succeed in hunting. The only time I heard them was when an old man was preparing to die. But although the medicine songs are seldom sung in public, they are always in a person's mind and in his dreams.

Ma yine carry a person's mind up and down the abysses of his subjectivity, but there are other gentler songs that reach out horizon-tally to touch the subjectivities of others through a sharing of com-mon experience. These are the songs a man sings in his camp when he is not out hunting, and the songs that bring people together to dance. They are called *ahata yine*, "God songs," or *nachene yine*, "Dreamer's songs," because they are brought back from heaven by a man who has died, a Dreamer or shaman. The Dreamer (*naáchin*) can bridge the gap between subjectivities because he has followed the vertical dimension of mind to its polar extremities and discovered that they form a circle into another dimension that links his mind to the minds of the people. He follows the inner path, led on by a song he hears in his dreams, to the point of death, the ultimate in subjective isolation but also the point of transformation, to find that beyond is a realm where all subjectivities merge into one. This is heaven (*yage*), from which Dreamers (actual men who are remembered by their descendants) have sent down a *nachene yine* whose turns are the path of heaven. If he can follow the song's path, "grab hold of it with his mind," in what we would call a state of trance or deep meditation and they call dreaming, he will return to the ordinary world as a Dreamer carrying a new song for the people.

Dreamers are the only men who may sleep toward the sunset. The ultimate source of Dreamers' songs is in the animal world, for they are the prayers that animals sing when they have hard times. The Dreamers in heaven have heard the animals dancing and singing and sent the songs down into the dreams of Dreamers on earth, who then give them to the people. Every song that the Beavers sing is both an animal's song and the song of a particular Dreamer. The songs bring people together to dance in prayer, and every man knows that when he dies he will follow the path of a Dreamer's song to heaven.

There is much more I could say about the penetration of dreaming and singing into every aspect of Beaver life, but in the short space remaining I would like to leave you with a description of a Beaver ceremonial. The Beavers dance, usually in a large tepee, clockwise or, as they say, "following the sun" around a fire. The fire is the center of the circle and its column of smoke joins heaven and earth, the axis of subjective experience. Extending horizontally out from the fire is a circle of people. The singers and drummers are mainly young adults, the hunters. They sit in the direction of the sunrise, just as they sleep in their own camps toward the sunrise. Older men sit toward the north, and the very old, as well as the Dreamer, if he is present, sit toward the sunset. Women and their children sit along the southern circumference of the circle, and the door is generally the dividing line between men and women.

The singing and dancing go on for three or four nights, and during the day the Dreamer may dream for the people or talk to them about his dreaming. The dance lodge is a ceremonial extension of the domestic camp, whose metaphor is extended to include all the people who have come together to dance. The singers sit to the east and sing, but instead of medicine bundles that bring medicine songs to their minds, they have drums that carry heaven songs out to the people. The dance is a hopping shuffle around the fire. They say it is walking to heaven. The rhythm is a steady, powerful beat, evocative of walking, and the melodic line with its intricate turns is the path that the animals, the Dreamer, and ultimately you, yourself, will follow.

The elements of Sekani religion that Jenness describes are not isolated culture traits, nor are they inaccessible to our understanding. Among the Beavers, personal medicines and public shamanism are parts of a single philosophy whose reality is grounded in common understandings about the meanings of dreams and songs. Both the hunter's personal medicine and the Dreamer's public medicine are songs that have been given in dreams. The hunter has learned through his vision quest to enter the cycle of death and creation that brings meat into camp to feed the people, while the Dreamer, through his own death, has been given the gift of guiding men through the experience of their anticipated death and creation.

Anthropologica, 1971

FROM HUNT CHIEF
TO PROPHET

Beaver Indian Dreamers and Christianity

At the time of contact with European civilization, Native people of the Canadian subarctic supported themselves by hunting and fishing. Their way of life was the product of adaptation over many millennia to the resource potential of the post-Pleistocene boreal forest environment. Their overall population density was among the lowest known, even among hunter-gatherers. In an area of two million square miles, aboriginal population may have been as low as sixty thousand (Helm 1981a: 1). People of the western and eastern subarctic spoke languages belonging to the Athapaskan and Algonquian families, respectively, but held many culture traits in common, suggesting that many "cultural core" features (Steward 1955: 93–94) were fundamental to the adaptive requirements of life in the boreal forest.

Despite their small overall numbers, northern forest hunters did not lead lonely or isolated lives. They were organized into small, kin-based bands of people who supported one another in their realization of the environment's resource potential. Hunting people of the North American boreal forest sensitively adjusted their activities to this resource potential. They maintained generally flexible patterns of association and a nomadic way of life as resources varied seasonally or from one area to another. They had (and retain) a clearly defined sense of territoriality in relation to local kin-based bands (Helm 1965: 380–382; Ridington 1969: 460–461; Riches 1982: 107–133; Ives 1985: 34–101).

The adaptive success of northern forest Indians depended particularly on the skill and knowledge of individual men and women (McClellan 1975: 66–67; Tanner 1979: 133–135; VanStone 1974: 121–122). Subsistence technology emphasized the possession of techniques rather than artifacts. The nomadic way of life placed a premium on the ability to create necessary artifacts from locally available materials. People generally found it more efficient to carry information from one location to another rather than to carry physical objects in their hands. Elsewhere I have suggested that

> in thinking about hunting and gathering people who must move
> frequently from place to place . . . technology should be seen as
> a system of knowledge rather than an inventory of objects . . .
> The essence of hunting and gathering adaptive strategy is to
> retain, and to be able to act upon, information about the pos-
> sible relationships between people and the natural environment.
> When realized, these life-giving relationships are as much the
> artifacts of hunting and gathering technology as are the material
> objects that are instrumental in bringing them about. (Riding-
> ton 1982a: 471)

Northern forest Indians were well aware that their means of production were mental as well as material. The world view of subarctic Natives reflected a complex and interdependent relationship between people and the natural environment (VanStone 1974: 59–60; Mc-Clellan 1975: 67–70; Tanner 1979: 108–111; Honigmann 1981: 724). In many subarctic cultures, children were sent out alone into the bush to gain "supernatural power" from animals or natural forces (Honigmann 1981: 718–719). This power symbolized the knowledge on which adaptive success depended. Among the Athapaskan-speaking Beaver Indians, people with power were said to "know something" (Ridington 1978a: 6–13, 1979: 3–6). McClellan and Denniston (1981: 385) report similar beliefs for Cordilleran Athapaskans, as do De Laguna and McClellan (1981: 647) for the Ahtna. Among both Athapaskans and Algonquians, mythical traditions about a transformative culture hero provided a model for the ability of humans to transform animals into food (Speck 1935: chap. 4; Ridington 1979: 5–7; McClellan and Denniston 1981: 385). Hunting was understood to be an essentially mental and spiritual activity that could succeed only through the hunter's special understanding of the environment and of the animal's state of mind. Animals, in turn, were believed to understand the hunter's state of mind and to give themselves only to people with whom they had made contact through dreams and visionary experiences (Honigmann 1981: 724; Tanner 1979: chap. 7).

Among the Naskapi (Speck 1935: chap. 6) and Mistassini Cree (Tanner 1979: chap. 6), divinatory techniques such as scapulimancy provided a means of contact between humans and the animate principles of their environment. Among the Beaver (Ridington 1971: 121–123), hunters encountered their game in dreams before the physical contact of the hunt itself. Dreaming was used as a way of visualizing and organizing the hunter's information about the complex pattern of potential relationships between humans and animals. A similar reliance upon dreaming the moment of contact between hunter and animal was deeply ingrained in the culture and experience of hunting people throughout the subarctic (Speck 1935: 91–92; Tanner 1979: 122–126; De Laguna and McClellan 1981: 647; Leacock 1981: 194).

Perhaps because our own culture is fundamentally dependent on the production, exchange, and possession of cultural artifacts, we are predisposed to overlook the artifice behind the technology of northern forest Indians and to disparage them for an apparent poverty of material possessions (Oswalt 1973: 150). A widely read survey of Native American cultures went so far as to contrast Inuit and subarctic interior Athapaskans as follows: "Unlike the Eskimo, whose mastery over their environment evokes great admiration, the interior Athabascans lack a precisely definable cultural base" (Spencer and Jennings 1977: 98). This view probably reflects our own culture's attention to material objects as defining characteristics of a culture's technology. We are predisposed to see artifacts and to ignore artifice. We tend to define technology as product rather than process.

Our bias is particularly pronounced when a culture's artifice is deployed in an environment that is totally unfamiliar to us. Such is the case with the knowledge and artifice possessed by northern hunting people. Rather than being deficient in their "mastery over their environment," northern forest hunters focused considerable attention on realizing the resource potential of that environment. They were perfectly aware that knowledge defined their technology. Although the ethnographic evidence of their adaptive reliance on knowledge has long been available to academic anthropology (McClellan and Denniston 1981: 377), this information has not always translated easily into our own organizational categories. These categories have sometimes led scholars to class knowledge associated with supernatural power as "religion" rather than "adaptation" (VanStone 1974: chaps. 4, 8).

Northern forest hunters, like other hunting and gathering people, depended fundamentally on knowledge and technique in their successful adaptation to the environment. Although they were capable of producing elaborate hunting implements such as bows and arrows, traps, and deadfalls (Oswalt 1973: 118–119), they also achieved complex interactions with their environment without having recourse to complex material artifacts. Northern hunters often carried out elaborately organized communal hunts with a minimum of material possessions. Artifacts as simple as snares, for instance, were deployed in communal hunts that required a number of people to work quietly and autonomously toward a common purpose. Coordination of their activities required complex mutual understandings of human and animal behavior in relation to environmental features. Although the physical artifact required for this form of hunting was minimal, success depended upon a complex and sophisticated form of artifice and understanding (McClellan and Denniston 1981: 377).

Activities of northern hunting people were not organized hierarchically or directed from above by a superordinate authority. Relations of power as opposed to those of hierarchical authority were highly elaborated. The cultural category of "supernatural power" or "medicine" reflected both overall competence and the social power that belonged to people of recognized aptitude and accomplishment (Ridington 1968: 1152–1154; Black 1977a: 141–151; Smith 1973: 10). In a classic paper on Native American concepts of power and authority, Miller (1955: 278–283) argues that ideas about supernatural power and an animate cosmos were important in coordinating collective actions among Woodland Indians such as the Fox. Even within the context of village life, they developed decision-making institutions based on consensus rather than coercion. They recognized the power of both ceremonial and secular leaders without giving over to them superordinate and coercive authority. The systems of government he describes for Woodland Indians seem to be elaborations of ideas and institutions deeply ingrained in northern hunting cultures (VanStone 1974: 74–76; Leacock 1981: 191; Honigmann 1981: 737).

People in northern hunting cultures expected one another to act with a minimum standard of intelligence in relation to mutually held understandings about the potential of any given situation. They expected their fellow humans to act with "sapient intelligence," using information coded into the "cultural intelligence" available to them (Ridington 1982b: 41). Observably unintelligent behavior was recognized and ridiculed. In defense against such ridicule or worse, a person invariably explained his or her misfortunes with an accusation that it was caused by another person's malevolent use of medicine power. Elsewhere (Ridington 1968), I have presented a full account of the "medicine fight" as an instrument of political process among the Beaver.

In accordance with their fundamental respect for personal autonomy (Honigmann 1981: 737), and lack of institutions based on superordinate authority (Leacock 1981: 191), the world view reported for many subarctic Natives was integrated by ideas we generally associate with animism and shamanism (Speck 1935; Tanner 1979; Smith 1973; Ridington 1971). They viewed the environment as being composed of sentient and living entities with whom humans could make contact through dreaming, visionary experience, or divinatory techniques. Such contact was seen as an extension of the mutual understandings through which individuals coordinated their activities. Humans were expected to share an underlying mentality with the powers and beings of their environment, just as they shared such an understanding with one another.

Shamanism may be seen as a technique for commenting on or even furthering mutual understandings. Shamans are described as knowing how to find the mental or spiritual pathways that connect all sentient beings. Eliade wrote that a form of "individual shamanism" was fundamental to all Native American hunting cultures. He described the shaman as a "psychopomp" or spiritual guide (Eliade 1964: 297, 182). He suggested that the more formal procedures of shamanic practitioners arose from an underlying assumption about the possibility of a spiritual and mental relationship between people

and the world of nature. Both individual shamanism and that prac-
ticed in aid of others in distress made use of "magical flights," in
which the shaman's mind slipped away from its body's physical location in time and space to encounter the mental and spiritual essence of other beings in other times and places.

DREAMING IN TRADITIONAL BEAVER INDIAN CULTURE

Dreams and the experience of vision quest training during childhood
were central to Beaver adaptive competence. Beaver men and women
obtained "supernatural power" from childhood vision quest encounters with the mythical representatives of animals and natural forces
(Ridington 1971: 120–123, 1983a: 70–71). As adults, they drew
upon these powers to assist them in hunting, healing, and success in
all other endeavors. Dreams, in particular, provided a means of ac-
cessing these powers and aided people in processing the culture's
store of information about the continuously unfolding pattern of
human and animal trails (Ridington 1980a).

The Beavers traditionally viewed hunting as a complex pattern of
connection between the trails of people, animals, and primary celestial bodies. Like many Native peoples (Whorf 1936: 57–64; Witherspoon 1977: 1–46), they believed that events must take place in
the mind before they can be realized in substance. They believed that
stories about the activities of supernatural beings in mythical time
provided essential information about the unfolding of events in ordinary time and space.

Dreams were essential to Beaver technology. The individual hunter
was expected to dream the point of contact between his own trail
and that of an animal. In order to facilitate this essential dream experience, hunters slept with their heads toward the place where the
sun was expected to rise in the morning. The sun's path was believed
to be the trail of Saya, the culture hero and a spiritual personification
of the sun. Saya's own vision quest is credited with first establishing
the relationship between hunters and their game. Beaver oral traditions describe Saya as the first man to follow the trails of animals.
The attitude of anticipation taken during sleep indicated the hunter's
hope that his dreams would reveal the pattern of his future hunt and
that he too would make contact with the trails of animals. By antici-

pating a point of contact with the sun's path across the heavens, hunters sought to give anticipatory power to their dream contact with the paths of animals.

The Beaver people understood that in their dreaming the mind was released from its task of processing information from the immediate perceptual environment. In the dream state, it could process internally generated information recalled from past experience and integrate this with traditional cultural knowledge to develop a strategy related to the environment as a whole (Ridington 1979: 8–9). A person with the ability to think and plan through dreaming was said to "know something." The essence of this knowledge was communicated in myths about the culture hero and his encounters with the various medicine animals in mythical times. Individuals came into possession of such knowledge through their own vision quest experiences, just as Saya came to "know something" from the first vision quest. Both men and women used dreaming to focus and activate the knowledge and power obtained through their vision quests (Ridington 1983a). Such knowledge may be seen as a form of cultural intelligence that instructed a person's own sapient intelligence (Ridington 1979: 9, 1982b: 41–42).

Communication between people hunting together required a high level of mutual understanding about time, season, and direction as well as about animal behavior and human relationships. Surround hunting, for instance, required that participants understand each other's movements without recourse to spoken communication. Even the modern rifle-hunting technique of circling back upon a game trail is often done by several hunters who coordinate their efforts in relation to shared understandings of the immediate situation. When weather conditions permitted, hunters took their physical direction by reference to the sun's position in relation to season and time of day, just as they took spiritual direction from dreaming and from their own vision quests, which were modeled after Saya's vision quest.

Mutual understandings were furthered by oral traditions. The meaning of the vision quest experience as a form of empowerment was conveyed most succinctly in the Beaver creation story and in a cycle of stories about Saya. These stories revolve around themes of shamanic transformation. They instructed people in the use of their culture as an empowering system of intelligence. The creation story, a version of the "earth diver" motif, tells how Muskrat brings up a speck of dirt from beneath a primordial body of water. The creator then places it at the center of a cross he draws upon the water's surface. Muskrat's action in the story suggests the shaman's ability to perform a "magical flight" to a hidden world. The story describes the physical world growing from a point where two lines meet, just as the hunt grows from a point where the trails of man and animal come together in dreaming. Both the moment of creation and the death of an animal are significant points of transformation that humans can understand through myth, visionary experience, and dreaming.

Another key story that suggests the importance of knowledge to shamanic transformation describes Saya's vision quest, which began when he was a boy named Swan. Through the intervention of a guardian spirit, the master of the migratory water birds, Swan lived through a winter of isolation to become Saya, the transformer who journeys across the sky as the sun and moon. Like the swans from whom he took his first name, Saya was empowered by his vision quest to fly between earth and heaven and from one season to another. Both creation and culture hero stories describe significant dimensions of the ideal shaman's personality. Muskrat dives down beneath the surface of an undifferentiated primordial water to bring up the seed of substance, while Swan flies up from this world to bring down the spirit songs of people in heaven.

The creation and culture hero stories taught generations of Beaver Indians how imagination and culturally instructed intelligence defined the place of humans as transformers of the world. They explained an association between personal transformative experience and the ability to control the transformation of the natural environment into a cultural one. The vision quest was a central, empowering, transformative experience in which the meaning of the creation and culture hero stories became central to the individual's personal sense of meaning. The stories provided a model for the adaptive artifice required of nomadic hunting people.

During times remembered by contemporary Beaver Indians, individual hunters were expected to use their personal powers to "dream ahead" in order to make contact with animals whose transformed bodies would give life to the people. Beaver oral traditions also recall a time, said to precede their involvement in the fur trade, when communal hunting was more common. In the communal hunt, special people known as Dreamers used their powers to "dream for everybody" (Ridington 1978a: 76). Like individual hunters, they used dreams to visualize a pattern of relationship between humans, animals, and the sun, but their dreaming also visualized a more complex social integration of the many people required for communal hunting techniques, such as drives or surrounds. The dreaming of these hunt chiefs represented an intelligence within the community, above and beyond the personal "knowing something" derived from the individual vision quest and accessed in the dreaming of a single hunter.

Like Dreamers of more recent times, the hunt chiefs are described as having an ability to travel in their dreams along Yagatunne, the "trail to heaven." The traditions suggest that their power was derived from vision quest encounters with Swan, the only bird said to "fly through to heaven without dying." The story of Swan-Saya suggests that a childhood visionary encounter with the power of swans could give a human the power of magical flight between worlds. An essential element of the Dreamer's power, according to Beaver tradition, was his initiatory experience of death, a journey to the spirit world and subsequent return to life in his same body. Thus, Dreamers may be thought of as "swan people," according to Beaver symbolism. Charlie Yahey, the Dreamer with whom I worked in the late 1960s, described swans as follows:

> Not only us pray to God. Even swans when they have hard luck in the fall time and they starve, they can just go right through to heaven without dying. Swans are the only big animals that God made that can go to heaven without dying. It is the only bird that can go right through without dying. Swans are hard to get for food. They go right through the sky. They catch them and want to make them go in big groups so there will be lots again. Saya wanted big groups of swans in heaven so there would be lots up there, and that is why there are only a few that he kept on earth. Most of them are up in heaven; only a few down here. In fall time the swans always go late. When they have a hard time in fall they pray to God in their own way and they go to heaven without dying. (Ridington 1978a: 87)

Swans are regarded as the masters of all migratory water birds. They fly with the seasons from one country to another. Although the Beaver people did not know of their wintering territory directly, they were able to infer that somewhere to the south a land of flowing water must exist. They reasoned that, similarly, a spirit world must exist beyond the sky because of the Dreamer's magical flight from his body and his subsequent return. Swans, like Saya, were seen to fly in a circle from one season to another. Like the Dreamer, they could fly to heaven and return in the same body.

Swans and other migratory water birds fly in organized groups behind a leader. The Beaver people viewed their Dreamers as spiritual leaders capable of seeing ideal patterns of relationship between people. They recognized a Dreamer's association with Swan as an appropriate metaphor of his ability to bring people into relationship. They operated under a metaphoric logic based on the deeply held cultural belief that animals only give themselves to people who are generous and cooperative with one another. By the logic of their belief that success in hunting follows collective action based on mutual understandings, the Beaver attributed lack of success to misunderstanding, disharmony, and a lack of generosity. The Dreamer exhorted people to be generous and cooperative. He urged them to live in harmony and order, like the swans and geese. He taught that easy access to animals depended upon a cooperative attitude between people.

The Dreamer was also a ceremonial leader who brought people together to sing and dance in the belief that an affirmation of interpersonal harmony and cooperation would further a giving relationship between people and animals. He warned that world destruction would result from selfishness and hostility. The prophetic oratory I recorded described the Dreamer's experience of the trail to heaven. The Dreamer made his way along this trail by holding onto the songs in his dreams. People could then dance to them along a common trail around the fire. Charlie Yahey described the experience of getting songs as follows: "They just go up, they just sleep and they get those songs. They go up there in dream. They go up there in dream and grab those songs. They haul them down and come back. Then they get up, just like right now when we sing, it is just like we knew that song before" (Ridington 1978a: 66).

MAKENUNATANE, THE DREAMER

According to Beaver oral tradition, an important Dreamer was alive at the time of their first contact with European technology and later made direct contact with European traders. His name was Makenunatane. This name was his special Dreamer's name. It means literally "his tracks earth trail" (*muh ke nun atunne*). A freer translation might be, "his trail circles around the edge of the world." The name suggests the trail of Saya, who circles around the world's rim as the sun. It refers to the Dreamer's ability to see the unfolding of events on a trail that circles ahead over the horizon's edge. It evokes the hunter's reference to knowledge of the sun's return as manifested in the direction of his sleeping.

In English, Makenunatane is referred to as the Sikanni Chief. (There is a Sikanni Chief River north of Fort St. John, British Columbia.) I assumed this name meant he was a Sekani Indian chief in reference to the neighboring Athapaskan Sekani, "people of the contoured rocks" (Jenness 1937: 5), until I read an excerpt from a 1799 North West Company journal from "the Rocky Mountain Fort . . . built on the south side of the Peace River near the eastern end where the river cuts its way through the mighty barrier of the Rockies." The author of this journal referred to a band chief who traded in the post as "the Cigne [Cygne]" (O'Neil 1928: 251, 255). Clearly, this man was being called the French word for Swan, but the orthography used by the journal writer, an Anglophone, indicates that he pronounced the name cig-ne. This is very close in sound to, although different in spelling from, Makenunatane's English name, the Sikanni Chief.

At the very least, the journal reference indicates that a prominent band leader trading into the Rocky Mountain Fort was called Swan. It seems likely that the name in French was a translation of his name or title in Beaver. He must, therefore, have been a Dreamer or someone associated with the swan's power to fly from one world to another and return as a guide. It is tempting to speculate that "the Cigne" and Makenunatane, the Sikanni Chief, were one and the same person. If such an identification is correct, it provides documentary verification of the Beaver tradition that Makenunatane was the first Dreamer to integrate European technology, institutions, and ideas into their existing traditions of shamanism and animism.

Beaver oral tradition relates that Makenunatane's dreaming gave him the power of prophecy. He is said to have known through dreams that the whitepeople would be setting up trading posts in Beaver territory. He is also credited with having been like Jesus in foretelling that he would die through the action of a person close to him. The stories about his life and death reflect both the traditional role of the Dreamer as hunt chief and his enhanced role as a prophet who integrates new experiences into traditional ideas of mythical and visionary empowerment. The following are segments of stories told by three elders in the 1960s about the life and death of Makenunatane.

The name of Makenunatane was called. Something is happening around here. They all look after it. One time Makenunatane went to sleep for a long time. The people looked after him always. Around noon the next day in his dream he went to heaven. It was a long ways back so he couldn't make it back soon. They knew he was still living but he was someplace, a long ways in his dreams. They looked after him and knew he was in heaven because they could see in his throat it was moving. They just kept watching him. His throat was still moving always so they just watched him and finally about noon he was himself again.

His dream came down again. In his dream he came down and he slept again. Then he sat up and started singing. He woke up and sat up and started singing. He sang that song and told about it. He told people about heaven. Everything what is wrong and bad. That person was called Makenunatane.

He told them to eat whatever has been killed by an axe. They told him, "They will listen to you if they do that." It was sure cold for them but some of them did not believe him. Some of them thought that he was just saying that. Some others thought, "He is the one who said this so let us go look for something with just an axe." They just took an axe and looked for something.

They followed a fresh moose track and from the tracks they knew it was a good moose. Some of them stood so as to form a surround, and one old man with an axe stood one place by the tree and saw the moose running toward him. He stood well behind that tree and held the axe. Then he threw the axe at the moose and it stuck in the moose. Pretty soon that moose fell down. He threw that axe and it stuck into him. Pretty soon that moose fell down and they all gathered around the moose, butchered it and took home lots of meat. (Ridington 1979: 78–79)

The story segments given above describe Makenunatane's initiation as a Dreamer. He gains the power to instruct people in communal hunting through a shamanic experience of death, magical flight, and return to earth in the same body. The image of killing an animal with an axe indicates that the moose allowed itself to be taken by hunters under the Dreamer's direction. The power attributed to him in the story is similar to that of the culture hero, in that both use their supernatural powers to assist others in hunting. Both are guides who know the trail ahead farther than ordinary people. Saya knows the sun's trail that circles the world. The Dreamer knows Yagatunne, the trail to heaven. Beaver oral traditions describe Makenunatane as both a hunt chief, with the ability to dream ahead for the benefit of an entire community, and a prophet, who informs people about the Europeans and their new technology. If Makenunatane is the same person as "the Cigne" of 1799, he could very likely have been the incumbent hunt chief in an upper Peace River band at the time of first contact.

Stories of Makenunatane's physical death describe a very different relationship between people and the environment than the one in which the hunt chief used his power to direct people in communal hunting. Significant elements of the story are as follows:

That man, that man who killed Makenunatane, he knew something too. That was his daughter's husband. He was a good man. In the winter he went up to the Sikanni Chief River. Makenunatane started to sing in the morning. "Just like the boss came to me," he said. "God came to me in the morning and he told me, 'You won't suffer anymore. Just like God's son, he will kill you too.'"

Makenunatane and his son-in-law started to hunt. Makenunatane went to a different place. He saw the fresh tracks of two elk. He went one way and his son-in-law went another. "Sazin! [my daughter's husband!] You go around the other way." The Sikanni Chief followed the tracks and saw them go up the mountain. He went up after them. He kept tracking the elk. He put his axe handle in the tracks to see if they were frozen. That way he could tell how fresh they were. He followed the tracks into a little stand of spruce.

Makenunatane was wearing a long coat made out of a Hudson's Bay blanket. His Sazin had come around below the spruce. He saw something move there and he shot. He shot Makenunatane in the stomach. He should have followed him but instead he went around. At that time there was not much food. Two people couldn't afford to hunt in the same place. People had to hunt just like the lynx. That way maybe one would be lucky and then everybody would eat. (Ridington 1978a: 101)

The story of Makenunatane's death contains several significant references to the profound changes said to have taken place during his lifetime. As a Dreamer whose initiatory power was reputed to have been acquired in the period before his people were directly involved in the fur trade, Makenunatane encouraged the cooperation and mutual understandings required for communal hunting. As a prophet who died after the fur trade had already profoundly altered Beaver technology, Makenunatane is portrayed as hunting alone, "just like the lynx." Makenunatane wore a Hudson's Bay Company blanket rather than the traditional shaman's coat. He used a gun. He tested an elk's tracks with the handle of what was probably a metal trade axe. The story says that because "at that time there was not much food," Makenunatane and his son-in-law could not afford to hunt in the same place. Both are described as hunting with the new firearms brought by Europeans. The game available to them is reported to have been seriously depleted, possibly as a result of increased hunting pressure associated with provisioning the fur trade.

The stories about his accomplishments as a hunt chief describe Makenunatane's ability to visualize the pattern of an ideal surround, in which people understood one another and their mutual situation perfectly. They describe his prophetic abilities in relation to communal hunting. The story of his physical death describes an opposite situation. The Dreamer died of a gunshot wound because of a single hunter's tragic lack of shared mutual understanding. During Makenunatane's life as a hunt chief, people followed his vision to bring themselves and the animals into an ideal relationship. At the time of his death, his hunting companion was unable to understand even the simple situation of his own position in relation to an animal and one other person. Firearms have the power to bridge a physical distance between hunter and game, but in so doing they diminish the spiritual relationship of knowledge and mutual understanding upon which success in hunting once depended. Makenunatane's life and death illustrate the profound adaptive changes people of his generation must have experienced.

FROM HUNT CHIEF TO PROPHET

According to the Beaver traditions cited above, contact with European artifacts and institutions brought an end to their communal hunting technology. Contact also challenged them to adapt familiar ideas and roles to new situations. During the fur trade period, they continued to live in autonomous nomadic bands and to derive most of their food and income from hunting and trapping on the land, but their means of obtaining a living during this period were radically transformed by new productive means and purposes. Later generations of Beaver Indian thinkers interpreted and perhaps elaborated on the life and death of Makenunatane, as passed on in oral tradition, in order to understand the changes that were being thrust upon them. They credit him with being the first in a long line of Dreamers known primarily as prophets. This assertion reflects their recent history and should not be taken as evidence that prophets did not exist in earlier times. Indeed, other and probably earlier generic stories refer directly to the prophetic powers of people not identified with the present prophet tradition (Ridington 1968).

European artifacts and institutions initially challenged the entire structure of Beaver thought and experience. Guns and snare wire and steel axes were objects that soon became essential means of production, but the Beaver people had no stories with which to explain them. The new artifacts could not be created from locally available materials using knowledge and power acquired in the vision quest and its associated instruction. They were not part of the cultural information contained in the stories of Saya and his travels. They were artifacts for which the Beaver people had no artifice.

When their common purpose no longer lay in communal hunting but in responding to the new European artifacts and institutions, the Beaver people turned to their Dreamers for new metaphors that would bring them together in common purpose once again. In particular, they looked for the story that would give meaning to the new artifacts and institutions. Rather than abandon their view that knowledge, power, and mythical authority underlie the world of substance, they turned to their Dreamers for information about the source of the whiteman's power. The story their Dreamers identified was that of Christianity. The whiteman's equivalent of Saya was Jesus, the culture hero who showed people a "straight cut to heaven" (Ridington 1978a: 67). Saya traveled to heaven in a circle like the sun, but Jesus could go straight through like a bullet. Charlie Yahey described his understanding of Jesus in relation to the creation and culture hero stories as follows:

> For a long time there was nobody going to his place. He was just up there by himself. God was alone there. On his earth there was nothing and he was alone in his heaven. God himself made one road but his son made a shortcut road. God made one that is a long way. And when Jesus got up he took a shortcut so he wanted some people down here to know which was God's road and which the one that Jesus made back to heaven, the shortcut. So he made some men to be prophets and dream about him and heaven. Before that prophets just knew the long road. When he made more prophets they took his dreams. He wanted them to dream about him so he wrote those things down on paper. That is the way he made some men to be prophets. (Ridington 1978a: 77)

Charlie Yahey sang "Dreamer's Songs" while playing a double-sided drum made by his teacher, a Dreamer named Kayan. The drum was painted with two designs. Both designs center on the image of an even-armed cross and show pathways leading toward a circular horizon. The Dreamer explained them as drawings of Yagatunne, the trail to heaven. He described his own experience of being a Dreamer:

> A person who is a prophet doesn't just dream for himself. He dreams for everybody. It would be good if someone helped the prophet try to tell the people to be good. Make them think about God always all along this road. Not long ago when I was small I started to get one song, the first one. I sang other songs

from other Dreamers too, when I was small. Now I know all these songs. I know how to make songs. When I was small I started to learn all those songs and I knew how to dream. After that when I got a little bit older I knew how to sing all those songs and after that I was able to dream, to know the things that will happen before me. Since I was young I didn't just start to sing. I learned it in my dream.

Even some people that can read don't know what is going to happen to us. After the first whitemen came lots of people have dreamed like me. God wanted some of the people to know what was happening through their dreams. Before that all the Indians used to kill each other. After that one of them started dreaming there was God. Some of them believed that man and there was no more war, no more killing. They stopped those wars. They didn't want any more wars or medicine killings to be done. They started to believe in God. Before that they didn't know there was a God. (Ridington 1978a: selections from 68–86)

Sometime in the nineteenth century, Dreamers began recording their experiences of the trail to heaven by drawing them on moose hide. These drawings were modeled after the "Catholic ladder," a pictorial catechism used by oblate missionaries to instruct Native people and others outside the literate tradition. The original catechisms depicted biblical history, from Creation to the institutional traditions of the Catholic Church, using a metaphor of lineal and progressive history. The Dreamers abandoned this lineal metaphor and used the medium to depict the Dreamer's shamanic flight to heaven. Many Dreamers even began conducting services modeled after the Catholic mass. The following story told by Augustine Jumbie illustrates a Dreamer's syncretic use of Catholic and Native images in the early years of this century.

One time some Chichodi [a band for whom Tuchodi Lake is named] people came to see Decutla. "Decutla, we're hungry." "All right," Decutla said. "You go to church. I will find game. Come on now. I'll see. Today I will have church. Next time, don't lie, don't steal, don't kill. People killing is no good. All right, I'll see now." Those Chichodi men were just skinny. All their dogs had died. Decutla sang a little bit and had church all night. Then he said, "Three men should try to go hunt. Maybe one man will get two cow moose, one will get a goat, one will get a moose, a fat one, too." "Sure?" they said. "Sure," Decutla said.

They went out and one man got two cow moose, one man got a goat, and one man got a big bull moose with lots of fat. It was wintertime and it had lots of fat. Nighttime came and the men went home. The man who got the bull moose came to see Decutla and shook hands with him. "Decutla, that's good," he said. "Bull moose I catch. All fat. Lots of fat on the legs." "Next time," Decutla said, "don't fight anymore. Don't make any more trouble." Decutla gave them something to put in their pockets.

One time the Indian Agent and the Bishop came to Fort Nelson. They had heard about Decutla and wanted to see him. Archie Gardner lived in Nelson and he could talk Slavey, Sekani, Cree, and English. He and my brother Joe Bigfoot and I took the Bishop and the Indian Agent to visit Decutla. We went by boat to where he was staying. When we got there he was smoking. The Bishop said, "Decutla, I would like to see something." "Aha, good. Too many roads now. Too many people in boats. Maybe tomorrow. Just quiet then." "All right, tomorrow. What time?" "Eight o'clock. I give you something to eat. Slavey come, too."

At eight o'clock the next morning they came again. They just talked and talked until one. All day, Decutla had church. He didn't eat. All day he sang. Finally it was time for the whitemen to leave. "Ah, good," they said. Then they shook hands with Decutla. The Indian Agent said to him, "You're just like my daddy. I'd like to see your letter." He wanted to see the moosehide Decutla had with a picture of heaven on it. That is the same moosehide I have now. Decutla told him, "All right. Everybody should be quiet. At dinnertime you can see it." He was just like a Father in church. Lots of people came to see it. Everybody knelt down, made the sign of the cross. Decutla talked. Then he showed the moosehide. "This is not this place, this earth," he said. "This is God's Place. Wherever you stay, God's Place is right here. It is just like the window in a house. Just like in sleep it came to me."

The next year the Bishop came. "That moosehide, I buy-em," he said. Decutla told him, "That is Indian's Church. I can't sellem. If I sell this, there will be no moose in this country, no chicken, no bear, no caribou, no sheep, no beaver. Everything will be gone. I can't sell it. How are we going to eat?" "All right," the Bishop said and shook hands with Decutla. That moosehide was just like this one [pointing to a Catholic ladder hanging on his wall]. (Ridington 1978a: 103–104)

The Dreamer continued to be an important figure in the Beaver Indian communities of British Columbia until the early 1970s, when Charlie Yahey died. Dreamer's songs are still being sung, and tape recordings I made of Charlie Yahey's songs and oratory are in wide circulation. During the last decade, several Beaver communities have been strongly influenced by evangelical Protestant sects. Many people have given up their identity as "Catholics" to become "Christians." They have not, however, given up their belief in the Dreamers and their teachings. Instead, people are reinterpreting the Charlie Yahey texts and taped oratory in terms relevant to their evangelical experience. My own presence as documentarian and supporter of the prophet tradition has certainly had some influence on the contemporary move to recontextualize the prophet's message within evangelical Christianity. "Christians" now study the recordings I made of Charlie Yahey's oratory in relation to their own knowledge of stories about Makenunatane and the other prophets in order to verify their new faith as genuinely Indian. Possibly, this new syncretism will be as effective as the one begun by Makenunatane.

CONCLUSION

Northern Athapaskan hunting people are flexible and resilient in their response to changes in the resource potential of their environment. Their culture at the time of contact with Europeans was undoubtedly the product of adaptive changes and adjustments spanning millennia. The fundamental and underlying principle of their adaptation was a reliance on artifice rather than artifact. They valued knowledge and information as the fundamental instruments of a successful adjustment to the demands of the nomadic hunting way of life. When European artifacts and institutions altered their relationship to the environment, they sought to adapt in ways that were familiar. Rather than give up their underlying assumption that technology derives from knowledge coded in mythical tradition and the quest for supernatural power, they sought out stories that explained the whiteman's power.

Hunt chiefs like Makenunatane became prophets and trading chiefs. According to Beaver oral tradition, people at the time of first contact turned to their Dreamers for knowledge of the newcomers and the artifacts they offered. Makenunatane is credited with foretelling the coming of the whitemen in his dreams. He redirected dream plans of communal hunting to the purpose of trading for the new resources brought by Europeans. He is also credited with beginning a tradition of prophecy based upon the "shortcut to heaven" associated with Jesus and Christianity. Oral tradition credits him with foretelling that he would die like Jesus. Although the full syncretism of Christianity and Native tradition undoubtedly took several generations and was only fully developed after contact with oblate missionaries in the later years of the nineteenth century (Faraud 1866), Makenunatane may very well have personally experienced the transformation from hunt chief to prophet. The prophet tradition is currently being reinterpreted in the language of evangelical Christianity. Only time will tell if new prophets will be called to speak about the new synthesis.

Arctic Anthropology, 1987

TECHNOLOGY, WORLD VIEW, AND ADAPTIVE STRATEGY IN A NORTHERN HUNTING SOCIETY

Anthropologists often refer to material culture as technology. They describe technology in terms of artifacts rather than by reference to the artifice that underlies them. I suggest that a culture's technology should be seen as a part of its overall adaptive strategy. In particular, world view and beliefs may contribute to the success of an adaptive strategy. Nomadic hunting and gathering societies seem particularly to value the possession of technical knowledge over the possession of material artifacts. Evidence for this argument is drawn from a description of Beaver Indian world view in relation to their adaptive strategy.

In the development of anthropology as a discipline, the study of technology ranks with studies of language, kinship, customs, and social organization as a central field of inquiry. As Fenton (1974) points out in an essay on the history of material culture studies in anthropological research, the involvement of many early anthropologists in museum work nourished a strong interest in what has been called (almost interchangeably) material culture or technology. Otis T. Mason's evolutionary approach to material culture studies, first published in 1895, was called *The Origins of Invention*, indicating an interest in both the product and the process of technology. By the middle of the twentieth century, the *American Anthropologist*'s decennial index had replaced its earlier separate headings of "material culture" and "technology" with a single category, the evidently more scientific-sounding term "technology" (Fenton 1974: 20).

More recently, studies of material culture in the evolutionary tradition begun by Mason were written by Wendell Oswalt in 1973 and 1976. In both of these, *Habitat and Technology* and *An Anthro-*

pological Analysis of Food-Getting Technology, Oswalt assumed that the complexity of food-getting techniques could be measured by rating the artifacts of material culture in terms of their complexity, according to what he called their constituent "technounits"—"an integrated, physically distinct, and unique structural configuration that contributes to the form of a finished artifact" (Oswalt 1976: 38). Oswalt's work is really a study of material culture from an evolutionary point of view rather than a more general comparison of food-getting techniques in relation to the evolution of overall adaptive strategies. He argues that "the elaboration of skills and the expansion of knowledge required to produce artifacts are undeniably among the most remarkable of all human developments" (Oswalt 1976: v).

One of the few writers to address directly the relationship between material culture and technology is Robert Spier. In *From the Hand of Man* (1970), Spier clearly states that material culture is a *product* of technology, not synonymous with it. Technology is seen as an activity or process, while artifacts are the product of that process (Spier 1970: 2–14). A similarly processual definition of technology is given by Lechtman (1977) in her essay "Style in Technology." According to her, "artifacts are the products of appropriate culture performance, and technological activities constitute one mode of such performance . . . technologies are performances; they are communicative systems, and their styles are the symbols through which communication occurs. The relationships among the formal elements of the technology establish its style, which in turn becomes the basis of a message on a larger scale" (Lechtman 1977: 12–13).

Another attempt to connect the material and mental aspects of technology was made by Miles Richardson (1974) in his introduction to a collection of essays on material culture, *The Human Mirror*. Richardson argued, "Tools, concepts and language are all made of the same stuff; all are symbols taken out of the mind and impressed onto material, behavior or sound waves . . . Material culture is at the final point in the process of extrinsic symbolization; it represents the fullest expression of man's efforts to objectify his concepts. Once this objectification takes place, material culture becomes a mirror that man may view to find out about himself—not only about his technical ingenuity, but also about how he, the symbol user, came to be, about the awful mystery of being human" (Richardson 1974: 4–5).

While it is now fashionable among students of technology to look at the symbolic meaning of artifacts, few recent writers in the field have thought seriously about investigating the technological meaning of symbol systems. Studies of technology still focus on artifacts rather than artifice. They focus on physical tools rather than on the strategic application of cultural knowledge as being at the heart of technology. The study of symbol systems is left largely to the mythologists and symbolic anthropologists, even though within that tradition there are strong suggestions that mythic beliefs and practices might be viewed as a form of technology. Throughout the writing of Lévi-Strauss, for instance, one may trace the thread of an argument, begun in *The Savage Mind* (1966), that mythic thinking is a "science of the concrete," but the idea seems to have intrigued students of myth more than students of technology.

Perhaps because our own culture is obsessed with the production, exchange, and possession of artifacts, we inadvertently overlook the artifice behind technology in favor of the artifacts that it produces. This artifactual chauvinism within our culture makes it particularly difficult for us to understand the technological artifice of many nomadic hunting and gathering people, for whom material possessions that must be carried are a necessary burden rather than "goods" of unquestioned value. Among such people, artifacts that must be carried from place to place have a high cost in that they compete with infants, clothing, and trail food for the very limited carrying capacity of the human body. For such people, techniques that can be carried in the mind and implemented using locally available resources are far more cost-effective than artifacts that must be carried in the hand.

In thinking about hunting and gathering people who must move frequently from place to place, I suggest that technology should be seen as a system of knowledge rather than an inventory of objects. The sophistication of such a technology might be measured by its cost-effectiveness in terms of a ratio of weight and bulk to productive capacity rather than by the number of "technounits" in a given artifact. The essence of hunting and gathering adaptive strategy is to retain, and be able to act upon, information about the possible relationships between people and the natural environment. When realized, these life-giving relationships are as much the artifacts of hunting and gathering technology as are the material objects that are instrumental in bringing them about.

Hunters and gatherers typically view their world as imbued with human qualities of will and purpose. The pervasive animism of such people may be viewed as a symbolic structure, within which life-giving relationships between people and their environment may be most effectively kept in mind. Hunting and gathering people study the life cycles of plants and animals carefully. They internalize detailed information about topography, seasonal changes, and mineral resources. They plan their own movements in relation to the information they hold in mind about the world in process around them. Often, information about the resource potential of the environment is processed and organized in their minds through the use of dreams and divinatory devices (Tanner 1979; Ridington 1978a). Their plans are central to an adaptive strategy in which control of information maximizes control over the relationship between people and environment. Unlike food-producing people who must transform nature "to make it reproduce the way they want it to," hunters and gatherers "live more or less with nature as a given" (Lee 1979: 117). Instead of attempting to control nature, they concentrate on controlling their relationship to it. Thus, they have developed highly cost-effective techniques for thinking about their own activities in relation to the world they see in process around them. The carrying device is an essential artifact of hunting and gathering technology (Lee 1979: 489–494), but the technique of being able to carry the world around in your head is even more fundamental.

To give substance to my argument I shall describe the traditional world view and adaptive strategy of the northern Athapaskan Beaver Indians, with whom I have done fieldwork. This will be followed by a review of the literature on the world view and adaptive strategy of other northern hunting people.

WORLD VIEW AND ADAPTIVE STRATEGY AMONG THE BEAVER INDIANS

The Beaver Indians call themselves Dunne-za, "real people," in their Athapaskan language. Traditionally, they lived in bands of twenty-five to thirty-five people in the prairie, forest, and muskeg country along the Peace River between the Rocky Mountains and Lake Athabasca. Hunting was far more important than gathering vegetable foods or even fishing. Because their territory included several different biomes, varied resources were available to them. The most important big game animals were mountain sheep and goats, moose, wood bison, deer, caribou, black bear, and grizzly bear. Smaller game that provided important food resources were beaver, rabbits, porcupine, and whistler (marmot). Whitefish and jackfish (northern pike) were plentiful locally but not widespread, particularly in the western half of their territory. Dolly Varden trout and grayling were taken in the rivers. In addition to these animals taken for food, the Dunne-za used a variety of fur-bearing animals for clothing. Bands moved seasonally from place to place, often covering as much as 400 kilometers during the course of a year. Each band was known as the people of a certain place, but territories were not held exclusively. Related bands came together during the summer for ceremonial and social activities.

The Beaver people had, and still retain, a rich and complex set of ideas about the possibility of meaningful human action in relation to the resource potential of their varied environment. They related to one another and to the animals with whom they shared the world on the basis of subtle references to mutually understood information. The importance of mutual understandings was evident, both in interpersonal relations and in those between people and animals. Relations between people were guided by their common understanding of a kinship system that made it possible for every person to establish a connection to every other. The system created a set of conceptual categories rather than kin groups (Ridington 1969). These categories divided opposite sex relatives in one's own and adjacent generations into people with whom marriage was possible and those with whom it was not. Common sex relatives were similarly divided into those who could and could not marry one's opposite sex sibling. The system was egocentric rather than sociocentric, in that there was no tendency for people to group themselves into moieties or clans on the basis of marriage categories defined by kinship. Relations between people were also strongly guided by the ethic of generalized reciprocity (Sahlins 1965), which required meat to be shared among all members of a band rather than being the exclusive property of the hunter.

Relations between people and animals were also organized by reference to common understandings believed to exist between hunters and their game. In order for a hunt to be successfully completed, the animal had to have previously given itself to the hunter in a dream. Both animals and hunter were supposed to have been known to one another before their physical meeting in the hunt itself. Animals were believed to be pleased by the hunter's respect for their bodies and to notice his generosity in distributing the meat. Hunters sought to develop an ability to think like game animals in order to predict their behavior. They were trained to interpret the environment from an animal's perspective. The hunter's understanding of an animal's thought process was believed to be mirrored by the animal's understanding of how humans fulfilled obligations incurred in the hunt.

In order to understand the animals, a person had to be well informed. People were also expected to be well informed about their relationships to one another. They believed that the quality of their interpersonal relations was reflected in the quality of their relations with animals. Animals were believed to know when people behaved badly toward one another and to withdraw from contact with them. When a person experienced consistently poor results in hunting, he would attribute his misfortune to the malevolent thought and action of other people. People accused of such malevolence responded by suggesting that the victim must have broken his obligations to the animals. These medicine fights (Ridington 1968) often accompanied personal misfortune. They revealed the complex associations between the thought and actions of people and animals.

Information about states of mind and states of nature was considered essential to survival. The possession of information was far more important than physical possessions. In order for a person to take effective action in the world, he or she would have to "know something." A person who "knew something" was thought of as a person with power. All normal adults were expected to have power to some degree or another. In the same way that hunters attempted to contact the thought processes of game animals by carefully observing their behavior in relation to their habitat, people also sought to learn what other people "knew" from behavioral observation. These observations began when adults encouraged their children to move independently from the security and protection of camp into the bush.

As children began to encounter animals and their trails on their own, adults watched for signs of their developing knowledge. The children's discoveries were guided by a cycle of stories about the relations between people and animals as well as by preparatory training by adults. Their forays out into the world of animals became more extensive as their knowledge and competence increased. At the same time, the quality of their encounters with the animal world became more intense, until finally the children came into direct visionary contact with the medicine powers of animals as recounted in the myths. These visionary encounters became the experiential basis of later personal medicine power. Alone in the bush, the children came to possess the germ of "knowing something." Later, they developed an identity around the powers represented by the medicine animals encountered in the bush. The visionary experience provided a point of reference to which a person returned throughout life. It was a model for later dream encounters with the real animals that would give themselves to people for food and clothing.

The Beaver people viewed human experience as a life-sustaining network of relationships between all components of a sentient world. They experienced their world as a mosaic of passages and interactions between animate beings in motion against the backdrop of a terrain that was itself continually in process through the cyclical transformations of changing seasons. They looked upon the trails of people and animals as a record of these interactions. Each trail, they believed, continued backward and forward beyond the point at which it could no longer be followed physically. The trails that lay ahead, as well as those that lay behind, could be followed by people in their dreams. The trail of every adult could be followed in the mind back to the point of visionary encounter with a medicine animal, just as the trail of a successful hunter could be followed ahead to his point of encounter with the spirit of an animal. Each actual point of meeting between person and animal was believed to be the manifestation of antecedent meetings in the medium of dream or vision.

In addition to visualizing the relative movement of people and animals, the Beaver people also paid particular attention to the daily and seasonal motions of the sun and moon. These, they symbolized as a single entity, *sa*, which, like humans, manifested itself in both dreaming and waking phases. In very practical terms, they took their direction by careful observation of the sun's position relative to their own movement, and they took advantage of the moon's light to extend their own travel into the hours of night. Success or failure in hunting depended upon a person's ability to conceptualize and control the mosaic of relationships between people, animals, and celestial bodies. The technology of subsistence required that a person be able to bring about a regular and coherent relationship between the trails of people, animals, and the sun and moon.

Traditional Beaver world view centered around their image of the trail. Every sentient being was perceived as existing at a particular point on a trail that could be imagined projecting forward and backward from that point. This projection was accomplished through the use of dreams. Success depended upon being able to make decisions about how best to move in relation to the complex network of trails emerging from the past and merging into the future. Hunters believed that in the dream state they could resolve a larger pattern of interrelated trails than would be possible in ordinary waking consciousness. In dreams, a person could draw upon his or her own personal relationship to the natural world established during the visionary experience of childhood. The power conveyed by that experience was believed to facilitate later dream contact between people and animals. The Beavers' beliefs about dreaming seem to have reflected an understanding that when the mind is released from the task of processing information from the immediate perceptual environment, it may concentrate on processing information generated internally and derived from past experience.

Hunters slept with their heads toward the place where the sun would rise, in expectation of being able to travel in dreams ahead of their physical trail on earth. They thought ahead to the places where their own trails might intersect those of the animals. In thinking ahead through dreaming, they sought to conceptualize the unfolding pattern of relationships between people and animals. Hunters knew that their lives depended on continuous regular contact between people and animals, but they also knew that the outcome of any particular hunt was inherently uncertain. They knew that if life was to continue they would have to be as certain of contacting animals on the trail ahead as they were of contacting the sun as it rose in the morning. Their practice of sleeping with their heads toward the sun's anticipated place of rising served sympathetically to class the two events together by association. The only uncertainty that remained was the actual time when the dream encounter would be realized in fact.

By reference to the sun's trail across the sky, hunters directed their dream experiences along the trail ahead, just as in the actual hunt they took direction by their positions relative to the sun. In order for life to continue, the trail ahead had to merge with those of animals. Similarly, the trails behind people with power allowed them to realize life-sustaining connections between people and animals. A person who "knew something" was believed to have the power to experience important points of contact in dreams and to realize them later in physical reality. The person with power could dream back to his or her childhood encounter with a medicine animal as well as forward to encounters with game animals in the bush. Power was symbolized physically by a medicine bundle that hung above its owner's sleeping place. The medicine bundle contained objects symbolic of the powers associated with a person's medicine animals. These powers were known publicly by reference to stories about the mythic times when giant medicine animals dominated the world and lived by hunting people. The bundle, hanging as it did between the owner's head and the bush to his east, served to focus power upon the dream trail ahead. It symbolized the connection between a childhood experience of visionary contact with medicine animals and adult dreaming about contact with the animals that gave life to the people.

The meaning of the vision quest experience as a form of empowerment was conveyed most succinctly in the Beaver creation story and in a cycle of stories about the culture hero and transformer who overcame the giant animals and brought culture to human beings. He was described as being like the sun and moon in the sky, a traveler who moved around the edge of the world. While other people ran away from the giant medicine animals, the culture hero turned to meet them. In each story, the culture hero overcame the giant person-eating animals by acting upon an informed understanding of his own abilities in relation to their particular habits. The stories illustrated that his power was derived from his knowledge. They made explicit the fundamental premise of Beaver life: that power lay in the controlled and intelligent application of knowledge. They showed by example how a person with power was one who "knew something."

The creation story, a version of the widespread "earth diver" motif, illustrated the underlying idea that important events came about because they were preceded by important images. In the Beaver version of the story, the world grew from a speck of dirt brought up from the bottom of a primordial sea by Muskrat. This speck of dirt was placed by the creator on a cross drawn upon the otherwise directionless chaos of the water's surface. The cross represented a point of articulation from which people could take their direction. It was like a meeting of trails. For the traditional Beaver people, the world as they knew it grew from this image of trails from the four directions coming together in a single point. The center of the cross was seen as the center of their world. For them, the trails of people and animals could not come together in fact until an image of the meeting had been experienced in the mind. The earth could not become real in substance and grow to its present size until the trails meeting at the center of the cross gave Muskrat his sense of direction.

In the creation story, Muskrat lost consciousness just as he touched the bottom of the water. When he floated to the surface, he took a great breath of air and came back to life. His experience brought about the transformation of an image into substance. His story provided a model for the personal transformation every Beaver child experienced during his or her vision quest. Muskrat's experience at the moment when image became substance also gave form to the hunter's dream contact with an animal on the trail ahead of him. The actual meeting between hunter and game was a transformation of image into substance, like the transformation that took place when Muskrat's speck of dirt became the world. His experience in the story was a metaphor for the child's vision quest experience and for the dreamer's contact with his game on the trail ahead of him.

In Beaver tradition, the story of Swan complemented the story of Muskrat. Muskrat was an animal who dove down to retrieve the world, while Swan was one who flew into a land beyond the sky to bring back the world of another season. The story of Swan was a description of the culture hero's own vision quest experience. In the story, a boy named Swan became the culture hero, Saya, after surviving a winter of isolation on an island world. As Saya, he turned to meet the giant animals that ate people. As he met each one, he used his knowledge of their weaknesses to transform them into the forms that people encountered on their trails in the bush.

The stories of Swan and Muskrat symbolized the transformative experiences of Beaver shamans known as Dreamers. Dreamers were people who symbolically died and returned to life. Upon their return to the world of everyday reality, they described their experiences on the trail to heaven. Like swans, Dreamers were believed to have traveled to a land beyond the sky and to have returned. Their return was like that of the sun to another day or season. Dreamers were thought of as prophets who could use their dreaming to see farther into the future than ordinary people. They were given names that symbolized their role as messengers from the trails that lay ahead. They were individuals with medicine powers, like the power that the boy named Swan acquired during his transformation into Saya, the culture hero. While ordinary people dreamed ahead on their own personal trails, the Dreamers could see ahead on the trails of an entire community. According to stories about Dreamers in times before the whitemen, they traditionally acted as hunt chiefs. In their dreams, they saw the pattern of trails made by people and game animals as they carried out communal hunts using drives and surrounds. In these stories, Dreamers are depicted as having the knowledge required to direct people's movements in communal hunting. Like Swan and Muskrat, they brought images to life. Their dreams visualized life-giving relationships between the people and animals. As people carried out their direction for communal hunting, these dream images were believed to come true.

The Beaver Indians directed their trails by reference to the sun's passage across the sky. They directed their lives by reference to the cycle of stories about Saya's power of transformation. They directed their hunts, both as individuals and collectively, by reference to information processed in dreams. The creation and culture hero stories laid out the structure of the physical world as well as the world of experience. In the physical world, people followed trails, seeking the transformation of animals in the bush into food and clothing in camp. In dream and vision, they left the places where their bodies were rooted and followed Muskrat and Swan into the places where image became substance.

According to the world view articulated by these stories and the practices surrounding them, success in hunting depended on the possession of knowledge rather than the possession of artifacts. The world view expressed an attitude toward technology that emphasized artifice over artifact. The vision quest effectively taught children that their survival as adults would depend upon knowledge rather than material possessions. Their vision quest experiences took place with the bare minimum of material goods. Children went out into the bush virtually empty-handed and returned with the germ of powers that would grow like Muskrat's speck of dirt to become the world. A group of people bonded together by ties of kinship and generalized reciprocity were expected to be in possession of all the knowledge required to bring about the life-sustaining potential of their environment. They considered their own mental powers to be the most significant carrying devices available to them. These mental powers were guided and informed by their stories and training techniques. The particular skills relevant to the production of artifacts were just one part of a larger complex relevant to the production of life-sustaining relationships between people and animals within the overall environment.

The Beavers seem to have viewed their overall relationship to the world of nature as an artifact of their technology. Their products were relationships rather than material goods. Their work was suffused with storied times and the dreamworld. They made their world in the same way that Muskrat made a world when he brought together the centering directions and a germ of substance. They made their world as Swan, who became Saya, did when he journeyed around its edge from day to day and year to year. They produced their world when they coupled will to intelligence. Although their work was very physical in its demands, their means of production were largely carried in the mind. Certainly, they viewed knowledge as a means of production more fundamental than any set of artifacts. They perceived their artifacts as products of knowledge and will. In the stories, Saya first used the skills and tools of human beings. He used some to overcome the giant medicine animals; others were acquired from them; all were passed down to the people who succeeded him. Humans who learned particular skills also took on knowledge of particular medicine animals and their stories. They enacted symbols of these stories in their lives by avoiding certain foods or forms of behavior. They also enacted the powers themselves through practice of their skills. Techniques and medicine powers were the same in their minds.

WORLD VIEW AND PRODUCTIVE FORCES IN HUNTING AND GATHERING SOCIETIES

The Beavers have traditionally been hunting and gathering people whose work and productive activity integrated human will and natural conditions rather than engaging human will in the task of transforming nature. Godelier described such an economy as one in which productive forces do not transform nature and "productivity depends above all on variations in ecological conditions" (1975: 8). According to Lee, "hunters live more or less with nature as a given. More than any other kind of society, foragers must fit their organization into the niches afforded by nature" (1979: 117). Although hunting and gathering people can do little to transform nature, they can and do devote considerable energy to understanding it. The Beaver concept of "knowing something" as a sign of empowerment typifies how many hunting and gathering people have directed their energies. Personal knowledge as a source of power is of practical and symbolic importance in very many hunting and gathering societies. Their references to mythic time and to the authority of shamanic experience touch upon common themes. Such people seek to control their relationship to the cycles of nature by studying them carefully. A person with knowledge derived from studying the relationship between people and natural environment is genuinely powerful. Such power is distinctively human. It is our ability to learn from the environment and from one another. It is the gift of information we pass on from generation to generation.

In small-scale, adaptively stable hunting and gathering societies, traditional knowledge becomes personal knowledge through training and observation. The person with knowledge is empowered to sense the life-giving potential of the environment and to act intelligently when making necessary decisions about how to relate to it. The pervasive animism and shamanism of hunting and gathering cultures may be viewed as systems of thought and practice that articulate associations between human will and environmental potential.

Rather than being unrealistic attempts to control nature, as Marx suggested (Godelier 1977: 181), the beliefs and practices of hunting and gathering animism and shamanism are eminently realistic techniques for controlling the relationships people bring into being between themselves and nature.

According to Godelier's interpretation of Marx, hunting and gathering societies have "a low level of development in productive forces" (1977: 183). Because they are said to lack control over nature, they are viewed as imagining the world as dominated by superior powers. According to Godelier, primitive man "spontaneously represents the world—the causality of invisible levels of nature and society, by analogy with his own experience—to a conscious being, endowed with a will who acts on himself and others intentionally" (1977: 183). Thus, "the mythic-religious consciousness of the world (ideological representation) is constructed by analogy, consciously or unconsciously, with the visible and intentional relations of men in society" (1977: 184). Godelier concurs with Aristotle, who says, "Why should we examine seriously the spurious wisdom of myths?" and Hegel, "The myth, in general, is not an adequate means for expressing thought" (1977: 184).

Through a little sleight of hand, it seems possible to retain Marxist concepts about the hunting and gathering mode of production in relation to shamanic and animistic ideology without necessarily accepting the stereotype that such people lack control over their relation to the environment. As I have attempted to illustrate in my description of Beaver world view, technology and adaptive strategy—the hunting and gathering mode of production—may be described as one in which knowledge of the environment is a genuine source of power that may enable people to regulate their relations to it. I have argued, in fact, that knowledge is a fundamental means of production in hunting and gathering societies. From this perspective, technology may be viewed as a technique for the application of knowledge.

Within a mode of production that controls human relationships to the environment rather than the environment itself, the possession of knowledge is more important than the possession of particular artifacts. Particularly among northern forest hunters like the Beaver Indians, artifacts were customarily made from locally available materials at the site of their use rather than being transported long distances. If knowledge can be accepted as the basis of technology in the hunting and gathering mode of production, then shamanic and animistic beliefs and practices are more like forces of production than illusory representations of productive forces. The social relations of production as seen in kinship and social organization would also be a part of the overall productive system. Artifacts themselves could again be referred to as elements of material culture. Rather than being mistaken for technology, they could be unambiguously described as the material artifacts and instruments of technology.

The preceding discussion of world view in relation to hunting and gathering technology has drawn upon information from only one society. In order to broaden that base, I will make reference to Adrian Tanner's study of world view and technology among the Mistassini Cree. In *Bringing Home Animals*, Tanner (1979) describes a relationship between religious ideology and mode of production. He concludes that Mistassini religion is

> a natural philosophy which addresses the realities of their life
> both in the bush and in the settlement . . . At the center it is a
> symbolic action available for the individual to use or to ignore as
> he wishes. Because the bush religion is not passed on by formal
> instruction and is not surrounded by secrecy, it is approached
> very much as a set of environmental phenomena, much like
> the natural characteristics of the various animal species. Just
> as a growing boy is expected to show a curiosity first to learn
> and then to make use of knowledge about animal habits, so the
> culture give rewards for those who assemble knowledge of reli-
> gious ideas, symbolism and practice through myths, stories and
> through the observation of others, and who gradually develop
> self-reliance in the face of the world of unseen forces. (1979:
> 213–214)

Tanner viewed religion and technology among the Mistassini Cree as being parallel to one another. In both the production and the social spheres, he says, practical action is paralleled by religious action. Cree religion has a direct relationship to the practical common sense reality of material production and to the organization of social relations. It is often assumed that religion and magic act to supplement actual control, which a group has through its technology, with a kind of illusory control in those areas of human actions where technological control is beyond its limits. For the Mistassini traditional religion, however, the ritual action parallels symbolically rather than reaches beyond actions performed at the physical level (1979: 212).

In Tanner's analysis, the hunting and gathering mode of production combines "technical conditions and the social relations of production, where it is recognized that the concept of production includes an economic, a juridico-political and an ideological level" (1979: 10). Cree ideology is viewed as concerned with "totalizing" the sense data that members of the group experience from their environment (1979: 208). Tanner comes close to saying that ideology is, in fact, an underlying productive force in Cree society. He certainly makes it clear that Cree ideology is not merely a fantastic reflection of their ignorance and powerlessness. In his analysis of Cree divination, Tanner says that the practice is used normally "as a means of thinking about their hunting activities" (1979: 100). In other words, he suggests that Cree hunters normally think ahead of themselves in an attempt to visualize the relationships between people and animals that make for a successful hunt. Although Tanner does not explicitly make the connection, one might argue from his data that divinatory practice, in this case scapulimancy, is part of Cree hunting technology.

CONCLUSION

Hunting and gathering people are not concerned with the overall transformation of their environment. This does not mean, however, that they feel any less in control of their lives than do agricultural people. It would be mistaken to view their shamanic and animistic religious beliefs and practices as fantasies indulged in because of their fundamental powerlessness. Rather, these beliefs and practices emphasize knowledge as the basis of power. Through them, individuals are trained to study the resource potential of their environment and to bring their own lives into life-sustaining relationships with the world of nature.

KNOWLEDGE, POWER, AND THE INDIVIDUAL IN SUBARCTIC HUNTING SOCIETIES

Native hunter-gatherers of the North American subarctic have consistently been described as valuing knowledge, power, and individual autonomy (Black 1977a; McClellan and Denniston 1981; Honigmann 1981; Feit 1986a; Rushforth 1986). Is there something distinctive about the adaptive conditions of subarctic life that brings about an association of knowledge, individualism, and power, or does this patterning suggested by the literature merely reflect a "culture and personality" tradition within North American subarctic scholarship? How do mutual understandings contribute to the communication systems of subarctic people? How can anthropology expand its own language to represent the ideas subarctic hunting and gathering people have about knowledge, power, and individual autonomy?

My reading of the literature on subarctic hunter-gatherers and my own field experience with the Beaver Indians lead me to suggest that (1) a complex of knowledge, power, and individualism is a distinctive feature of subarctic adaptation, (2) the social theory of subarctic people themselves has exerted a powerful influence on several generations of anthropologists in formulating their own theories about the individual in society, and (3) an interpretive language (Geertz 1973; Marcus and Fisher 1986; Keesing 1987) is best suited to make sense of the ideas subarctic people have about knowledge and power. I suggest that anthropological theory may, and in some cases should, reflect the thoughtworlds of the people we study as well as those of our own academic traditions. (See Martin 1987 for a discussion of Native thoughtworlds and the writing of history.) Conversely, the careless and uncritical application of ideas from academic traditions to the thoughtworlds of subarctic people may produce bizarre and ethnocentric results. For example, such uninformed ethnocentrism dominated much of the debate about the causes of a "windigo psychosis" that was believed to be a culture-bound syndrome peculiar to the eastern subarctic (Ridington 1976a; Preston 1980). Marano's "Windigo Psychosis: The Anatomy of an Emic-Etic Confusion" (1982) carefully documents how social science theory may become ethnocentric when it removes ethnographic information about subarctic people from the context in which it is known, learned, and communicated.

TRADITIONS OF SCHOLARSHIP IN THE SUBARCTIC

Despite the relatively small number of ethnographers who worked in the subarctic until recently (Rogers 1981: 22 lists only fifty-eight for the entire subarctic shield and Mackenzie borderlands area through 1969), many of the first ethnographers made original contributions to anthropological theory in addition to their descriptive ethnographic work. Some of the best-known subarctic scholars wrote about individual knowledge and understanding in relation to culture and the environment. Frank Speck (1935) was one of the earliest of these. His student A. I. Hallowell (1955) similarly used information about the northern Ojibwa in writing about "the self in its behavioral environment." Later scholarship has continued to describe the individualism of subarctic peoples (Henriksen 1973; Christian and Gardner 1977; Scollon and Scollon 1979; Tanner 1979; Honigmann 1981; Brody 1981; Rushforth 1986; Feit 1986a).

Speck's classic, *Naskapi* (1935), describes a complex Native theory of individual thought and action. Speck suggests that, in the anthropology of his day, "thought concerning the effect of environment upon culture-imagination may be scientifically outlawed" but asserts that he will discuss cultural categories and the environment, because "in native esteem it calls for consideration" (1935: 242). Speck explains that Naskapi theory is focused on the individual's possession of knowledge about the environment and on his or her personal experience of transformation. He says, "Existing conditions, the forms and behavior of animals and the geography of the country, are largely the result of *transformation*. Consequently, transformation becomes an abstract principle in the system of thought of the nomads" (1935: 49).

Speck argues that Naskapi hunters experience a powerful transformation in their contact with animals. He refers to the hunt as "a holy occupation" because "the animals pursue an existence corresponding to that of man as regards emotions and purpose in life" (1935: 72). Hunter and animal, he says, share an experience of transformation when they come into contact through empowering visions and "hunt dreams."

> The hunting dream is the major object of focus—*kunto' pwa'men*, "he hunt-dreams" (*nto'pwata'm muckw*, "I hunt-dream a bear," *kunto'hun*, "I hunt"). It is part of the process of revelation by which the individual acquires the knowledge of life. It is the main channel through which he keeps in communication with the unseen world. His soul-spirit speaks to him in dreams. (1935: 187)

In Naskapi theory, as described by Speck, a person's "active soul," which guides him through life, is called Mistapeo ("great man" in Speck's translation). Mistapeo reveals itself most directly in dreams. "Every individual has one," says Speck, "and in consequence has dreams." Because dreams are integral to Naskapi hunting technology, practices such as "fasting, dancing, singing, drumming, rattling, the sweat bath, seclusion, meditation, eating certain foods, as well as drinking animal grease, [and] various kinds of medicine" are used to induce dreaming. "When dreams are obtained," Speck explains, "interpretation is required" (1935: 188). This interpretation takes the form of divination. A person's Mistapeo directs the interpretive process through *mutone'itcigun*, which Speck translates as "the power of thought." This power allows a person to focus his or her thought on the complex and ongoing pattern of transformations of which each individual's life is a part.

Speck's account of Naskapi divination and hunting strategy examines both its logic and its practice. He consistently presents this and other ethnographic information as part of an organized Native system of intelligence that may be apprehended through Naskapi linguistic categories. Speck suggests that Naskapi religion, their "soul philosophy," is integral to their overall adaptive technology. He shows how Naskapi ideas and practices constitute a system of information that guides and empowers the thought, will, and intelligence of individual men and women. According to Speck's presentation of Naskapi theory, human thought and action are part of a more general animating principle of the universe, *tce'mentu*. The spirit of an individual human being, *nic'tu't*, represents the "intellect, comprehension [or] mind" (1935: 33) through which he or she may take intelligent action within this animating intelligence of the world at large.

Speck describes Naskapi customs and actions as indications that they experience the world as having an internalized, culturally defined "soul." He says that the Naskapi "perceive the objects of nature . . . as tangible embodiments of volitional beings" (1935: 50). Although later scholars (Preston 1975; Tanner 1979; Armitage 1987) point out alternative interpretations of the Naskapi metaphysical vocabulary, Speck's portrait of Naskapi world view remains an important contribution against which others may be measured. Tanner's *Bringing Home Animals* (1979), for instance, advances Speck's ideas by presenting scapulimancy as part of "a specific ecological and decision-making context" (1979: 124), in which the oldest hunters practice divination to "make use of their knowledge of animals and of the environment, a knowledge which is analogous to, and spoken of as, a spiritual power" (1979: 134–135). Feit (1986a: 176) similarly describes the world of the James Bay Cree as "analogous to that of some ecological scientists" but based on "a personal metaphor" rather than the organic one of biological science.

Speck's own intellect and comprehension are revealed in the language of his rich ethnography. His work sets out both Naskapi theory and his anthropological understanding of the Naskapi world. He crafts the two into a single statement through the language of his interpretive description. His own theory is implicit in the language through which he represents Naskapi theory. Rather than attempting a theoretical language that would distance the reader from the Naskapi mind and spirit, Speck has adopted one in harmony with Naskapi intellect and comprehension as he understands them.

A. I. ("Pete") Hallowell is being discovered, or, more correctly, rediscovered, as the brilliant thinker he has always been. Brian Morris, in a 1985 *Man* article, described him as "a much neglected scholar, whose work has come to be recognized only in recent years" (1985: 736). According to Morris, Hallowell is important because he viewed "self and society" as "aspects of a single whole." "Thus," he says, "'social' existence was [for Hallowell] a necessary condition of the development of the self (or mind) of the individual" (1985: 738). Hallowell's generalizations about "the self in its behavioral environment" grew out of his work on the individual in northern Ojibwa society (Black 1977a, 1977b). His theoretical language seems to have emerged effortlessly from the language of his ethnography.

Hallowell stated explicitly what was understood and implicit in the work of his former teacher. In an essay written for *Culture and History* (1960), he develops the argument that "in the metaphysics of being found among [the Northern Ojibwa], the action of persons provides the major key to their world view." In Ojibwa thought, as described by Hallowell, the concept of a person "is not in fact synonymous with human beings but transcends it." Because he viewed the Ojibwa concept of person as more inclusive than that of the culture that produced anthropology, Hallowell warned that "a thoroughgoing 'objective' approach to the study of cultures cannot be achieved solely by projecting upon those cultures categorical abstractions derived from Western thought" (1960: 21).

Brown points out that Hallowell described thought categories of the Manitoba Ojibwa as leaving "open the possibility of animation in and communication with the totality of the surrounding universe." Ojibwa experience as Hallowell described it, she says, "was individualized, changing, and cumulative." Hallowell's ethnography, Brown states, shows that Ojibwa "concepts of persons and of the world in general" explain why "the private vision or dream was the prime means of access to significant knowledge and power among Northern Algonquians," who treat dream encounters "as seriously as did the Freudian psychologists who 'discovered' the importance and relevance of dreams" (1986: 222).

The abstractions that constitute anthropological theory are, according to Hallowell, "a reflection of *our* cultural subjectivity." But the security of anthropological objectivity may be maintained, he says, by seeking "a higher order of objectivity." This higher order is realized "by adopting a perspective which includes an analysis of the outlook of the people themselves as a complementary procedure"

(1960: 21). This statement suggests that Hallowell derived his view of culture and personality from the people he studied in the field as well as from the scholars he read during his university education. His focus on self-awareness in the context of a culturally mediated behavioral environment indicates that he found a complementarity between northern Algonquian phenomenology and that of Western phenomenologists.

Black cites several pages selected from Hallowell's work that "document his conviction that the ethnographer should strive for an 'inside view' of a people's phenomenal world" (1977b: 92). She argues that Hallowell appeared "to have solved the phenomenological dilemma in a manner similar to the ethnoscientists" (1977b: 93). She says that Hallowell may have been "particularly sensitive to 'cultural factors in the structuralization of perception'" as a "result partly from his Ojibwa experience" (1977b: 99). In effect, Hallowell rationalized and objectified what Speck was doing implicitly through the rich language of his ethnographic description. For both Speck and Hallowell, accurate and objective understanding of northern hunting peoples requires entering their thought categories rather than imposing our thought categories to describe their behavior. True objectivity must integrate the perspective of northern hunting people with our own.

Like Speck, Hallowell viewed transformation (which he calls metamorphosis) as a key to the northern Algonquian perception of human and nonhuman persons. Transformation helps explain the Ojibwa concept of causality, which, he says, "directs the reasoning of individuals towards an explanation of events in personalistic terms" (1960: 45). Mythic beings are as much causal agents as are the physical instruments of causality. Similarly, "dream visitors" influence the turn of events as much as do the circumstances of waking experience. For the Ojibwa as described by Hallowell, "all the effective agents of events throughout the entire behavioral environment . . . are selves" (1955: 181). The relations a hunter has with his game may thus be seen as interpersonal ones and therefore subject to the moral obligations that pertain between human persons in Ojibwa society. Success in hunting depends "as much upon a man's satisfactory relations with the superhuman 'masters' of the different species of game and furbearing animals, as upon his technical skill as a hunter and trapper" (1955: 120).

Black (1977b: 95) points out that Hallowell's category of "persons . . . turns out to be what ethnoscientists would term a 'covert category'" because "the Ojibwa do not recognize this class as such, but the belief system structure is more truly represented by inferring it from his data" (1977b: 95). Feit cites Hallowell as a reference when he says that knowledge is "centrally important in Cree hunting practice" and is "encoded and highlighted by Cree concepts . . . in what we might call their science of hunting" (1986a: 176). The Cree concept of power, he says, "is a coincidence between an internal state of being (thought) and the configuration of the world (event), a congruence which is anticipated by the inner state and which this anticipation helps to actualize . . . Power . . . is a relationship in thought and action among many beings, whereby potentiality becomes actuality . . . We might say that power is truth, rather than that power is control" (1986a: 178).

Like Speck, who describes northern Algonquians as being "egoistic" but not "egotistic" (1935: 245), Hallowell speaks of Ojibwa "ego-involvement" as "the identification of the self with things, individuals, and groups of individuals" (1955: 102). Hallowell generalized from his knowledge of northern Algonquian thought to argue that "the self and its behavioral environment" is a fundamental "feature of human adjustment" (1955: 75–110). Although Hallowell grounded his ideas about self-awareness and culture in a phenomenological tradition of Western scholarship, he also credited his Ojibwa friends and informants, particularly Chief William Berens, with teaching him about the phenomenology of northern hunting people (1955: 120; Black 1977b: 91–92). Hallowell's classic 1937 paper, "Temporal Orientation in Western Civilization and in a Preliterate Society" (Hallowell 1955), which strikingly parallels Whorf's "An American Indian Model of the Universe" in its attempt to translate Native phenomenology (Ridington 1987a), is personalistic rather than positivistic in its point of reference. Hallowell writes: "During the summer of 1932 when I spent most of my time up the Berens River with the Pekangikum Indians, I lost track of the days of the month, since I did not have a calendar with me; the days of the week became meaningless . . . the significant fact is that since I remained associated with human beings it was a very simple matter to make their temporal reference points my own" (1955: 218–219).

Several later Algonquianists have related their own field experiences to the work of Speck and Hallowell. One of these is Richard Preston, whose monograph *Cree Narrative: Expressing the Personal Meanings of Events* (1975) is a rich and thoughtful presentation of James Bay Cree ideas about shared meanings expressed in narrative form and ritual practice. Preston, a student of John Honigmann, writes that, like Hallowell, "my point of view and method of approach is not only derived from my intellectual background," particularly Sapir's "insights into the relationship of culture and personality," but is equally a reflection of "the tendency of Cree individuals to emphasize meaning more than form, to view events personally rather than objectively" (1975: 9). Preston consciously attempts to understand Cree narratives "in their meaningful Cree context." This context includes "conjuring power, autonomy, self-control, hardships and their associated emotional responses, and the shifting contingencies of the environment" (1975: 13).

Cree Narrative is both more detailed and more reflective than Speck's *Naskapi*. It includes extensive and well-contexted narrative texts and a close description of the shaking tent performance. These serve as vehicles for approaching the Cree meaning of concepts such as Mistabeo (Speck's Mistapeo). Preston suggests that Mistabeo is best thought of as an "attending spirit" related allegorically to the spirit of the conjurer, rather than as a direct manifestation of that person's "active soul" (1975: 92–93). While acknowledging that *Naskapi* is a "pioneering work of creative ethnology" and that Speck "is on to something of great importance," Preston feels that Speck's use of a language that contrasts the Indian "mystical" world with Western "rationality" took him away from fully entering the world of northern Algonquian thought and experience. This limitation, he feels, did not constrain Hallowell, whose greater understanding is apparent in papers such as his "masterpiece," "The Role of Conjuring in Saulteaux Society" (Hallowell 1942, cited in Preston 1975: 162–163).

Preston argues that the key to understanding fundamental Cree practices, such as conjuring, lies in coming to grips with what he calls, after Sapir, "the psychological reality of the culture pattern" (1975: 164). Because Mistabeo is experienced as a psychological reality, it is literally conjured into consciousness through the media of narrative and ritual performance. In Preston's view, the psychological reality of Cree knowledge contributes to its power. Because Cree knowledge is thoroughly contexted in experience, Preston argues that it is most appropriately communicated (following Cree tradition) in the language of narrative. Cree psychological reality "is not simply an uncritical (prelogical) hodgepodge of unconscious patterning, but rather a mixture of partially understood, partially related events, narratives, beliefs, and suspicions . . . it is not a matter for critical analysis and generalization in the fashion of an ethnologist" (1975: 168).

As an ethnologist attempting to understand Cree culture from the inside, Preston concludes that while Mistabeo may appear to the outside observer as a "mental construct," to the insider it is a "mental percept" that is experienced directly (1975: 262). Black uses strikingly similar language in explaining her own and Hallowell's Ojibwa data. She argues that a key to Ojibwa individualism may be seen in what she calls their "percept ambiguity." The Ojibwa belief system, she says, "allows the expectation that individuals will 'see' different objects in the same landscape, will 'hear' different sounds; it also allows the expectation that the same entity may appear in different forms from one *time* to another; and it respects the individual's privacy and veracity as to what he has seen or heard, and as to which of the entities has appeared to his senses alone and thus in a certain class for him" (1977b: 101–102).

ATHAPASKAN PERSPECTIVES ON KNOWLEDGE, POWER, AND THE INDIVIDUAL

Ethnographers have consistently described Athapaskans of the subarctic interior as being individualistic (VanStone 1974; Christian and Gardner 1977; Scollon and Scollon 1979; Brody 1981; Rushforth 1986) but until recently have written little about a rich, culturally based phenomenology (Krech 1980). Honigmann's classic *Culture and Ethos of Kaska Society* (1949), for instance, forcefully presents a portrait of Athapaskan individualism but contains none of the complex Native phenomenology that one finds in the work of Speck and his successors. Honigmann's chapter on Kaska ethos concludes that the Kaska personality is motivated by "egocentricity, utilitarianism, deference, flexibility, dependence, and emotional isolation" (1949: 249), but he provides very little information about the cultural context of these psychological characteristics. It is significant, therefore, that even an ethnography that makes little reference to Native phenomenology or personality theory describes individual freedom of thought and action as being of paramount adaptive significance.

Honigmann uses the language of an outside observer's "mental constructs" rather than what his student Preston calls "mental percepts." It is not surprising that he begins a brief account of Kaska religion with the statement that "religious beliefs are of minor importance in Kaska life" (1949: 217). Rushforth suggests that traditional Dene religion is less well known by anthropology than are other aspects of Dene culture because of "the general difficulty anthropologists have in translating the meaning of religious experience," as well as "the relative lack of formal religious institutions among Dene" and "the deeply personal nature of their religious beliefs, which makes many people hesitant to discuss them in any detail" (1986: 252). From his own experience with the Bear Lake Dene, Rushforth concludes that "belief in a mythological past within which the world was formed" and "belief in an inherent power that pervades the world" explain the knowledge and power required for both hunting and dreaming. "Through dreams," he says, "individuals come to 'know a little bit about' things" (1986: 253). The Dunne-za, in my experience, say that a person with power obtained through dream and vision "little bit know something."

A recent paper by Jean-Guy Goulet, "Ways of Knowing with the Mind" (1987), explores the difference between belief and knowledge in Dene thought. Goulet argues that the ethnography of Athapaskan religion has been relatively undeveloped because "among Athapaskans a person with religious experience is described not as a believer but as someone who 'knows'" and "generally, anthropologists do not share in the kinds of experiences—dreams, visions, power of songs, ceremonies—that are at the foundation of aboriginal religious experience and knowledge" (1987: 4). Goulet describes how he developed a deeper level of communication with Dene elders by sharing his own experience of knowing through dreaming in a discourse conducted in the idiom of Dene linguistic categories. He says, "As I progressed in the world of the Dene . . . the Elders continued to instruct me in increasingly greater depth, through stories, accounts of their own experiences, interpretations of objects and songs, and so on. As they did so, they would often conclude a session of several hours with the words *wondsdele ndedassi edaondihika* 'I tell you a little bit so that you may know'" (1987: 25).

The classic literature on northern Athapaskan individualism has been well summarized by Jane Christian and Peter Gardner (1977). The word "individualism," they say, "has been used over and over again in the literature to characterize interpersonal relations in the Subarctic." Beginning with J. Alden Mason's comment in 1913 that among the Great Slave Lake Dene, "individualism seems to be the keynote to the interpretation of this culture," they cite similar statements about the individualism of interior subarctic Athapaskans from Honigmann, Helm, and Nelson, indicating an "accord as to the emphasis on individual autonomy in the Subarctic." They use information from their own Slavey ethnography to ask a key question about "how cognitive sharing is developed and maintained among such concertedly self-reliant people [who are] quiet, uninterfering, and independent almost to the point of anarchy" (1977: 3–5).

Their observations about Slavey individualism are similar to Savishinsky's statement that among the Hare "the successful person is . . . a flexible one, an individual who can alter materials and rely on inventive procedures when his situation calls for such adaptations." The Hare, he says, clearly value "the freedom to live as one chooses, to move when and where one pleases, and to schedule, order, and arrange one's life as one wishes." The value they place on freedom "is cognate not only with flexibility, but also with the people's stress upon individualism, anti-authoritarianism, and independence." Savishinsky compares his observations with "the variously individualistic, or 'atomistic' ethos that Honigmann . . . Hallowell . . . Landes . . . and others have found to be characteristic of both Northern Athapaskan and Northern Algonquian groups" (1974: 80–81).

The individualism of Athapaskan people has been particularly striking to ethnographers because it differs so from their own socialization into the authority of an academic tradition. Scollon and Scollon focus on this difference when they contrast what they call the Chipewyan "bush consciousness" to the "modern consciousness" of their own academic way of thinking about information. The Scollons comment that "we felt, as others must have felt before us, that we were unable to explain our presence with any conviction except to other Euro-Canadians." They conclude that they, as social scientists, and the Chipewyans, as hunter-gatherers, have profoundly different expectations about the need "to encode knowledge for storage but not for immediate use" (1979: 177–209).

Academic knowledge, they say, following Gumperz (1977), is a "decontextualized [form] of knowledge." In contrast to themselves as academics, they describe the Chipewyan individual as "a fully viable unit of survival." They even go so far as to describe themselves as "a hired sensory apparatus for a knowledge organism." In contrast to their own academic trust in the written word and the documentary evidence of history, the Chipewyan, they tell us, regard the written word as hearsay. "Knowledge that has been mediated is regarded with doubt. True knowledge is considered to be that which one derives from experience." "Far from rejecting order," the Scollons say, bush consciousness "seeks a fully integrated view of world order in which there are no elements felt as foreign. What cannot be assimilated to its worldview is rejected as irrelevant or useless knowledge" (1979: 185).

Other scholars (Smith 1973, 1982, 1985; Jarvenpa 1982a; Sharp 1986, 1987) have written about cultural categories of Chipewyan phenomenology, in particular the Chipewyan idea of Inkonze as an empowering "secret knowledge." Sharp interprets Inkonze as a "subjective paradigm" representing "a pan-Chipewyan system of knowledge." He says that "relations between men who possess *Inkonze* and the creatures that reveal it to them appear to be controlled by reciprocity." Thus, in Native theory, an individual's power is believed to reflect his reciprocity, both with supernatural creatures and with other humans. "As a plant taken for magical use must have a return given to it in the form of a gift . . . a man with an established reputation for more than the normal amount of *Inkonze* . . . must be paid by those he cures" (1986: 258). The individualism so evident in observation of how subarctic people behave suggests that similar mental percepts operate as unstated assumptions throughout the subarctic.

UNSTATED ASSUMPTIONS AND MUTUAL UNDERSTANDINGS IN NORTHERN INDIAN COMMUNICATION

Jane Christian's chapter on "Some Aspects of Communication in a Northern Dene Community" (Christian and Gardner 1977) is particularly informative in addressing the apparent contradiction between northern Athapaskan individualism and the obvious human need for community and communication. She points out that, among the Slavey, there is an unwritten cultural rule: "Don't interfere with someone engaged in a line of thought, a task or other endeavor, but allow him to finish out his intention." The Slavey, she says, will not "stop someone in work or travel without good cause," nor will they "interrupt a speaker or interrupt a deliberate silence" (1977: 25). These rules indicate that the Slavey value listening because of a respect for one another's skills and knowledge. Christian concludes with the suggestion that Slavey communication is supported by complex cultural "beliefs, values and attitudes" that are not amenable to quantitative analysis. Although, to an empiricist, these may appear to be a "Pandora's box," she argues that "failing to open this [box] leaves us with a superficial and misleading study" (1977: 100–101).

Christian presents the empiricist's dilemma as she sees it with considerable candor. The dilemma she identifies is inevitable unless attention is paid to the unstated assumptions or mental percepts deeply embedded in the culture and experience of subarctic Native people. Subarctic people assume that the events of individual experience are connected to an empowering wealth of cultural tradition. Behind the individualism, flexibility, and autonomy so widely reported for northern Indian people, there is a widely held implicit assumption that the individual receives power by acquiring direct knowledge of sentient beings referred to in the mythic language of oral traditions (Ridington 1979; Rushforth 1986). People in subarctic Indian communities share knowledge about these beings as part of communicating what they know about the resource potential of an environment they hold in common. They explore their place in a complex world of other sentient "persons" by following the multiple possibilities of this fundamental mental percept. They are both autonomous in these negotiations and considered responsible for any consequences that may result. Animals and natural forces know and respond to humans in the same way that humans are assumed to know and respond to them and to one another. Because their category of "person" includes sentient animals, animal masters, and forces of nature, northern Natives negotiate social relations in the same way they negotiate relations with animals and natural forces.

The individualism of subarctic people is fundamentally different from that of people in a system of social hierarchy. It is very like the individualism Woodburn (1982) describes in what he calls "immediate return" egalitarian societies. In such an egalitarian society the authority of individual judgment requires respect for individual autonomy and nonintervention, while in a system of social hierarchy individualism is viewed as the mechanism by which some people gain the power to intervene in the lives of others. Leaders in the subarctic demonstrate knowledge and the ability to negotiate with human and nonhuman persons, while leaders in hierarchical societies often demonstrate an ability to command and control others. The individualistic form of leadership found among subarctic people is easily misunderstood as a lack of leadership. Leaders communicate by articulating what is commonly known rather than by giving orders.

Henriksen gives a particularly good account of reciprocity as a basis for leadership among the Naskapi. The leader, he says, must "be aware of deviating opinions among his followers" and must "voice his own opinion in relation to that of others" (1973: 48). "No one," he says, "will either give or take orders from others . . . they are even reluctant to give advice, and when consulted usually answer, '*mokko tchin*'; that is, 'it's up to you'" (1973 : 44). Autonomy is equally important for both leaders and followers. In order to be well informed, the follower "wants to know all the alternatives." Consequently, "in any Naskapi camp, people are continually 'spying' on each other, trying to find out what everyone is thinking of doing" (1973: 48).

My own experience with the Dunne-za illustrates how a leader may instruct without giving orders. After I had spent several years in Dunne-za communities of the Peace River area, their Dreamer, Charlie Yahey, let it be known in one of his talks about heaven that "the people in heaven," with whom he was in contact, knew about me. He said that I could expect to join them there sometime. He said it was good for me to dance during the summer powwows. The message he conveyed was complex and "multivocal." It acknowledged that I had spent enough time among the Dunne-za to accumulate a certain amount of shared experience. The story of my life had become one of their stories. The Dreamer's statement articulated our mutual understanding that should I die my shadow would walk back in the dark of night along the trails I had taken in life. It would not be light enough to rise along Yagatunne, the "trail to heaven," until it had passed back through negative events and experiences.

In Dunne-za theory, the presence of a shadow trail near those of the living is considered to be dangerous, especially to the lives of small children, whose own shadows are very light and easily dissociated from their bodies. The ghost's journey backward can only be shortened by dancing with others around a common fire to the "Dreamers' Songs" (Ridington 1978a: 24–26). Dancing is a way people demonstrate good will to one another and to the other non-human persons of their environment. Charlie Yahey's statement that the people in heaven knew me thus made sense as part of complex cultural assumptions about the responsibility individuals have in relation to all sentient persons. The statement was his way of explaining to me why I should dance.

It is a common experience of subarctic fieldworkers to "find it virtually impossible to follow a discussion or argument" (Scollon and Scollon 1979: 186) because a context of shared experience is missing or because the culture's mental percepts are not known. But it is possible also to follow Hallowell's suggestion that a "higher order of objectivity" may be obtained "by adopting a perspective which includes an analysis of the outlook of the people themselves" (1960: 21). Such an order of objectivity requires that the observer understand both the mental percepts of subarctic people and at least something of the mythic and personal stories within which their subtle and ongoing communication is embedded. He or she must be willing to accept that social life and communication among subarctic hunter-gatherers include a wider range of "persons" than the language and culture of social science generally admit. The ethnographer must discover concepts within his or her language of description that resonate with those of subarctic people.

Communication based on assumed mutual understandings has been described by sociologist Basil Bernstein (1971) as a "restricted" as opposed to an "elaborated" code of discourse. Although Bernstein developed his distinction in reference to class differences within a modern urban culture and there are serious problems with his application of the idea, his terms may be adapted to describe an important quality of communication among northern hunting people. Restricted discourse refers to communication in which the context is taken for granted. A social setting where the context of communication is assumed provides ample opportunity for references to mutually shared knowledge and experience. When applied to the oral communications of highly individualistic subarctic Native communities, Bernstein's "restricted" code might better be called a "reflexive" code, in that discourse depends upon each person placing him- or herself within a mutually understood context. Bernstein's distinction would then refer to differences between systems in which the context is assumed and those in which it must be specified.

Edward Hall has described a similar phenomenon in the distinction he makes between "high and low context messages." According to Hall, "the more information that is shared . . . the higher the context" (1983: 56–57). Discourse in small subarctic communities would, in Hall's terms, be highly contexted because of the shared mutual understandings on which it is predicated. Hallowell's "higher order of objectivity" would then be required to develop an interpretive language capable of translating such a highly contexted form of communication.

Ethnographers have described northern hunting people as individualistic because they correctly note that each person is expected to inform, and thereby empower, him- or herself within the mutually understood context of shared knowledge and a shared code of communication. Their individualism is not, however, at odds with their social context. Indeed, the individualism of northern Indian people is based upon a fundamental social compact, a trust in the individual's social responsibility and informed intelligence. Northern hunting people trust the individual to be responsible not only to him- or herself but also to all the other human and transhuman persons of a sentient social environment in its widest possible context (Hallowell 1960; Scollon and Scollon 1979; Goulet 1987). The intelligence of individual human judgment and the system of cultural intelligence that informs it thus define a fundamental resource on which all other adaptations depend.

NORTHERN HUNTING KNOWLEDGE AND TECHNOLOGY

Subarctic hunting people depend fundamentally on knowledge and technique for their successful adaptation to the environment. Although they have been capable of producing elaborate hunting implements such as bows and arrows, traps, and deadfalls (Oswalt 1973: 118–119), they also achieve complex interactions with their environment without having recourse to complex material artifacts. Northern hunters have, for instance, traditionally carried out artfully organized communal hunts with a minimum of material possessions. Using artifacts as simple as snares, they have relied on knowledge held in common to work quietly and autonomously toward a common purpose. In some cases "hunt chiefs" (Ridington 1987b) visualize and direct the overall hunt plan through dreaming, but success ultimately depends upon the individual's understanding of human and animal behavior in relation to environmental features. Although the physical artifacts required for this form of hunting are minimal, success depends on a complex and sophisticated form of artifice and understanding (Ridington 1983b). It is easy for an outside observer to interpret information about dreaming and knowledge differently from information about material culture because of an unexamined assumption that technology *means* material culture. Such an assumption could disguise the full adaptive significance of knowledge for subarctic people and result in what Christian called "a superficial and misleading study."

In their *Handbook* article on "Environment and Culture in the Cordillera," McClellan and Denniston (1981) describe the technology of Cordilleran Athapaskans as "admirably adapted to mobility." They say that "people carried little with them, since many things could be made rather quickly with materials close at hand." They cite snare and surround hunting to illustrate the mobility, economy, and essentially mental quality of subarctic technology:

> What was absolutely critical was the knowledge of how to use the equipment effectively in varying situations, where best to set

the snare or deadfall or to build a caribou surround, where to go
on one's snowshoes to locate a moose, how to bait a wolverine
deadfall or to disguise the human odor on a beaver net. The successful hunter had to know the landscape, the habits of his prey,
and the probable course of the weather. *Equally essential to his
mind was the knowledge of how to behave in a personalized universe
in which many animal spirits were thought to be more powerful than
humans.* (1981: 377, emphasis added)

Northern forest Indians are well aware that their means of production are mental as well as material. Their subsistence technology
has emphasized the possession of techniques rather than artifacts.
Elsewhere I have suggested that

> in thinking about hunting and gathering people who must move
> frequently from place to place . . . technology should be seen as
> a system of knowledge rather than an inventory of objects . . .
> The essence of hunting and gathering adaptive strategy is to
> retain, and to be able to act upon, information about the pos-
> sible relationships between people and the natural environment.
> When realized, these life-giving relationships are as much the ar-
> tifacts of hunting and gathering technology as are the material
> objects that are instrumental in bringing them about. (Riding-
> ton 1982a: 471)

CONCLUSION

Knowledge, power, and individual intelligence are keys to understanding the adaptive competence of northern hunting people. The
individualism of these people is intelligible only in relation to *their*
understanding that an individual's sentient intelligence must make
contact with an intelligent organization of the environment at large.
Their individualism is sustained by their closely contexted communities, in which a great deal of information about social and natural
conditions is held in common. The phenomenology of northern
hunting people may be seen as integral to their overall adaptive
strategy. Their "religion" may be viewed as social and psychological
dimensions of their technology.

Although the traditions of scholarship among Algonquianists and

Athapaskanists differ in the attention they pay to Native phenomenology and psychology, both indicate that northern Native individualism must be understood in relation to empowering cultural beliefs. A significant number of the anthropologists who studied people of the subarctic have made contributions to anthropological theory. Many of these contributions seem to have transformed elements of Native theory into the language of social science. These contributions correspond to what Hallowell called a "higher order" of objectivity that adopts "a perspective which includes an analysis of the outlook of the people themselves" (1960: 21).

Subarctic ethnography is important to anthropological theory as a whole in that the adaptive conditions experienced by the subarctic Native people of North America are in many ways similar to those of northern hunter-gatherers in much earlier times. Fundamental traditions of human thought and practice may have evolved and been sustained in the cultures of northern hunter-gatherers. Their cultures may be understood as systems of information that guide and sustain the intelligence of individual thought and action. The cultural and individual intelligence they have developed are complementary products of a long coevolutionary process.

American Anthropologist, 1988

THE POLITICS OF EXPERIENCE

Eskama in camp, Doig River, 1968

As I studied Dunne-za stories and the artifice of hunting technology I also thought about how hunting people negotiate relations with one another in the absence of a system of social hierarchy. I have called this section "The Politics of Experience" because in these papers I go back to my fieldwork experience and to Dunne-za stories as a source of information about the context in which these negotiations take place. Being with the Dunne-za led me to adopt a view of culture as process. The Dunne-za, I learned, do not relate to one another by giving orders; rather, they create a mutually understood social and natural order. All persons, human and nonhuman alike, seem to be equally responsible for bringing that order into being.

In writing "Phases and the Moment of Transformation," I looked at the phenomenology of Dunne-za culture and experience. I particularly wanted to think about how experiences in a medium of dream and vision can be instrumental to the adaptive technology of hunting people. I also became interested in the evolutionary question of how culture itself changes and transforms. How has culture evolved as a system of information that simultaneously informs and is informed by the intelligence of individuals? How do individuals negotiate with their own culture as well as with one another? How do these negotiations bring about culture change and adaptation?

"The Medicine Fight: An Instrument of Political Process" was my first published paper. It resolved a contradiction between what I had come to expect from my reading and what I observed in the field. From reading anthropology I expected a well-integrated culture to have a single coherent theory of explanation. In the field, I heard two different explanations for personal misfortune. One said that the misfortune is caused by another person's malevolent use of his or her power. Another said that misfortune results from a breach of taboo. Were the Dunne-za poorly integrated, or was there something wrong with the view of culture I brought to the field? The resolution came when I looked at the context in which one or another explanation is given. The explanations turned out to be situational and relative to whether a person was a victim or the potential instrument of misfortune.

The final paper in this section, "Wechuge and Windigo," compares the Dunne-za image of a person transformed into a cannibal by becoming "too strong" with the classic windigo complex of the eastern subarctic. The paper complements and expands upon information about the politics of the medicine fight. I have added a note of reference to a recent paper on windigo by Robert Brightman (1988).

SEQUENCE AND HIERARCHY
IN CULTURAL EXPERIENCE

Phases and the Moment of Transformation

Activity at biological, linguistic, and cultural levels proceeds sequentially and is meaningful hierarchically. Experience, too, is sequential, and its significance depends upon a hierarchy of cultural forms that serve as collective memory. The meaning of experience is fundamentally relational. The here and now is meaningful only in relation to a person's culturally instructed representations of the there and then. These cultural representations are themselves brought into being through reflexive negotiation with the experience of individuals. Cultural hierarchy and individual experience feed backward and forward to reflect and instruct one another.

Although possessed by the phenomenological moment, human experience derives its meaning from its place in a superorganic hierarchy of information. The meaning of individual experience is a product of an ongoing process of negotiation with an objective, artifactual, superorganic system of information traditionally identified by anthropology as culture. Culture as an organized information system reflects, instructs, and synthesizes the moments of human experience. It is the relational hierarchy through which experience becomes meaningful.

Humans have redirected the phylogenetically ancient animal capacity for modifying the present moment by reference to memory of the past. This is what Laughlin and D'Aquili (1974) have called the "cognitive extension of prehension." In the human case, learned responses have become coded as cultural representations and are passed on from generation to generation. We orient ourselves by reference to the superorganic information of our culture as we have come to know it internally. Human experience is meaningful because it takes place within a culturally constructed environment. The hierarchy of information that is our culture may be generated internally without reference to immediate sense data. Culture does not come to us from our senses but only through them. Sense data are meaningful to us only through the mediation and instruction of our culture. It is through culture that individual experience makes sense. Without the organizational template of culture, human experience would deteriorate into mere sensation.

This paper explores the channels through which experience and culture are interrelated in a traditional small-scale hunting society, the Dunne-za, of Canada's Peace River region. It contrasts their culturally defined phenomenology with our own. In Dunne-za phenomenology, unlike our own, the experiential states of dreaming and vision are systematically integrated into the cultural mosaic. The paper will present ethnographic evidence to show how this integration is achieved. The purpose of the essay will be both to reveal the terms of another culture's phenomenology and to reflect upon the terms of our own. An explanation will be suggested for the question of why modern Western phenomenology has given so little importance to subjective states of dreaming and visionary experience.

PHENOMENOLOGICAL PHASES

The concept of phenomenological phases developed by Shearer, Laughlin, and McManus (n.d.) will be used here. Their general terms of reference are those of biogenetic structuralism (Laughlin and D'Aquili 1974). According to these authors, phases are categorically distinct "cognized strips of experience . . . lying between points of salient transformation." These various phenomenological categories process information in different ways. The ordinary waking phase, for instance, is dominated by information entering the brain as sense data, while the dreaming phase is dominated by internally generated information. The ordinary waking state is concerned with immediate orientation and decision making, while the dream state deals with the "reorganization and reintegration" of information processed initially during waking phases. The transformation from the waking to the dream phase is regular and cyclical, generally following a circadian biorhythm.

Within the waking phase, there may be transformations in the way in which information is processed. Casual inattention to the environment in general may be suddenly transformed into intent concentration on a particular object. This has been called a developmental transformation by Shearer, Laughlin, and McManus. Attention may shift again from object to myth (a surface transformation) or from one object to another (a sensory transformation). A more profound transformation in the waking phase occurs during visionary experience. Shearer, Laughlin, and McManus suggest that a phenomenon such as shamanism may be described as an institutionalization of a transformation from the ordinary waking phase to a nonordinary one, in which internally generated information comes to dominate and override the ordinary decision making and orientation function of the waking phase.

Phenomenological phases and the information they process are organized hierarchically. Although phenomenological moments are inherently located in a sequential order, "cognized strips of experience," their meaning is relational within a hierarchical structure of plan (Miller, Galanter, and Pribram 1960). The sequential flow of information is hierarchically organized at the level of neurophysiology and general motor behavior (Lenneberg 1967; Miller, Galanter, and Pribram 1960), language (Chomsky 1957), and culture. The transformation of experience from one phenomenological phase to another may be viewed as a shift in the point of reference or level within a hierarchical structure.

The moment of experience, although part of the sequential flow of events, is also like the center of a sphere of influence casting its organizational pattern concentrically upon the surrounding environment and receiving information from all directions. It is not simply point Y in the sequence X, Y, Z; rather, it is influenced equally by the memory of X and the anticipation of Z which reflects and is instructed by a pattern of organization that is hierarchical rather than linear, taxonomic rather than enumerative, synthetic rather than additive. In our cognitive construction of a given point in sequential time, we refer it to a plan of organization that stands above the momentary event and yet paradoxically is inherent in the experience of the event if that experience is to be meaningful. Experience flows sequentially but is meaningful hierarchically.

A neuromotor, linguistic, or cultural event is more than the consequence of its immediate antecedents. It is equally connected to subsequent events as part of a larger coordinated unit of organization. A word's meaning derives not only from its dictionary definition but also from its place in a hierarchically organized syntactic structure. Subsequent words and events in a sequence of words and events have a reflexive relationship to their own antecedents. The meaning of word or event depends upon its relationship to subsequent as well as antecedent units within which it is integrated to form a pattern or mosaic of meaning. By the same principle of hierarchical organization that applies to neurophysiological and linguistic events, individual experience, too, is meaningful only within the higher cultural domain of which it is a part.

Cultural forms exhibit more generally the organizational principle found in neuromotor and linguistic activity. Culture is the central hierarchy of organized information that brings together the experiences of people removed from one another in space and time. It is the symbolic mediator of intersubjective relationship and the hierarchy to which subjective experience must be related in order to become meaningful. For human beings, meaningful experience is cultural experience. Intersubjective relationship must be culturally mediated. Culture is the whole through which we, as parts, relate to one another. It is the central hierarchy in relation to which experience has meaning.

CULTURE AND TRANSFORMATIVE EXPERIENCE AMONG THE DUNNE-ZA

Our own phenomenology gives little cultural representation or reinforcement to phenomenological phases other than those of the ordinary waking state, while that of the Dunne-za takes other phases very seriously. Dunne-za culture places particular emphasis on the experience of individual transformation from one phenomenological phase to another. In experiencing transformations from the ordinary waking phase to the dreaming or visionary phase, the Dunne-za draw upon an overall cultural mosaic of meaningful relationships. Although they recognize that information is processed very differently in different phases, their culture integrates information from all phases into a single central system of meaning. In particular, it provides channels for the cross-referencing of information from one phase to another. Thus, control of information in the dream phase is derived from a previous visionary experience which is, in turn, instructed by information presented in myth.

For the Dunne-za, events in the ordinary waking phase are systematically related to information or "knowledge" contained in myth and individually acquired in dream and vision. Every child undergoes vision quest encounters with supernatural powers from mythic times. These encounters activate, in a person's life, powers represented by the myth. These powers return to his or her experience in dreams throughout life. Peter Chipesia described the vision quest experience as follows:

> When you are close to something, an animal, you are just like drunk. You don't know anything. As soon as this happens you have trouble thinking straight, like being drunk. Everything is just like when you see this animal it is as if he were a person. If you take water then, everything will get away from you and you will be a person again. You won't see anything. That is why you can't drink water before you go out into the bush. When kids are about the same size as Joe [about five], when they are just old enough to think, to talk, to walk . . . when they are older, the animal shows them how to make a medicine bundle. Asah [grandfather] kept one for himself. One time he showed me that frog. He moved on his hand. It's kind of a rubber thing, but he moved, he jumped . . . Their parents know ahead of time. They dream about it. Lots of times, the kids they raised, they're gone about ten days, fifteen days. The parents start to worry and pretty soon the old man starts to look for them, dream where they are, where to find them. This thing that talks to them, he stays with them about that long. Then he tells that boy, he tells him, "Your parents are worrying about you. I'd better take you home." He puts him back close to home where the people can find him. Then he goes back, that thing goes back. [Question: Do they forget how to talk to people?] Yes, they look strange. When you see your people you start to run away. Even Mom was like that that time. Long time ago, she told us about that time. She said she traveled about sixty miles, I think. She said that the man, those people who raised her, left an axe that far

away just on purpose and told her to get it. They told her to get the axe. So Mom starts traveling in the wintertime I guess. She said, "There was a wolf traveling ahead of me. I keep following that wolf, just keep following. Then there were some hunters, some people just camping out hunting. They were about that far away. As soon as I came close to that place where their camp was, maybe about a mile there was a trail, the bottom trail or something came close to that place and that wolf walked on, you know, just a shadow, and he was kind of like saying things." It was old wolf tracks she saw, but she saw the shadow of the wolf in them. "That thing is still going on ahead of me so I keep on going too. As soon as I saw the fire of that hunting camp," she said, "I can't go near it." But those hunters spotted her. She said, "That one woman in the camp spotted me and started toward me and I ran away. I was knocked out for two days." I think that animal kind of made her mad. And that one old man he started dreaming and for two days she didn't know anything, just knocked out. After two days that old man covered her with his coat and she went to sleep. Next morning she woke up and the old man gave her water and she was all right. If those people hadn't camped there she would have caught up with the wolf and they would have stayed together in real life.

Through experience in phenomenological phases other than those of ordinary waking reality, the deep structure of their myth becomes real to the Dunne-za. In dream and vision, their cultural plans or hierarchies may be experienced directly. In them, the sequential flow of experience is overwhelmed by direct apprehension of the plans to which the experience of events relates. These plans are symbolized by the structural relationships of mythic and supernatural times and places. They are supernatural not because they are unanalyzable mysteries but because they are representations of the hierarchy by which the meaning of natural events is defined. In them, the form and structure of the sequential flow of ordinary events is brought to conscious attention. In them, a person becomes conscious of the reflexive relationship events have on the meaning of their own antecedents. In them, pattern dominates process; syntax dominates segment; hierarchy dominates sequence.

When a person dreams or has a visionary encounter, his or her mind is described as being freed from the body's situation in time and space. In dream and vision, the mind may travel across a conceptual landscape whose contours are already known through myth and symbol. There, freed from the sequential constraints of a perceptual mode dominated by immediate sensory information, the mind is free to process information generated internally. Although this information becomes phenomenologically real within individual experience, its source is the intersubjective superorganic system of information we call culture. Its organizational plan comes naturally to mind in the experience of dream and vision.

Although we, as observers from another culture, can never know directly the quality of Dunne-za dreams and visions, we can understand the structure and content of the cultural mosaic with which they are informed. The symbolic representations of Dunne-za reality found in their myths instruct us about their phenomenology, just as they instruct the dreaming and visionary experience of the Dunne-za themselves. Even their songs are viewed by the Dunne-za as symbolic representations of the trail to heaven, the beat of the drum being the rhythmic fall of feet on the trail, and the melodic line the turns and contours of an intricate conceptual landscape. Their symbolic representations are both objective artifacts of past relationships and internally generated images giving meaning and instruction to their subjective states of dream and vision. Because they are objective and superorganic, they are not dependent on the immediate flow of sensory information, as is the ordinary waking state. The relationships known through myth, dream, and vision are abstract and imaginary, but they function as plans that are vital to the accomplishment of adaptive activity. In Dunne-za philosophy, as articulated by their myths, substantive reality must be underwritten by a plan or design representing the relationship inherent in the world as it is experienced. Their creation story makes this point clearly.

He made this world and at first there were no animals. There was just water and no land. Then he started to make the land. He finished all the land. Finally this world started to move, started to grow and kept growing. That is what the old people said. Just the water and no land, there were no animals. Where are they going to stay with no land? Only God stayed someplace where he made it for himself, maybe boat or just water, no land. There was just water and God made a big cross that he floated up on the water. He floated the cross on the water. He floated that cross on the water and then he called all the animals that stay in the water. He sent them down to get the dirt, but they just came out. They couldn't get it. Too far down. The last one was rats. He sent him down to get the dirt and he stayed down for how long. Finally he just brought up a little dirt. He put that little piece of dirt on the cross and he told it, "You are going to grow." From there it started to grow and kept growing, every year and year like that. Finally it was getting bigger and pretty soon it was big. That is what the old people say.

And stars, everything, animals, just like animals coming down, landing down. Pretty soon sure lots. Where people stayed there were some great big animals coming around. He made those giant animals from the stars that he sent down to this earth. There was just one person in this world. He wanted to put everything together. He traveled along looking for all those bad animals, the giant ones that kill people. He looked for every one of them. Everybody ran away from those giant animals that ate people, but that one person only looked after them. He followed them instead of running away. Everyone ran away from the camp but this one man just went after them and killed them. He just kept on like that. He looked for those bad ones. The old people heard that. That man Saya started to work on the world so everything would be straight for today. Some of the animals he didn't kill. He just chased them under the ground. That is why you can see some of them where there is high ground.

In order for meaningful action to be possible in the world of substance, cultural plans must be impressed upon the flow of events. The Dunne-za accomplished this impression through dreaming. Just as in the creation story, where a plan of articulation precedes the emergence of substance, in the course of events the revelation of a plan is believed to be a necessary precondition of meaningful experience in the ordinary waking phase. Thus, the Dunne-za set up their camps so that people sleep with their heads pointing in the direction of the sun's return across an expanse of bush unbroken by human trails. In dreams that come symbolically from the direction of the sun's anticipated return, the plan of future substantive events is revealed. These dreams are prophetic, not because the dream state has a mysterious compulsive influence on the course of events but because it reveals the overall plan or hierarchy within which all events are meaningful. When, in the ordinary waking phases of experience, events are realized through physical sensation, they are expected to be understood as manifestations of a plan whose general form has already been experienced in phases where information is generated internally. The events of ordinary waking experience are familiar to the traditional Dunne-za, because the categories to which these events belong have already been represented in a cultural code brought down in dream and vision.

Events proceed sequentially to the realization of an expected pattern with the certainty of the sun's return to the eastern horizon. Because the Dunne-za are hunters, they know that if the people are to continue to live, the trails of their hunters must continue to make contact with the trails of animals in the bush. Elsewhere (Ridington 1980a) I have written at length concerning the image of the trail in Dunne-za symbolism. With the certainty that the sun will return to the sky in the east each new day, the Dunne-za know that if their life as a people is to continue, the hunters will realize in substantive reality the images of relationship that come to them in their dreams. Thus, the world of sequential sensation and that of a plan held in mind are viewed as transformations of a single reality rather than as separate worlds of reality and imagination. The image of a future trail held in mind, like the image of a world to be brought up by Muskrat and placed at the center of a primal point of articulation, reveals the meaning inherent in the sequential course of events.

While the trail that the body must follow is necessarily sequential, its meaning can only be found in a relational hierarchy permanently coded in the superorganic structure of myth. The creation story may thus be seen as being like a metalogue, itself an example of the phenomenon it describes. It not only reveals the Dunne-za view of the relationship between image and substance, it also functions as a plan for the organization of substantive experience. It is both a plan and a story about plans. Every point of articulation brings the world into being. Every moment is both a speck of dirt under Muskrat's nails and a self-sufficient universe. Every vision connects the symbols of realization in a myth with their substantive realization in a person's life. Every dream places future events within the pattern of relationship represented in myth and experienced directly during the vision quest.

The symbols of myth experienced in the dreaming or visionary imagination articulate the meaning or hierarchy inherent in the sequential events of ordinary waking reality. Phenomenological phases dominated by sequential sensory information, and those in which internally generated information is processed, are known by the Dunne-za to be systematically related to one another. The different phenomenological phases are not viewed as being real versus unreal but rather as systematic transformations within a single overall reality. In this knowledge they give special significance to the moment of transformation from one phenomenological phase to another. To them it is normal for a person to control and manipulate the experience of transformation from one phase to another. Through transformative experience, the knowledge on which basic subsistence skills depend may be activated as the realization of a cultural plan within a person's life.

The death of an animal that brings life to the people is a natural transformation, brought about through cultural control and competence. Before a person can bring about this fundamental transformation of nature, he or she must have already undergone the transformative experience of a vision quest encounter with a mythical power. In this encounter, the powerless child is overcome and transformed by a powerful mythic animal-person. Upon his or her return from this vision quest encounter, the newly empowered child must be brought back into the life of the camp by an adult whose own personal powers are socially recognized. It is the child's personal transformative experience that gives him or her the power, later in life, to bring about the transformation of animals in the bush into food for the people in camp.

The moment of transformation from one phenomenological phase to another is given special status by the Dunne-za. It is seen as the point of entry into another world closer to the meaning of things. It occurs when the child encounters his or her medicine animal on the vision quest, during dreaming, and in ritual. In the creation myth, it is the plunge of Muskrat down beneath the superficial appearance of everyday reality to retrieve the germ of substance that will become the world. In his plunge, he passes out of one consciousness into another. It is an act of creation. The myth describes not only the creation of the physical world but also the creation of the world of experience. Through the experience of personal transformation a person may, like Muskrat, penetrate beneath the appearance of ordinary waking experience to retrieve the germ of substance from which a new world will grow. Through transformative experience, a person is enabled to bring about transformations in the natural world.

Within the logic of the creation story, Muskrat's penetration of the world beneath the surface of sensation implies its structural opposite, the penetration of a world above its surface. Within this shamanic cosmology, the possibility of a journey to the nadir is balanced by the possibility of an ascent to the zenith. These extremities of shamanic penetration are not physical places but representations of the polarities of human cognition. Together, zenith and nadir represent the *axis mundi* of a shamanic cosmology. Their significance lies in their relationship to one another.

In the creation story, as in Dunne-za phenomenology, the mind is represented as having access to worlds above and below the level of everyday reality. The transformation of experience from the surface world to that of the zenith is represented by Swan. Swans are believed to be the only animal capable of flying through to heaven (*yage*) and returning in the same body. The transformation of experience from the surface world to that of the nadir is represented by Muskrat. Muskrats are believed to be the only animal capable of diving down to the earth below the water and returning in the same body. The down feathers of swans metonymously represent their ascendant quality as they are apparently released from the gravity that possesses other bodies. In the sky, the constellation of the swan flies across the Milky Way's celestial field. With the transformation of summer into winter, swans fly through to a life-sustaining land otherwise unknown to the people, and with the return of warmth and the sun the swans also return. Swans travel in formation, their relationship to one another resolving a form in the sky. Even the single celestial swan in the summer sky forms the cross in evocation of the image of articulation that precedes an emergence of substance.

Together, Muskrat and Swan represent transformative phases of the shamanic personality. The meaning of ordinary waking experience emerges from the relationship between them. As beings who have traveled beneath and beyond the appearances of the world of sensation, they reach out to the extremities of conceptual possibility. It is inconceivable to the Dunne-za to go beyond their respective phases of experience. Together, the deepest diver and the highest flier represent the world to them as they imagine it to be through dream and vision. The world of everyday experience exists at the center of the cross, the resolution of these phenomenological polarities. Their shamanic cosmology represents the limits of conceptual possibility rather than physical places.

The Swan is used by the Dunne-za as an image of the Dreamer, or prophet. Dreamers are people who have symbolically experienced the transformation of their own death but, like Swan, have returned in the same body from a journey to the land beyond the sky. Swan is also the childhood name of Saya, the Dunne-za culture hero transformer whose later name means "sun-moon in the sky." The story of his life, along with the creation story, is a key to the meaning of transformative experience among the Dunne-za. Through the phenomenological phases of dream and vision, the plans they represent become instructions for a person's life experience. In the moment of transformation, a person enters these stories and they become real for him or her. In dream and vision, the plans of the stories instruct the ordinary course of events as they are experienced through sequential sensation.

When a person has experienced transformation, he or she becomes capable of bringing about substantive transformations of nature. This equation of personal transformative experience with transformations in the natural environment is exemplified in the life of Saya, the culture hero transformer. As a child, he was called Swan, a name associated with the seasonal north-south migration of water birds and with the seasonal migration of the point at which the sun rises and sets. In winter, both swans and the sun are in the south. In summer, they are in the north. Swan is also a metaphor for Dreamer, the person whose mind is able to fly through to heaven and return to the same body on earth. As an adult, the Swan child takes the name of Saya, sun-moon in the sky. His transformation comes about through a vision quest isolation on a tiny island replicating the world in its germinal form. A supernatural helper tells him he can live through the winter by placing pitch on the island's rocks heated by the sun to snare the migratory water birds on their way south. Thus, in his name, he realizes a plan for substantive survival.

Just as the cross preceded Muskrat's retrieval of substance in the creation story, the name of Swan precedes the actual appearance of migratory water birds on the island at his visionary isolation in the culture hero story. Elsewhere (Ridington 1978a) I have analyzed the symbolism of this story in greater detail. In the myth, Swan's experience of personal transformation in his vision quest isolation leads to his ability to transform the giant animals that in mythic times hunted people. The empowerment of Swan's vision quest transformation into Saya, the culture hero, is a prototype for the vision quest empowerment of every child into a competent adult, capable of transforming the bodies of animals into food, tools, and clothing. The Dreamer is a person whose understanding of the mosaic of meaning allows him or her to "follow [the giant animals] instead of running away."

The primary celestial bodies, sun and moon, are key symbols in Dunne-za phenomenology. They call both sun and moon *sa* and discriminate between them as daytime and nighttime *sa*, respectively. These bodies are used metaphorically to represent transformative phases of a single personality. Through observing the daily progression from horizon to horizon of the daytime *sa*, the nomadic hunting Dunne-za take their sense of direction. By noting one's own relationship to its arc across the sky, taking into account time of year and an estimate of the passage of time, the Dunne-za hunters and travelers accurately determine their position in an otherwise featureless terrain. The daytime *sa*'s passage across the sky provides information relevant to a person's passage across the physical terrain of the boreal forest. In the phenomenological phase dominated by the daytime *sa*, information from external sources determines what is integrated into the pattern carried internally. Both symbolically and literally, the Dunne-za find their direction in the daytime world in relation to Saya's passage across the sky.

The nighttime *sa* is Saya transformed into a shadow of his daytime self. This phase is dominated by internally generated information experienced in the dream state. The nighttime and daytime phases of Saya's personality are related to one another as a person's shadow is related to his or her body. The body must move step by step through sequential time, but the shadow can leave the body in dream and move within a purely symbolic world of internally generated information. Each phase processes information relevant to experience in its transformational counterpart. Each component of Saya's personality relates to the totality represented in the creation and culture hero myths. In the dreaming, the Dunne-za orient their bodies to the place of the daytime *sa*'s return; awake, they retain the significant images of their dreams. Together, the two phases apprehend the mosaic of meaning represented in their myths.

The world and the phenomenological moment of experience in which it is apprehended are always centered by the center of the cross. The creation story represents a continuous creative process of bringing the world into being. In hunting, a person goes out in the four directions but always returns to the center that is camp. Conceptually, every hunt must begin in the east, the direction in which the hunter sleeps, awaiting a dream that will come to him with the certainty of the daytime *sa*'s return in the morning. In dream or vision, a person, like Swan and Muskrat, penetrates reflective imaginary worlds above or beneath that of the ordinary waking phenomenological moment that always returns to its point of balance at the center of the cross. The point at which the four directions and the three worlds come together balances the polarities of other states of mind. The center of the cross is the point of reference through which dream, myth, and vision are brought into meaningful relationship within ordinary waking experience. Transformative experience proceeds from this symbolic point of articulation. In Dunne-za phenomenology, as represented by their creation story, the physical world grows from the center of an image of lateral articulation and vertical penetration. The world of substance brought up from the deep by Muskrat is also an image of the human body with its physical senses. The world, the human body, and the celestial bodies of sun and moon are experienced sequentially but are meaningful hierarchically. At the center of the cross, the moment of experience is meaningful only in relation to culturally instructed representations of other imaginary worlds.

The ability to conceptualize other times, places, and subjectivities removed from the phenomenological moment appears to be part of the biogenetic program, Laughlin and D'Aquili's (1974) "cognitive extension of prehension." In the absence of cultural information, however, this biogenetic capacity can only result in a kind of autism. The ability to conceptualize subatomic particles, black holes, or distant galaxies stems from the same biogenetic symbolic function apparent in Dunne-za conceptualizations of creation and transformation, as represented in their myths. Biogenetically, humans are as well adapted to conceptualize scientific abstractions as they are to conceptualize imaginary worlds beneath and above the surface of everyday reality. In both cases, the imagination, instructed by cultural information, postulates conditions outside the realm of ordinary perceptual experience. In both cases, the mind brings into subjective experience information from the superorganic realm of culture. The difference between the two conceptualizations lies not in their biogenetic basis but in the adaptive conditions that underlie their cultural content. Among the Dunne-za, an adaptively stable hunting society, cultural information coded in mythic symbolism instructs the experience of the moment through dream and vision, while in adaptively unstable modern technological society, cultural information coded in scientific constructs and procedures instructs the moment through informed conscious insight. Dunne-za cultural symbols focus on personal transformation in the vision quest, dreaming, and shamanic experience, while modern Western cultural symbols focus on transformations in the culture's own system of information.

To the Dunne-za, sun and moon represent regular cyclic transformative phases of the mythic culture hero's personality. In acquiring power through the vision quest to control the mind's activity during dreaming, the normal Dunne-za personality comes into contact with Saya's power of transformation. The Dunne-za know that their lives depend upon the transformation of animals, alive in the bush, into food, clothing, and tools in camp. Their myths and symbols instruct them to use the experience of personal transformation of nature on which their lives depend.

In *Swan People* (1978a), I have described in detail the role of a Dreamer or Swan Chief as a person whose personal shamanic experience gives him the authority to organize the communal hunting. The same basic formula of Dunne-za logic underwrites both the vision quest–based power of individual hunters and the shamanic experience of Dreamers who organize the communal hunt. Both derive the authority to transform nature from their knowledge gained through individual transformative experience. Relationships between people and the natural environment remain more or less constant and have been coded into the cultural symbolic mosaic. There is virtually no knowledge, experience, relationship, or technique that is not represented in the cultural code of mythic symbolism. The entire fund of Dunne-za adaptive information is reflected and transmitted in their oral tradition. Through dream and vision the basic structure of this information becomes part of an individual's experience even before it is put into effect. In Dunne-za phenomenology, a substantive experience cannot take place until its form or image has been experienced previously in the mind. Just as the world's body is preceded by the image of the cross, encounters with an animal's body in the bush must be preceded by a dream image of the person's relationship to it. The dream is itself directed by an image of the daytime *sa*'s return, which is, in turn, instructed by the myth of Saya, the transformer.

All information and all relationships known to the Dunne-za are coded by their oral tradition, so that when they are encountered by an individual in his or her own life they are experienced as transformations of a familiar pattern. Knowledge of traditional adaptive relationships is preserved from generation to generation. Relationships between people and nature move with the regularity and recurrence of the daily, monthly, and seasonal cycles of sun and moon, personified as Saya, the transformer. The experience of personal transformation from one phenomenological phase to another is represented metaphorically by the cyclical transformations of nature. Dunne-za culture thus makes use of phenomenological phase transformation to introduce information and meanings that will be of adaptive value in understanding the course of events. Through transformative experience, the sequential progression of events is constantly referred back to a mythically represented cultural hierarchy of information.

In modern Western experience, under conditions of adaptive instability and lineal progressive transformation of both society and nature, information of adaptive significance is constantly being revised and modified. The scientific paradigm emphasizes falsifiability rather than absolute knowledge. Because of rapid culture change from generation to generation, and even within the lifetime of a single individual, an adaptive cultural program must retain a high degree of flexibility and receptiveness to new information. Where, in traditional Dunne-za culture, every possible human experience or technique is precisely indexed in oral tradition and made accessible through dream and vision, in modern historical culture it is assumed that in the course of a person's life he or she will experience dramatic transformations of past cultural experience. The historical culture's program therefore emphasizes symbols of historical transformation rather than those of individual subjective transformation.

Our fields of knowledge, and even the very paradigms into which information is organized, are known to have changed dramatically within relatively short spans of recorded history. Within a few years we have become aware of our place in a galaxy of galaxies in a universe that has been expanding for fifteen thousand million years. We have seen the surface features of other worlds, thus transforming forever their metaphoric potential for us. We know that the most fundamental energetic relationships of modern global adaptation are based on nonrenewable resources. We have reason to believe that even our own culture may be a nonrenewable resource.

While Dunne-za cultural information has been collected and integrated over many generations and millennia of boreal forest hunting adaptation, our own cultural information is continually being added to and repatterned in a linear transformative progression. Dunne-za myth and oral tradition provide accurate and highly patterned information relevant to a person's anticipated life experience. This information is brought into relationship to the ordinary, waking, sequential, phenomenological phase through dream and vision. Phenomenological phases that depend on internally generated information are useful to Dunne-za adaptive strategy because the information they draw upon is the very basis of the culture's plan of organization. Although this information is internally generated from the point of view of the individual, it is superorganically generated from the point of view of society at large. The intelligence that comes to a person through dream and vision is the intelligence commanded by millennia of boreal forest adaptation.

Dream and vision are not themselves inherently revelatory, without a fund of culturally coded information to back them up. They are merely biogenetically given phenomenological phases through which fundamental relationships and information may be processed abstractly. They reveal the meaning inherent in the course of sequential experience because that meaning is articulated clearly in cultural symbolic structure. Nonsequentially dependent phenomeno-logical phases allow for direct apprehension of the deep structure of information that already exists in a cultural code. They have no power to conjure information or structure where none exists. Colin Wilson makes essentially the same point in *The Philosopher's Stone*. He says that what he calls the "value experience" is like a flash of lightning. "What is important is not the lightning, but what you see by it. If lightning explodes in empty space it illuminates nothing. If it explodes over a mountain landscape it illuminates a great deal" (1969: 83).

Revelatory experience is informative only where a system of in-formation is waiting to be revealed. In modern historical experience, information is revealed only as it comes upon us. Our culture has not had time to organize information relevant to current adaptive conditions in a form that can be usefully apprehended through dream and vision. Thus, although the biogenetic capacity for expe-rience in these phenomenological phases is universal, the meaning of this experience is dependent on a culture's adaptive context. In an adaptively stable culture, the experience of phenomenological phase transformation allows cultural information to be processed abstractly and integrated effectively into the ongoing course of events, while in an adaptively unstable culture, information derived from dreams and visions risks being anomalous or even misleading.

Shearer, Laughlin, and McManus conclude their paper on phe-nomenological phases with a question about why the phenome-nology of Western culture does not integrate dreams and visions significantly into its information-processing system. I suggest that phenomenological phases that process internally generated informa-tion are dependent upon systematic and intelligible cultural data in order to function effectively. The experience of a vivid dream or heightened sense of meaning is useful only when it can be integrated meaningfully into the culture's adaptive program as it is carried out in an individual's life. Modern historical experience is carried on through continual negotiation with new information and emerging patterns of meaning.

Although dreams and visions may reveal for an instant the con-tours of a darkened, unfamiliar landscape, we may only come to know our world directly through the ongoing unfolding of our ex-perience of it. We are denied the quality of familiarity engendered through myth, vision, and dream with which the Dunne-za experience the course of events. Our experience becomes familiar to us only after the fact, seldom before it. Things are as they are for us because they happened to come together that way, not because Saya the transformer gave them their present form. Sequential progressive evolution corresponds to our experience better than the unexplainable authority of special creation. The progressive transformation of a changing historical culture is more salient for us than is the experience of personal phenomenological phase transformation. We must attend to information about a changing world and make it intelligible for ourselves. The superorganic hierarchy of information available to us is coded in our written, artistic, and artifactual record of life in other times and places. The patterns inherent in this record are complex, sometimes contradictory, and beyond the apprehension of any one individual.

Because our culture's knowledge is beyond the experience of any single individual, we institutionalize the processing of information according to conventional disciplinary categories. It is up to each individual to integrate as much or as little of this information into his or her reality as seems possible or worthwhile. There is both a wide variety of roles and occupations available to people in modern society and a wide range of information also potentially available to them. No single system of symbolic representations in modern culture can provide the kind of adaptive instructions that are coded into Dunne-za myth and symbol. The meaning of individual experience in modern culture cannot be represented by the metaphor of a transformative culture hero. Although we do experience dream and vision, these transformative experiences tend to reflect the polarities of universal archetypes and the events of idiosyncratic life history rather than an articulate cultural program in which the experience of past generations is revealed to be the plan of one's own personal experience.

Our culture's internally generated phenomenological phases cannot be realistically prophetic because our cultural past and future are linked lineally rather than in a cycle like that of the seasons. Significant figures in our past are meaningful relative to their particular time and place and do not return like Saya with the return of the seasons. Although we may—indeed we must—learn and profit from our knowledge of history, our knowledge is bereft of figures like

Saya who come to us whenever we close our eyes. We delude ourselves if we believe that dreaming and visionary phenomenological
phases, in and of themselves, have ever had an unanalyzable mystical
power. Their power has always been in their ability to make fundamental cultural information available to immediate experience. To
the extent that an adaptively stable culture has accumulated a coherent superorganic cultural program that reflects and instructs an experience of life common to all people over many generations, it is to
be expected that this information may be apprehended directly
through dream and vision. To the extent that an adaptively unstable
complex historical culture depends upon the apprehension and synthesis of information by individuals or groups within society for its
meaning, it is to be expected that dreams and visions will reflect
archetypal and idiosyncratic information rather than an informed
cultural program. Jung and Freud respectively recognized archetypal
and idiosyncratic symbolism in dreams, but there has been very little
systematic cultural symbolism apparent in Western dream analysis.

There is currently a revival of interest in dreams, visions, and non-
Western phenomenology among people in our culture who feel restricted by a classification of the ordinary waking phase as real and
internally generated phases as unreal. Unfortunately, many of these
people have transformed the dominant dogmatic repression of nonordinary phenomenological phases into an equally dogmatic assertion of their mystical efficacy as causative agents in the substantive
course of events, failing to perceive the dependence of these phases
upon a developed cultural program of information. The prophetic
function of dreams and visions for the Dunne-za does not guarantee
that all dreams and visions must be prophetic. It is the information
processed in the dream and visionary states that is meaningful, not
these states alone. It is mistaken to confuse the phenomenological
medium for the information content available to it in traditional,
adaptively stable societies. Our culture provides us not with absolute
answers but rather with procedures for the exercise of intelligent
judgment in processing information that will generate answers.
Dream and vision may suggest to us possible connections between
fields of information we hold in mind, but the proof of these intui-
tions rests upon our culture's procedures of validation.

It would be mistaken to assume, because people like the Dunne-
za traditionally used dream and vision successfully to anticipate the

future course of events, that these people possess a mysterious power kept from us only by our repressive phenomenology. It would be even more mistaken to attempt to emulate their prophetic uses of dream and vision out of the context in which they are meaningful. Their transformative experience is meaningful because of the cultural intelligence to which it gives them access. Deprived of that cultural intelligence, some Dunne-za have been seduced by the destructive and meaningless phase transformations made possible by drugs and alcohol.

Our own phenomenology can only be enriched by an understanding of the phenomenology of another culture, but it is well to remember, as a first principle of anthropological analysis, that the meaning of any cultural practice depends upon its relationship to the cultural whole in its adaptive setting. Our culture provides us access, for the first time in human history, to information about the fundamental structure of the universe. Apprehension of this information requires the exercise of an informed imagination. We are coming to see the universe as a progressive self-transforming system of physical relationships. In our myth of evolution, we conceptualize animals undergoing physical and cognitive transformations over time. We may have lost the sense of familiarity with the past that characterized Dunne-za thought and experience, but we have gained a sense of time and process of awesome proportions if only we can find the cultural intelligence to internalize it meaningfully. We are the first people to dream among the galaxies.

Anthropology and Humanism Quarterly, 1979

THE MEDICINE FIGHT

An Instrument of Political Process among the Beaver Indians

This paper describes political process among the Beaver Indians of northeastern British Columbia and analyzes the medicine fight as a style of discourse that defines the roles assumed in Beaver competition for the validation of supernatural power. It suggests that the medicine fight is related to the ecological imperatives that make success in hunting unpredictable and relatively infrequent: conditions opting for a projection of causation onto others rather than acceptance of guilt. It concludes that complementary theories of explanation are held by members of the same society and that the theory an individual will use is dependent on the needs of the political role he is playing. The roles played are, in turn, determined by an individual's success or failure relative to others, and success or failure is unpredictable and subject to chance.

Anthropology has traditionally studied culture as a set of institutions, beliefs, and techniques that are superorganic and transcend individual utility and strategy. It has therefore described government in almost Hobbesian terms, emphasizing social control, the institutional and ideological constraints on an individualism that is assumed to be potentially chaotic and disorderly. Radcliffe-Brown defined political organization in his introduction to *African Political Systems* as "the maintenance and establishment of social order, within a territorial framework, by the organized exercise of coercive authority through the use or the possibility of use, of physical force" (Fortes and Evans-Pritchard 1940: xiv).

Following Durkheim, anthropologists have tended to focus on the sovereign collectivity and the norms and institutions that regulate individual behavior. The common denominator used to analyze a wide variety of human societies has been the concept of authority—in the British tradition, the authority of institutions; in the American tradition, the authority of norms.

Political scientists, on the other hand, have defined government in terms of the distribution of power within a society. In this frame of reference, authority becomes simply an institutionalized application of power (Bierstedt 1950: 733). They assume that power has an almost universal utility and are puzzled by seemingly negative cases, like the Zuni as described by Ruth Benedict, who reports that they profess no interest in power (Benedict 1934: 96). Swartz, Turner, and Tuden (1966) attempted to reconcile these two positions by defining politics as the study of processes involved in determining and implementing public goals and in the differential achievement and use of power by members of the group concerned with these goals. They replace the concept of institutionalized political structure with that of "political field," but their definition still gives precedence to collective goals rather than individual motivation.

In this paper I describe the system of power politics in a society that has no institutionalized authority structures. It is not a society without political relations but simply one in which political positions are in a constant state of flux because they are contingent upon the vagaries of hunting. The society is a reasonably representative group of North American hunters, the Beaver Indians of northeastern British Columbia. Northern Athapaskans like the Beavers have sometimes been described in negative terms: no clans, lineages, or corporate groups; no full-time political, economic, or religious specialists. Because of the simplicity of their institutions, a condition directly related to ecological constraints, hierarchical authority structures have not developed, yet the Beavers are an intensely political people. Theirs is a society in which political process operates in the almost total absence of formal hierarchical political structure. I propose to make a virtue of necessity and use the Beavers to demonstrate the possibility of a purely utilitarian political analysis. The focus is on individual strategy and the transactions that distribute social power rather than on collective goals or formal political office.

Utilitarian political analysis must begin with a schedule of utilities—in anthropological terms, the values and motivations shared by members of the society. It assumes that political action can be analyzed in terms of competition for scarce and hence valuable resources as defined by the culture.

The Beavers live under considerable ecological pressure and highly value success in hunting, good health, and security; but these commodities are far from free, and their value lies in their scarcity as well as in their practical utility. The vagaries of hunting during the difficult winter season subject individuals to many hazards beyond their control. To the Beavers, control itself is the ultimate scarce and valued resource and assumes a greater utility than the actual physical resources over which it is exercised. The quality of control, of freedom from risk, is symbolized by the focal value of Beaver culture, the concept of supernatural power, *ma yine*, literally "his song" or "his medicine."

The Beavers value supernatural power because actual individual risks are high. This statement is a version of the familiar Malinowskian proposition that magic is used in uncertain circumstances, for supernatural power can be seen as an elaborated form of hunting magic, but the value placed on supernatural power, its utility to the individual, extends beyond functionally specific hunting activities to affect the strategy behind all other social behavior. Because it is scarce and of top priority in the schedule of utilities (i.e., a focal value), supernatural power is a bone of intense political contention.

To an outside observer, success or failure as a Beaver Indian depends on a combination of abilities and luck. Luck is probably of paramount importance. But to a Beaver Indian, success is a sign of supernatural power and power is seen as the means to success. It is like Calvinist grace, known through outward worldly signs of which it is in theory the cause but in fact the effect.

Supernatural power forms the basis of political action in that to demonstrate it one must have social power: the ability to change the actions of others to one's advantage. It is more than culturally patterned wish fulfillment, Malinowski's magic as substitute for actual control, because of social transactions through which it is acquired. Supernatural power is based on social recognition and goes beyond a naive attempt to link subjective desires with objective reality. Because there is no permanent social hierarchy and no substantive means for assuring more than temporary superiority, the Beavers must continually jockey with each other for social power and its supernatural tokens.

Claims to supernatural power are based on vision quests experienced between weaning and puberty. Through these quests, an individual is expected to acquire animal friends, songs, medicine bundles, and abilities and taboos related to the species-specific behavior of the animal friend. Vision quest experiences are not used as political capital; they are not publicly announced until the individual is in a position to assure the validation. Hence, a young man who has not yet achieved adult status is reticent and secretive about his animal friends. He only brings forth a claim when he can substantiate it publicly.

For a younger man, the opportunity to validate a claim comes most often through his hunting ability. In a system of generalized reciprocity (cf. Sahlins 1965), the hunter distributes meat to other members of his residential group, and these gifts lay an obligation on the recipients, who in turn recognize the power of the giver. After a successful hunt, the hunter can present his claim for validation. He can reveal the dream that led to success or the animal that showed him the game. By validating such a claim from a position of strength, the hunter has exerted social power and effected an exchange of food for status. The exchange is mutually beneficial, in that good hunters are welcomed rather than being resented because of their power. The more urgent the need for food, the more power is granted. A man who makes a kill that saves people from starvation claims, and is given, greater power than a man who brings meat into a well-supplied camp. The value of a given claim to power is directly proportional to the scarcity of the commodity for which it is exchanged. When resources are scarce, the person who controls them receives a high price; when they are plentiful, control is not concentrated in the hands of a single fortunate individual. Thus, less supernatural power can be bought with the same amount of substantive resources. The Beavers value highly their ability to feed people, to control resources for the benefit of others. The highest respect they can bestow is to say, "He looked after orphaned children"; that is, he had sufficient supernatural power to control resources on behalf of others.

As a person grows older, the basis of his claims to power and control begins to change. Young men initially establish their credit through the actual control of substantive resources and the market of generalized reciprocity. Their power grows as they distribute meat to others. Each distribution places them in the role of provider and the others in the role of dependent. Of course, they accept meat and bestow status as well. Within the circle of meat distribution there is a mutually beneficial flow of material and immaterial commodities. Those who need meat buy it with status; those who have meat exchange it for status. Older men do not lose status when they lose their strength to hunt, for they take on the new status of shaman or Dreamer (*naachi*). People who have lived past maturity have amply demonstrated sufficient supernatural power to protect themselves against the ecological and supernatural perils of being a Beaver Indian. They are accorded the power to kill and to cure, to dream and to divine, symbolically to provide for the well-being of the whole group. Old people are surrounded by mine fields of personal taboos that must be meticulously respected by the members of their band. Every interaction with an old person (*kwolan*) is tinged with deference and a tacit recognition of his demonstrated ability to control the uncontrollable. As an individual grows older, he begins to dream of and make public the songs, medicine bundles, and behavior taboos garnered from his vision quests. The public acceptance of these attributes of *ma yine* marks recognition that he can cure or kill others with his power.

THE MEDICINE FIGHT AND CONSERVATION OF MA YINE

Because humans do not, in fact, have supernatural control over the world of nature, a person's socially recognized *ma yine* is contingent upon the ebb and flow of his fortunes. Although positive thinking and a belief that he has supernatural aid may improve a hunter's efficacy, illness and misfortune can strike down even the most confident. The best hunters can still expect to fail three or four times as often as they succeed. Such failures are seen as direct attacks on the hunter's supernatural power because they undermine the social recognition on which it is based. A Beaver's life motion is built around a complex interaction between objective reality, public image, and self-image. The environmental context of Beaver behavior calls for both internalization of confidence in one's power and the assumption of roles that optimize the social validation of the valued status. Individuals capitalize on success and rationalize failure in an attempt to increase and conserve their stores of validated and internalized *ma yine.* These capitalizations and rationalizations have become institutionalized into a set of mutually reinforcing roles that form the fabric of the medicine fight.

The medicine fight is an institutionalized instrument of competition for supernatural power. (Medicine is an English word commonly used by Indians to refer to supernatural power.) It is a contest between two individuals to determine whose *ma yine* is greatest. But since the inequalities in fortune that instigate a medicine fight may be reversed, the superiority established at one time may later be lost. It can never be assumed that victory over one individual implies supernatural and social superiority over all those he has bested in the past. Misfortunes and the social losses they may bring are seen as temporary setbacks rather than permanent defeats. The medicine fight does not produce permanent hierarchical offices. The fights seldom result in open physical combat but are waged in dreams between the animal friends of the participants. The fights that take place in dreams are, of course, not themselves complete interactions but provide the background for actual contact between antagonists. Each person dreams that he has bested, or at least temporarily thwarted, his antagonist, but his claims to success in his dreams can only be validated by subsequent substantive success in hunting, health, or marriage.

Through medicine fights, individuals attempt to explain adversity or capitalize on good fortune. When a hunter experiences good luck he believes that his power is strong, but when his luck turns bad he rationalizes the contradiction between his wishes and reality in an attempt to deny any loss of substantial power.

Failure in love or hunting, death, disease, or any other personal misfortune experienced by an individual or his dependents is rationalized, just as personal fortune is seized upon as a demonstration of power. The culturally established explanation for misfortune is that unknown others have been using their supernatural power against one. When an individual feels that others have made such surprise attacks that prevent him from finding game, deflect his shots, or cause him other misfortune, he dreams to discover his opponent's identity. He is then ready to initiate an accusation and thus declare a medicine fight. The fight becomes a social interaction rather than an individual conceptualization when the person who has suffered accuses the adversary revealed in his dream. The accused adversary responds either with a counter-accusation that lays the blame on a breach of taboo by the accuser or with a declaration of his intention to carry the fight through to the death. In the former case, the accused denies the validity of the dream in which the accuser was attacked by his adversary's guardian spirits; in the latter case, he concentrates on dreaming a pitched battle between his guardian spirits and his accuser's. Only occasionally do the adversaries do physical battle, in which case each mentally summons his animal counterparts by silently singing his songs.

The environmental condition to which medicine fight role playing is relevant usually consists of a temporary inequality in the fortunes of two individuals (or groups represented by individuals). The roles played are specific to the actor's immediate fortunes. The successful individual plays a different role from the unsuccessful one. Medicine fights tend not to occur under conditions of equality unless it is an equality of penury or between individuals with markedly different status, for example, a young man and a venerated old man or shaman. Ego accuses only in relation to an alter whose immediate fortunes are superior to his own. The environmental conditions that cause an unpredictable distribution of success and failure set the stage for a play of opposing and complementary roles relevant to one's access to resources, success, or failure. An individual's acceptance of one role or the other is contingent on his immediate fortunes, and as fortunes change individuals typically slip from one role into the other. The following Beaver story about the trials of a small family band during a difficult winter illustrates the logic of medicine fight interaction and the environmental conditions to which the roles apply.

THE STORY

A family band, consisting of an old father, three sons, the wife and children of one son, and another dependent sibling group, are the protagonists of the story. The group's well-being depends on the supernatural power of the old man, as demonstrated through his dreaming and prophecy. One summer, the old man has a premonition. "Something's going to happen. Every time I hunt I can't get anything but tracks." Because of his worry, he dreams of an anthropomorphic intermediary between the supernatural and earthly realms (Achudunne, literally "Nowhere Man") who tells him, "Don't worry, yours is the only family that will be saved from starving to death. This coming winter will kill every Indian in the country, but if you do what I say from now on, you will be spared. If you move from this camp and kill a really fat moose you will know that you are going to make it." The old man tells his dependents of the dream, and shortly one son kills the fat moose. Later, he dreams that they will kill a skinny moose as a sign of hard times to come, and that dream comes true as well. Thus, the old man's prophecies cover every contingency. Both fat moose and thin moose validate his oracular powers.

After this introduction establishing the supernatural power of the old man, the story enters directly into its main theme, an extended medicine fight relationship between the father (henceforth called protagonist, P) and another old man whom we shall call antagonist, A.

The father, P, and his band join a larger group of people in the late summer. P tells another old man in this group, A, that he has only been able to get skinny moose: "We hunt all the time but we can't get anything, while in here every boy hunts and they get every animal they can see. There is lots of game, but I don't know what is wrong with us." This statement is the opening move of a medicine fight dialogue in which P indirectly identifies A as the person responsible for his misfortune. To contrast one's own misfortune with another's fortune in a direct confrontation is taken by the Beavers as an accusation and the beginning of a medicine fight.

A responds to the challenge with a counter-accusation that P has broken taboos and is responsible for his own misfortune: "Why don't you talk to your wife and girl and ask them why they don't look after the meat right?" To drive the point home, A tells his own wife to give meat to P: "I don't know what's wrong with you. There's lots of game there—caribou, moose, sheep, beaver. What's wrong with you?" A then gives P meat and fat and tells him to stay with him. P stays with A but soon has a dream in which Achudunne tells him, "Stay away from that man. He thinks he is the best hunter, but he is going to find out what will happen to him this winter."

The events of the story to this point may be summarized as follows: (1) P has relatively poor luck but claims power because events verify his predictions. His behavior is a rational attempt to resolve the cognitive dissonance created when misfortune threatens his stores of internalized and validated *ma yine*. (2) When P's poor luck contrasts with A's success, P accuses A of using his power against him. (3) A defends himself by (*a*) accusing P of breaking taboos and causing his own misfortune and (*b*) claiming superior power over P by offering him food and treating him as a dependent. A clearly attempts to take advantage of P's need by forcing him to accept food and thus admit A's temporary superiority. The story does not make explicit the accompanying medicine fight dreams of P and A, since this is assumed by every Beaver Indian.

P decides to listen to his dream advice and to move away from A. The smaller "family" that has been camping with him is in a quandary about whom to follow but finally decides to stay with P. P says, "We're moving off. You fed us good but we're going to try again," to which A replies, "That poor fellow. I told him to stay with us so they could eat well. His boys won't hunt for him but he went off. Poor fellow. They're going to starve to death." Crocodile tears and fawning "generosity" are conventional dramatic devices in the stories about medicine fights as well as in the actual fights themselves.

It is fall when P leaves the larger camp. He dreams that winter will soon come and his prediction is, of course, verified. (Many of the Beaver dreamings or prophecies that my wife and I actually observed were of this nature.) There is a period of very cold weather and then a chinook followed by even more severe cold. Many animals die of cold, but P's dream friend warns them not to eat carrion. They move from place to place following P's dreams, but game is hard to find. The story says, "There was only one of every animal." The only tracks they see are human. P concludes, "All the game in this world is finished." His next dream instructs him to go to a river, and he is finally able to get enough fish to last the little band through the winter.

At this point, A reappears, starving. The economic tables are turned and the medicine fight resumes, with P shedding crocodile tears of generosity. P's wife gives A some fish. A has been starving and the price of salvation is total surrender. He says, "Why do you bring me a fish when I wanted you to die? Was it hard for you? How easily did you get it?" P's wife replies, "Don't say anything. Don't blame anything on us. Just cook the fish and eat it."

This statement refers to their last interchange, which began with P's accusation against A. Now, A has no choice but to accept his life from P, and P's wife makes the conditions of acceptance clear. If A wants to live, he must renounce his option of accusing P of his misfortune. In the first round of this medicine fight, A appeared to win, but P managed to retain his autonomy and freedom of action. In this second round, A is clearly forced to capitulate and admit that his life is in P's hands. P then presses home his advantage: "Come with me and I'll show you how to fish." He treats his opponent like a helpless child. As if this state of affairs were not bad enough, A uses a broken fishing pole that his wife has given him and frightens away all the fish. The story earlier pointed out that in such hard times one must be careful to keep women who may be menstruating away from fishing spots and fishing implements. Here, the disappearance of the fish is seen as the result of A's violation of taboo. A's power is thus doubly invalidated.

The group continues to have hard times as a result of A's breach of taboo. They move to a cache from the previous summer but find it empty. They find another river with fish in it but are unable to catch any. One son begins to despair and talks of going to the mountains by himself for sheep, but P has another dream about fishing at a certain lake. At the lake, the loons help him to get fish and the group is once again saved by P's supernatural power. Summer comes and the hard times are temporarily over. The story does not have a definite ending but simply leaves the little group still moving from place to place according to the dreams of the old man.

INTERPRETATION

The story illustrates most of the significant features of actual Beaver medicine fights. Good fortune is taken to be evidence of supernatural power, and bad fortune is both rationalized ("I knew that this was going to happen") and projected in the form of an accusation ("How come you're lucky and I am not?"). Generalized reciprocity, or the norm of "sharing" food, may be used aggressively as a demonstration of superior supernatural power. The medicine fight style of discourse typifies much of daily noncrisis interaction. The story analyzed above and others like it reflect a form of interpersonal relations and explanation that is familiar to every Beaver.

The Beavers commonly use two major theories to explain illness and misfortune: (1) adversity is caused by the aggressive use of supernatural power; (2) adversity is caused by a breach of taboo. These theories are not contradictory, since they are not formal, philosophical absolutes; rather, they are contingent upon one's role as accuser or defendant in a medicine fight exchange. If one is the accuser and attempting to explain one's own misfortune, theory 1 will be advanced, while if one is the defendant accused of causing harm, theory 2 is the appropriate defensive move. (There is also another move that is occasionally resorted to. The defendant may not only admit to theory 1 but will exult in claiming power over the accuser. In this case, the defendant's response to an accusation is, "Yes, I have caused your misfortune. You are in my power and are going to die." This kind of discourse takes place both in stories and in real life.)

Among the Beaver Indians, a system of belief and explanation provides alternative hypotheses appropriate to complementary roles. A given event is usually interpreted in several ways, depending on the role of one's informant. Every death, illness, accident, or misfortune has the potential of developing into a medicine fight if someone makes an accusation of responsibility to another.[1] Few misfortunes or successes take place without concomitant adjustments of power relations. It is the accuser's role always to subscribe to theory 1. Theory 2 is rarely accepted by the victim of misfortune; that is, one seldom admits to being responsible for one's own troubles. If one is forced into the role of defendant, however, theory 2 is the obvious recourse. Theory 1 is specific to the role of accuser, while theory 2 is specific to the role of defendant.

EXAMPLES FROM DAILY LIFE

In daily life, most misfortunes get an airing in terms of these two theories. Most members of a coresident group are forced to identify themselves with one role or the other. Of course, many misfortunes pass without generating actual confrontations, and the theories of explanation merely circulate as gossip. There is also an option of preventing face-to-face confrontation by agreeing on a distant outsider to stand in the role of defendant. Accusations are generally made within the group along the lines of already existing latent hostilities.

The medicine fight style of discourse and explanation may pattern relations between individuals over long periods of time. Many interactions have at least an overtone of medicine fighting about them. The following example illustrates the tenor of a relatively permanent stable competition between two factions in a Beaver community. X and Y have headed rival factions in a particular band for some years. They seldom camp together during the summer but live on the same reserve in winter. A competitive equilibrium is maintained by both sides refusing to request meat from the other.

Any Beaver will assert the norm that it is good to give meat to every member of his camp, but he generally neglects to point out that the recipient must send his wife to where the donor's wife has laid out the meat in order to get in on the distribution. On the reserve, Mrs. X seldom shows up for Mrs. Y's distribution, and vice versa. Thus, neither side puts itself in the other's debt and both complain of the other's stinginess to anyone willing to listen. There is a continual flow of gossip, lies, half-truths, and innuendo between the two groups. Certain families have ties to both groups, and the gossip is often directed at these people. (Although we were associated with the Ys, we had close ties with the Xs and thus received a full dose of gossip from both sides.) When X family fortunes fall, they implicate the Ys, while the Ys invoke the Xs' violations of taboos and norms. Y family fortunes, of course, receive the same treatment from the Xs. Hunting, trapping, money, health, style of life, behavior of children, even behavior and fortunes of their dogs are used as evidence in the ongoing current of competition between the two factions.

An interesting episode brought about by a temporary disparity between their respective fortunes occurred during the summer of 1965. Y and X were camped about seven miles apart, and Y had experienced a frustrating stretch of bad luck. Despite persistent efforts, Y had run out of fresh meat and seemed unable to get a moose. At the same time, X had a stroke of the remarkable good luck for which he has a flair and shot three moose at one place. He could not resist capitalizing on the disparity between their respective efforts and rewards by (1) asserting that Y was an impotent old man who had brought his misfortune upon himself (theory 2), thus assuming the role of defendant in anticipation of the other's accusation, (2) revealing a dream that had given him power over the three moose, and (3) breaking the tacit mutual nonexchange of meat by taking a box of meat from his kills to Y's camp and shedding crocodile tears of mock pity and generosity. Y, obviously put out at his rival's coup, complained that X had given him bad meat, a form of accusation. X's behavior in this interchange exactly parallels that of the antagonist in the first round of the medicine fight story cited earlier, while Y's reaction parallels that of the protagonist. The roles of accuser and defendant that are outlined in the story reflect the actual roles that Beavers play in daily life.

In the course of fieldwork with the Beavers, we inadvertently found ourselves involved in a number of medicine fights. Although we were hardly aware of the pattern behind the events as they happened, in retrospect it is possible to analyze at least the Beavers' side of the interaction. During the winter, both my wife and I came down with flu and responded to the illness by staying in bed for several days. During this period we abandoned our usual daily visits to various households. When we recovered, we noticed that a young friend was withdrawn and avoided contact with us. We inquired about his change in behavior toward us but could not get a clear answer. Only much later it became evident that he had thought that our cessation of regular visits during the flu was an accusation that we thought him responsible. The reason he, rather than some other person whom we had also slighted, gave our actions this interpretation is that he felt a good deal of latent resentment against us because we were close to his father and because we had a vehicle and other assets he lacked. Thus, he projected his actual hostility toward us by thinking that we felt (and expressed) hostility toward him, and were accusing him of causing our illness by not visiting. If we had been Beaver Indians, his reading of our behavior would probably have been more or less correct. Since illness requires some explanation and since the accuser never subscribes to theory 2 (breach of taboo), he had good reason to believe that our change in behavior toward him constituted an accusation. In this particular case, I did not think to ask whether he defended himself by applying theory 2 to us. It would have been an easy defense, since we had inadvertently broken many taboos.

CONCLUSION

The Beavers believe that supernatural power allows one to kill and to avoid being killed, an assertion at a fantasy level of the ideal qualities of actual power—as a political scientist might define them. Strategically, the Beaver individual seeks not to kill indiscriminately as a demonstration of his power, for this kind of power cannot in fact exist, but, rather, to validate a claim of immunity from supernatural attack. Every misfortune is seen as an attack on one's power and must be met with counterattacks couched in terms of medicine fights with adversaries who have been discovered through dreams. Personal misfortune is explained in terms of interpersonal hostility, but personal fortune does not imply that another person must lose.

The Beavers' ecology poses a serious motivational contradiction that is resolved in their system of belief. Success can only come through the efforts of the individual. Game is only killed by the hunter who has the confidence to try, but in contradiction to this need for positive motivation there is no assurance that any attempt will be successful; rather, the chances of success in a given hunt are at best 25 percent, and real hardship is a common experience. Man must hunt to live, but even his noblest efforts do not guarantee success. Out of this imbalance between the imperative to action imposed by hunting and the lack of any reciprocal imperative that the hunter can exert on the game has arisen a system of belief through which men seek to control nature by controlling each other's actions. The end of Beaver competition for supernatural power is to make people (including oneself) believe that one has the ability to kill and not be killed, precisely the opposite from real life, where the hunter may not always kill and always runs the risk of losing his own life if he cannot take the lives of animals. In the Beaver schedule of utilities, the value placed on control is a function of its actual scarcity.

The high odds against success in a given try make projection rather than guilt a useful response to failure. Guilt is effective in making a person consciously shy away from making mistakes, but when failure is unavoidable projection takes the onus from the person and allows him to try again. The Beavers approach life with strengthened confidence in the face of often discouraging odds by projecting external aggressive powers rather than taking responsibility onto themselves. The medicine fight can be seen as an institutionalized means of defense against an environment that is motivationally trying. Although there is no place in Beaver society for authority and the hierarchical institutions and offices in which it must reside, a system of competition for social power thrives as the cultural resolution of a natural dilemma.

The Beavers see almost every event, ordinary and extraordinary, fortunate and adverse, in terms of supernatural power and the discourse of the medicine fight. From the subjective point of view, fortune is caused by a person's own power, while misfortune is caused by someone else's. An ally is someone with whom a man agrees in accusing a third party, while an enemy is someone who, with his allies, has accused him.

What might appear to be a general zero sum theory of explanation (the gains of one are another's loss) is actually used only by a person whose fortunes have fallen. The zero sum theory (theory 1) is specific to the role of a loser. It is in the interests of the person who suffers misfortune to blame his loss on another's gain, while it is in the interests of the person who is doing well to attribute his success to his own powers and the failure of others to their own mistakes. The Beavers do not gain status by actually causing others harm; rather, power is validated through gifts, the amount of power one can claim being directly proportional to the need of the recipient. A starving man may even be asked to relinquish his option of playing the role of accuser; that is, be forced, at least for a time, to subscribe to theory 2 (admission of guilt). The Beavers have invented guilt culturally but seldom experience it individually.

Every Beaver has played both roles and subscribed to both theories of explanation. That the society as a whole holds to two explanations of adversity indicates not that their thoughts are poorly integrated but rather that an individual's thought reflects the utilities that govern his behavior in a particular context. These utilitarian patterns of behavior and belief have become institutionalized into the roles played in the medicine fight.

NOTE

1. The Beaver Indians have two further explanations of death that do not apply to difficulty in getting meat: (1) that the individual's soul is stolen by a ghost and (2) that a person's soul is taken by

relatives who are living in heaven. The former explanation is used almost exclusively to explain the illness or death of a child, who, it is assumed, is too young to have engaged in medicine fights. If a patient is diagnosed as suffering from soul loss, the shaman uses his ecstatic powers to go to the underworld, where he does battle with the ghost who has stolen the patient's soul, and sometimes recovers it. This is a special and important type of medicine fight. The second explanation—desire for a person to join the community in heaven—has been adopted only in the last hundred years, during which time the Beavers have added to their traditional shamanism the belief that ordinary people can go to heaven after death (this was previously the prerogative of shamans who had made the journey to heaven during their life). Everyone is expected to rejoice in the good fortune of someone whose death means acceptance into the sky world. This is the only explanation of death that is divorced from the discourse of the medicine fight.

American Anthropologist, 1968

WECHUGE AND WINDIGO

A Comparison of Cannibal Belief among
Boreal Forest Athapaskans and Algonquians

Belief in a cannibal monster known as windigo has been reported by most students of boreal forest Algonquian culture. A number of authors (Cooper 1933; Hallowell 1955; Landes 1938; Parker 1960; Teicher 1960; Hay 1971) have linked belief in the windigo monster to a behavioral complex involving threatened or actual cannibalism, considered to be a culturally patterned form of psychosis. The literature on the windigo phenomenon generally assumes that it represents psychological weakness and breakdown of the normally functioning personality. This diagnosis of windigo behavior as psychotic has not been seriously questioned in the literature, even though all authors recognize that in none of the reported cases has there been first-hand information on individual and case histories, let alone analysis of subjects' lives by observers with experience in psychiatric diagnosis.

In reading through the literature on windigo one is struck by a repetition of the following two statements: (1) The diagnostic feature of windigo behavior that automatically makes it psychotic is the intense unsocialized desire to eat human flesh. (2) Native explanation of the behavior is that the person has been the victim of sorcery or possession by the windigo spirit. Teicher says, "The outstanding symptom of the aberration known as windigo psychosis is the intense compulsive desire to eat human flesh. In many instances, this desire is satisfied through actual cannibal acts, usually directed against members of the individual's immediate family. In other instances, before authentic cannibalism takes place, the individual is either cured or killed . . . The individual who becomes a windigo is usually convinced that he has been possessed by the spirit of the windigo monster. He therefore believes that he has lost permanent control over his own actions and that the only possible solution is death" (1960: 5). Hay says, "The windigo psychosis has long been regarded as a disorder specific to the people of the northern tribes of Algonquian-speaking Indians. The disorder is marked by the desire to eat human flesh, a desire to do something which is ordinarily extremely repugnant and horrifying to these people. . . . To the Indians, the desire to eat human flesh was incomprehensible except as the result of sorcery or possession by the mythical windigo spirit" (1971: 1). Parker describes it as "a bizarre form of mental disorder involving obsessive cannibalism" and regards the victim's belief in his possession by the windigo spirit as an obsession "with paranoid ideas of being bewitched" (1960: 603).

In the course of fieldwork among the Athapaskan Beaver Indians of the Peace River area, I have become acquainted with a form of cannibal belief and behavior associated with this belief that are clearly related to the Algonquian windigo and yet are central to a sense of cultural and individual strength rather than weakness. The cannibal figure Wechuge is as feared as the Algonquian windigo, but because he has become "too powerful," not because he is in some sense psychotic. Comparison of the two phenomena leads one to ask, Are Athapaskan and Algonquian cultures so different that the same cannibal monster belief can have almost opposite meanings in the two different contexts? If the complex does indeed mean something different to the two groups, why is this so? Is it possible that the idea of windigo as psychosis is more a function of our own categories of thought than that of the Indians themselves? This paper will describe the Dunne-za concept of Wechuge in terms of its meaning within the context of their ideas about supernatural power and then compare Wechuge to windigo as it has been described, concluding with an examination of the three questions posed above.

WECHUGE AMONG THE DUNNE-ZA

Before I begin to describe Wechuge I must emphasize that the Dunne-za take it very seriously and believe that to discuss it frivolously is both foolish and dangerous to oneself and others. I trust that the reader will receive this information in the spirit of serious inquiry into the human condition in which it was received from the Dunne-za.

The idea of giant man-eating monsters is deeply ingrained in Dunne-za mythology, as it is in that of the Algonquians. Dunne-za myth cycles tell of a time when giant animals hunted and ate people. These animals behaved like people, and the people were compelled to be their game. They are referred to as Wolverine Person, Spider Person, Beaver Person, Frog Person, etc. Although they were all overcome and transformed into their present form by the culture hero, their power is still in existence. Indeed, it is these giant people eaters who confer supernatural power on the child during his or her vision quest. Contact with this power gives a person the ability to find and transform animals into food. In the context of an underlying belief that animals are sentient, volitional creatures like ourselves, the idea of personlike animals who eat animallike people is a logical transformation of the economic fact that people must eat animals in order to live. Both Algonquians and Athapaskans share a common mythical background of belief in giant person-eating animals, a transformative culture hero, and some form of association between supernatural power and the eating of creatures who are sentient and volitional.

The behavioral characteristics attributed by the Dunne-za to We-chuge are remarkably like those attributed to the various person-eating giant animals of mythic times. The giant animals do not pursue their victims with inchoate frenzy but rather use artifice and a knowledge of their game's desires and weaknesses to bring them down. They hunt people with the cultural strategy and intelligence that people use to hunt animals. Similarly, Wechuge lives apart from the people and uses their desire for food to lure them to him. He is like one of the giant person-eating animals of mythic times come back in human form. The following stories illustrate this quality of the Wechuge monster.

WECHUGE STORY TOLD BY JUMBIE

One time a long time ago a whole bunch of people were camped together. It was wintertime and lots of families camped one place. They didn't move around. There must have been

about a hundred people camped there. One night one young
man heard somebody calling him outside his tepee. The person
outside called in to him, "Somebody wants you to visit him." It
was the middle of the night but the young man thought, Maybe
somebody got a moose. Maybe they want to feed me. That must
be why they are calling me in the middle of the night. He got up
and went outside.

Wechuge, the man who had called him, was standing there.
Wechuge came forward and choked the young man so fast that
he didn't have a chance to scream. Then Wechuge carried him
back where he was coming from. Nobody knew a thing about
what had happened. Wechuge was a bad man. He didn't live
with those people. He stayed by himself and then followed
people's tracks.

The young man that Wechuge carried off was married. His wife
had heard somebody calling her husband, but she hadn't really
woken up and she didn't go with him. Lots of time went by and
her husband didn't come back. She began to worry. She went
outside. It was still nighttime and there wasn't a fire in the camp.
Everyone was asleep. The woman went to some people and
woke them up. She told them, "Somebody called my husband
and then he went out. That was a long time ago. I don't know
where he is."

They got up and started looking around. They woke up every-
one in the camp, all the people, but they didn't find that man.
Then they lit torches, big sticks, and started looking for tracks.
Soon they found the tracks of the big bad man, that Wechuge.
They knew darn well that he had taken that man. "If he's taken
one, he will take every one of us," they said. All the men and
young men gathered together. They had to decide what to do.
They are going to follow Wechuge.

One young man who was crazy thought that he was a little
bit tough. "I'll be the first one to go after that man," he said.
One middle-aged man thought he wouldn't make it. He thought
that the boy wasn't as tough as Wechuge. He said, "I'll try him
first," but the boy said, "No, I want to." So the middle-aged
man said, "All right." He knew he would come second anyway.

All the men and boys went out after Wechuge. They followed
his tracks. Not too far away they saw him. He was sitting by the

fire, spitting the young man he had killed. He had opened him
from neck to ass and taken out his guts, and he was roasting the
whole man.

The men and boys circled around behind Wechuge in the
bush. When they got close, the young boy jumped on Wechuge's
back. He took his shoulders in his hands and tried to pull him
back. Wechuge sat there just like a rock. He didn't budge. Then
he reached around behind his back with one hand and grabbed
the young man's hand. Then he threw him in the fire.

Just then the middle-aged man jumped on Wechuge. They
wrestled for an hour. Then the middle-aged man grabbed the
cannibal by the neck and by the leg and broke his back. He
threw him in the fire. But that Wechuge was tough. He didn't
die from that. All his stomach and back had turned to ice. That's
why they couldn't kill him easily. They could see the ice melting
out of him as he lay on the fire. For the rest of the night and all
the next day they kept the fire going. At last he died. Until all
the ice had gone he still wanted to get up and kill people.

WECHUGE STORY TOLD BY AKU

I don't know this story well. There's someone I don't know.
The people knew that one lake always had lots of fish. Whenever
they were hungry or starving in the wintertime they would go to
that lake. There was one man who was eating people. He was
Wechuge. He knew that all the people would be coming to that
lake, so he went there and made himself a great wooden tepee
and put holes through the logs so he could see when people
were coming. He was a very tough man, big and tough. He
didn't kill those people with a gun or bow. He would dream
about dirty stuff. Then he would take green logs and carve plates
and spoons and cups from them. Then he would carve something on them, monsters and things like that with a stone knife.
When people came he would ask them if they would like to eat.
The people were hungry so they would say yes. He caught lots
of fish for them and he fed them from those plates. The people
ate what he gave them. In not more than a minute they would
be dead. That man was a good medicine man, really strong [*ma*

yine natsut]. He went on like that, killing those people and eating them for a long time. He ate lots of people.

One summer one boy and his grandmother were really hungry. They had heard about the man who was eating people, but the only way they could eat was to go to that lake. They decided to stay at a different place on the lake from the cannibal. The boy wanted to visit him all the same. "I think I'll go see that man," he told his grandmother. She told him, "Don't go," but he said, "I'm just going to visit him." Twice more she told him not to go. That boy knew something. Since he was a baby, the buffalo raised him. Finally his grandmother agreed, and the boy went to the cannibal's camp.

The boy sat down and the cannibal offered him fish on a plate he had carved. The boy took the plate and finished it off. He didn't die. That boy was not really a man. He was from the buffalos. He was half-animal, half-man, a different person [*gradi-dunne, achu-dunne*]. The cannibal told his wife, "You'd better give him another plate." So they gave him another plate filled with fish. The boy finished all the fish on his plate, but still he didn't die. "How come you don't die?" the cannibal said. "All the other people have died." The boy said, "Why, I'm not filled up yet." That old lady had found the boy in the buffalo hair. He was like Aghintosdunne [the moosehide scrapings boy]. "Grandfather," he said, "I thought you were just feeding me. I didn't know you were trying to kill me."

The cannibal got his arrows. He couldn't kill him with the plates, so he was going to kill him with arrows. The boy was still licking his plate. He told the boy, "You'd better throw up the food I fed you. I want to eat it." The boy made ready to throw up in the cannibal's hands. The only thing that came out in his hands was a little green frog. The cannibal swallowed that frog and sat down. The little boy sat down, too. He looked at the man. He was sitting still, just looking at one spot on his foot. He didn't feel very well. The boy knew what was going to happen so he went back.

Not long after that, the cannibal's wife came after him. "Your grandfather tells you to come and fix him up. Something's the matter with him. I don't know what."

"I don't know, either," the boy said, but the woman said, "Just come and take a look," so they went back. When they got to the cannibal he was lying still. He didn't know anything. The boy took some black sticks from the fire and put them on his neck. The black went right through him and he died. "I can't fix this man up. He's already dead," the boy said. That's how he killed Fish Man.

In the first story, Wechuge is described as a bad man who "stayed by himself and followed people's tracks." In the second story, Wechuge placed his camp along a well-known people's trail. In other stories, he makes a trail leading to his fortified camp by bending grass stems, the sign used by the Dunne-za to tell others who are hungry that they have found food. Wechuge, as portrayed in these stories, is not a psychotic obsessed with the desire to eat human flesh but rather is a human who behaves like one of the man-eating animals of mythic times, hunting people by taking advantage of their desires and weaknesses. It is in this context of Wechuge as a person who behaves like one of the giant animals before the culture hero's transformation that the common description of Wechuge as someone who has become "too strong" becomes intelligible. For a real person to become like wechuge in the stories would be for that person to behave like the giant animal that is the basis of his supernatural power. Indeed, the cannibal in the story of Aku is called Fish Man, implying that he is the giant animal in human form.

The Wechuge concept of the Dunne-za is more than a set of stories about people who act like the giant animals before the culture hero's transformations. There are times and circumstances when people actually begin to become Wechuge. I know of only one instance of more or less authenticated cannibalism, and that was said to have been perpetuated sometime in the late nineteenth century by a man named Tsekute. However, real people that I knew personally were said to have begun the transformation to Wechuge and been cured.

BECOMING WECHUGE

To become Wechuge is to become "too strong." Wechuge is not an unspecified person eater but is always the particular person-eating monster that is a person's animal friend and the source of his super-natural power. The integration of Wechuge with ideas about super-natural power is very clear in Dunne-za thought and practice. Al-though Algonquian cultures also have a vision quest–based concept of supernatural power, the ethnographies do not give a clear picture about the degree of connection between belief in supernatural power and the windigo phenomenon.

The possibility of becoming Wechuge underlies every situation in which a Dunne-za person with supernatural power finds himself. Older people are generally acknowledged to have more power than younger people, or at least give out more obvious signs of their medicine powers to those around them. The space around a power-ful person is to be respected. One must learn the proper respect for the space around such a person so as not to violate one of the per-sonal taboos that go with his power. These taboos are actions relat-ing to the action of the giant animals who hunted people in mythic times. I learned about some of these taboos by inadvertently violat-ing them or seeing them infringed upon by other whitepeople. I never saw one consciously violated by another adult Dunne-za, but I was told of occasions when such a violation occurred. It was this type of conscious violation of a person's medicine taboos that was said to bring on the appearance of Wechuge.

Once in the camp of an old man named Jumbie a whitewoman who has lived in the Peace River area for many years and claims to know the Indian people well attempted to take a picture of the old man with a flash camera. She did not ask permission to take the picture, and when the camera was raised some of the younger people in the camp told her not to take the picture: "Old man he don't like that kind." Although Dunne-za do not like to have their pictures taken without having been given the opportunity to give their con-sent, the issue in this case was more serious. It was the flash that the old man "did not like." The whitewoman persisted in attempting to take the picture, and Jumbie, seeing that she would not respect his personal space, dove beneath a sleeping robe in the back of the tent. To the whitewoman this was an act of fear and reinforced her belief that Indians are childlike and superstitious. To every Dunne-za pres-ent, however, Jumbie's action demonstrated his power, not weak-ness. It showed bravery rather than fear. To have been exposed to the flash would have made him "too strong." It would have risked bringing down to earth the power of Giant Eagle, whose flashing eyes still penetrate from heaven to earth in time of storm. The power would have compelled the man to become the person-eating monster, and the man would have lost his own will and judgment to that of the all-consuming monster inherent within himself by virtue of his encounter with it during the experience of visionary transformation as a child.

On another occasion I was driving with the Dunne-za prophet or Dreamer, Charlie Yahey, and turned on the car radio to country and western music. A young man in the car with us reached over and turned off the radio, an action I found most unusual since most Dunne-za enjoy this kind of music and normally would not interfere with another person's choice. In reply to my question, I was again told simply that "old man he don't like that." I did not understand the meaning of what had happened for more than a year. I was able only to learn that Charlie Yahey could not hear any sound made by a stretched string or hide, and hence he could not hear guitar music. Indeed, in town he had once been in a cafe when the jukebox began playing guitar music and he began to get "too strong." He was hustled out of town and into the bush, where another person sang his medicine song to overcome the emerging monster within the old man. Just what this monster was became clear to me when I connected the events I have related with a story about giant Spider Man who lured people to a mountain top by swinging a sort of bull roarer around his head. The sound made by this stretched spider thread attracted the natural curiosity of passing humans, and when they approached they were killed by the Spider Man, who sucked their body fluids. To make a similar sound in a similar way would bring the mythic monster back from then and there to here and now. The Spider Man within the human would become too strong, and all the people would be in danger.

For every power there is a myth, and within each of these stories is the information relevant to the personal taboos demanded of a person who has encountered that power in a vision quest. To act in a way that evokes the behavior of the mythic monster associated with a person's medicine is to activate the myth and bring it into reality. The space around a person with recognized supernatural power cannot be taken for granted. One is expected to know and respect the mythic role into which he would be forced to step at the appropriate signal. Although at times I inadvertently violated personal taboos and thus became aware of them, these violations were not interpreted as intentional affronts and hence did not trigger the otherwise automatic response. My behavior was viewed as that of a child. Certain missteps were accepted as part of the learning process. When children talk too loudly and out of place they are told, "Naa-za wontlon," literally, "Your lips too much." The import of this everyday admonition is loosely equivalent to "shut up," but its more subtle implication is "with your excess of lips you are consuming our common space."

Adult Dunne-za are reasonably expected to know the taboos and hence the supernatural powers of the people with whom they come into contact. When in doubt, they are expected to ask if it is all right to act in a certain way or offer a certain food to a person whose powers are unknown to them. Peter Chipesia told me about the taboos associated with medicine power as follows:

> If I know something [i.e., have supernatural power] and you feed me meat and I know there's fly eggs in it, I have to eat it. When Asah [grandfather] was alive, Mom was always careful when she fed him. When we fed him we always told him, "Look through the meat." If there's fly eggs he doesn't want to eat it. But lots of people make a mistake. That's why lots of people have gotten strong. They make a mistake. I wouldn't be like that, me. I wouldn't be like that now. I know it helps lots to know something, but you have to watch all the time. People are scared of you. Even when I go down to Rose Prairie, they're afraid to feed me. They have to ask me first if I like to eat that. Even beaver meat, they ask me if I eat that kind of meat. I say, "Sure, I eat it." Lots of Indians are afraid of any kind of man. You never know if, me, if I know something. You wouldn't know. Just like that, you don't know with another kind of person.

Anyone other than a child or whiteman is expected to know and observe the medicine taboos of their fellow Dunne-za. To violate these taboos is to bring Wechuge among the people. The account quoted above came up because I had been told previously that the person's grandfather (Asah) had not too long before begun to get

"too strong" after being given meat with fly eggs in it by some
thoughtless people from another community. Briefly, the story as I
was told goes as follows.

Asah, a man in his early seventies, had been married to a woman
in her early thirties about ten years previously and had had several
children by her. Recently she had left him and taken up residence
with a younger man in the same community. The old man now had
his own house and was fed by whichever other family had fresh meat.
His youngest daughter, a girl of about five, lived with him and slept
in the same bed. He was, in a sense, everybody's grandfather and was
called Asah by most of the younger people. Whenever meat was being distributed, the hunter's wife always made sure to send a portion
over with some child to Asah.

According to the story I was told, some people from another
community were visiting the reserve where Asah lived. Perhaps they
were from the group to which his former wife belonged, although I
was never told outright who these people were. A woman or women
among the visitors sent Asah some meat that had been hanging for
a time. There were fly eggs on this meat. Because the meat was a gift
and because he had not been asked by the visitors if he could eat it,
he had no choice but to accept the gift. He ate the meat and began
to get "too strong." He was a tiny man, but his behavior was fright-
ening to the point of throwing the whole community into a panic.
The little old man had climbed up onto his bed and begun jumping
up and down like a frog, singing his medicine song. It was well
known in the community that one of his medicine animals was Frog.
One sign by which they knew this was that he did not play drums
and did not even like to hear the sound of drums. When the people
were singing and dancing or playing the stick game, he would retire
from the scene. His grandson told me:

> You know that a long time ago Asah didn't like even to hear
> the sound of drums. You know those frogs? Even now you can
> hear them making lots of noise back and forth, and when some
> night the bottom stream they don't make any more noise, that's
> when they lose. That top one making lots of noise, they're the
> winners. It just goes back and forth. Old man told me about
> that. That's why he doesn't like to hear drums long time ago.
> Asah said, "I've been staying with those people on the bottom of

the lake. You can't beat me gambling." He heard that drum on the bottom of the lake long time ago. That's why he doesn't like to hear that drum. When he was younger he was like that. But when he got older he got used to it. He didn't like to hear the drum because he heard it down there. He couldn't play the drum and he couldn't see people throw it. He stayed with them and they gave him his power. Those frogs gave him his power, their power, and they heard that drum up there in the same time. They play. Up here on land that's different. That's why he doesn't like it.

To the people in camp, the little old man bouncing up and down on his bed was becoming the person-eating monster, Wechuge. To an outside observer his behavior would have appeared ridiculous and deranged, an object of pity rather than fear, but to his fellow Dunne-za he was becoming the Giant Frog, a warrior and gambler of super-human power. The people could no longer relate to him as a person. Some gave way to their fear and prepared to flee from him. Unless the power growing stronger within him was returned to its proper place, he would begin to eat his own lips. In this first act of the self-consuming monster the people could see themselves consumed, for he had been one of them. Once the flesh of his lips had lodged within his body, he would be the all-powerful invincible Wechuge monster of mythic time and space. When he had consumed his own lips, he would no longer be able to speak to them and could be reunited with them only by eating them. Once he had eaten his lips, his internal organs would turn to ice and he would be beyond them in power and cunning. Unless the Giant Frog could be sent back to its home beneath the lake, the people would be in mortal danger.

The old man's froglike performance began only when the women and children were in camp. To attempt to cure him, they turned to the person closest to his power, the five-year-old daughter who slept as he did under the medicine bundle containing, among other things, tiny images of frogs that were alive and moved when the bundle was opened. The young girl took down his medicine bundle and brought it close to him. She who had been closest to him physically and had slept under the influence of his medicine was able to approach him and gently pass the bundle over his body. According to the story I was told, this action had the desired effect, and he began to grow calm. The cure that she had begun through the application of his own medicine was completed when other people arrived on the scene and used their own powers to bring him back. I was not told directly the logic of the cure, but it seems to have been that she was able to entice the power of the giant frog to leave his body and return to its place within the medicine bundle. Neither was I told exactly why giving the old man meat with fly eggs in it would cause him to go Wechuge. I do not know for sure if a taboo against such meat was something peculiar to his medicine power, but there is an obvious connection of eater/eaten between frogs and flies, so that it would make sense that to eat the eggs of flies, the food of frogs, would intensify his medicine power and effect his transformation into Giant Frog, whose flies were people.

I was told another story of the Wechuge performance that comes when a person's medicine is violated. In this case my informant was a five-year-old girl who had been directly involved in the affair. All the other people were well known to me. One long-time member of the band in question was a lame widower in his early sixties. Because he had not taken up permanent residence with a woman, his house had developed into a place where teenage boys and young unmarried men stayed. One of his medicine powers was Wolf. This was unknown to me until I learned of it through the young girl's description of the Wechuge incident. One of the young men who stayed with him from time to time, a grandson of the old man with frog power, had gotten into a pattern of violent, destructive, and "crazy" behavior. He was fascinated with guns and knives but disclaimed traditional medicine power. Some time after the events herein described, he was killed in a fire.

On this occasion, for reasons unknown to me, he had taken the medicine bundle of the lame widower from where it hung above where he slept and hidden it somewhere in the bush. This happened when the people were camping in tents during the summer. The lame man began to grow "too strong" at a time when most of the adults were in town for a stampede. On the afternoon in question he was alone in camp with three children under six years old. Because he did not often go out into the bush, he was frequently called into service as babysitter.

During the afternoon the children, my five-year-old informant among them, saw him working quietly by himself sharpening something. They noticed uneasily that he was carefully filing a long nail to a sharp point. The children knew well the story of Giant Wolf whose teeth are like bright metal and who, when sent out to measure the extent of the world by the creator, came back with a human arm in his mouth.

According to my informant's account, the lame man then began to "act strange." He sang something over some water, and then told a boy around six years old that he should drink it. He told the boy he would like it and it would make him strong. This is significant in that traditionally, before being sent out on a vision quest, the child must fast and particularly abstain from drinking water. Water has a number of other symbolic associations in the context of supernatural power and medicine acquisition. The boy drank the water and then he, too, began to "act strange." At this, the lame man seized him and drove the sharpened nail into his hand. The boy then went berserk, grabbed his father's rifle, loaded it, and began firing wildly around the camp. The two little girls remaining fled the camp and went to where the grandfather of one of them was passing the time of day in a cafe on the highway. He returned to camp, disarmed the boy, and overcame the lame man—first with force and later with his own medicine song and by using his coat as a medicine coat. (These are the traditional curative practices used when a child comes in from the bush after the vision quest unable to speak human language and shy like an animal of the human camp, when a person is sick, and when a person has been brought back from a Wechuge performance.)

Although I have never seen a Wechuge performance first-hand, I have been told of episodes involving people I knew well. Perhaps these accounts were actually more meaningful than the impressions I would have had as an outside observer, since they describe the events in terms that are symbolically significant to the context of Dunne-za belief in medicine power. I cannot say what "really happened" in these two cases, but I can clearly say more than that Wechuge is caused by "possession by a cannibal monster."

Although I was not told this in so many words, I think it would be an accurate abstraction from the nexus of events and symbols to say that Wechuge is seen as a return of the person-eating monsters of mythic times. A person begins to act like the mythic animal (jumping up and down, making shiny metal teeth, etc.) when an action by others violates the taboos inherent in the possession of a particular medicine power. The sound of a stretched string will make a person with spider power too strong; eating fly eggs or contact with drums will make a person with frog power too strong; cooking food in an electrical storm, eating red berries, or seeing a flash camera will make someone with Giant Eagle power too strong; stealing or violating a medicine bundle will make its owner too strong. Snake medicine is an interesting case which I do not have time to explain here, but part of the complex is that having daughters is the tabooed event that will make the person's power too strong.

In each case, the violation of a symbolic taboo associated with the mythic charter of a medicine power will make the person possessing that power too strong, the first stage in becoming Wechuge. If the person is not cured and his power put back into the myth and the medicine bundle, he will begin to eat his own lips, which will turn to ice within him. From this point on, it is believed that the person will have become the invincible Wechuge monster that appears in the first two stories cited in this paper. Thus, the Wechuge complex among the Dunne-za involves at least the following points of focus: (1) myths about the ways in which the giant animals of various species hunted and consumed people; (2) the mythically patterned experience of the vision quest, in which an all-powerful animal gives a human child the power to hunt animals; (3) violation of personal medicine taboo, activating power inherent in the myth; and (4) transformation of a person whose medicine has been violated into Wechuge, a monster that eats people. These points of focus integrate into a meaningful symbolic pattern.

The myth of giant animals is a precondition for the transformation of the vision quest, and the transformation induced by a violation of the taboo brings back the myth. The myth is a charter for the vision quest transformation experience, subsequent taboo, and Wechuge performance. Both vision quest and Wechuge performance are transformations of a person's experience into the mythic mode, but whereas in the vision quest the transformation must take place outside the social circle, in the Wechuge performance the transformation takes place in the presence of others. Alone, the child who must be fed by others is given the power to transform the lives of animals into the life of the people; within a social setting in which this power is not respected, the hunter turns upon the human beings (Dunne-za) who have become like animals to him. He becomes the hunter who follows the tracks of people. After meeting a giant animal in the bush on his vision quest, the child returns to camp with his power. After meeting with this power in camp, the adult is forced to return to the bush.

The person becoming Wechuge is not demented but simply a person compelled to act upon the logic of his experience in the world. Certainly, his behavior is motivated by a need to validate a status claim that is being publicly challenged, but presumably for the person himself the mythically patterned experience of the vision quest is sufficiently authentic to validate his own belief in his medicine powers. The Dunne-za strongly believe that you cannot fake medicine power, and they do not practice its sale or transfer by inheritance or any other means.

I do not know the intricacies of interpersonal politics among the Dunne-za well enough to say why a challenge to someone's medicine power would be precipitated in the first place or how those said to have violated a taboo would feel in a group swept by the real terror of a man-eating monster at large in their midst. The social drama, of which the Wechuge performance is but a small segment, has other issues besides those to which I have addressed myself in this paper.

SUMMARY AND CONCLUSION

The summary and conclusion I draw from the scene among the Dunne-za I have described are as follows: The Dunne-za are a people who have long lived in large part from the bodies of animals they have hunted. In the round of Dunne-za experience people follow the tracks of animals, meet them, take their lives, and take them into their own lives and into the life of the camp (*kwon*), a social as well as physical space. Animals are known to be creatures of volition and experience, and so their distinctive habits, preferences, and specific behavioral characteristics are in many ways brought into the life of the camp. Diet, clothing, movement, and even mood are conditioned by the life experience of the animals. The myths provide examples of distinctive and recognizable animal behaviors transformed into cultural terms; the vision quest gives experiential instruction and validation of the connection between life in the bush and life in camp, the realms of animal and human social experience.

Wechuge becomes "too strong" when the world of his everyday experience tips the balance into the animal mode of experience, translated into human social terms. In the vision quest, the person is alone and the animal medicine moves within him, the possession of a benevolent spirit. His subsequent return to the social circle will bring the power of the benefactor's experience of life into line with the purposes of the people. If, instead of receiving his return as the return of benevolent power to the camp, the people consume the space inhabited by his medicine power, it will come back to them only as an image of self-opposition. When a child's voice consumes the social space they say to him, "Naa-za wontlon," "Your lips too much." When the people within the group, for whatever reason, refuse to provide the social space within which a person's essence can manifest itself, the group consumes itself and projects this in the person of Wechuge, the role that must be played by the logic of the one whose taboo has been violated. Wechuge must consume them all, unless a benevolent power once again befriends the person. Wechuge must consume his lips, his means of communication with the minds of humans and the bodies of animals. Wechuge must consume himself as seen in others, unless others see themselves in him. Wechuge, myth and actor, is a performance required of the social logic in human (Dunne-za) experience.

There is no "Wechuge psychosis," even though every participant in the drama becomes somewhat crazed by the intensity of it. The Wechuge performance is more terrifying than mere deviance. It is experienced as the reality of the social body consuming itself, the Giant Animal consuming the people in their childhood. It is a sickness borne by the people of the camp as a whole and cured only by the benevolent application of supernatural power from within the group. The ice within a person who cannot return to the social circle can only be overcome through his death and the application of fire, the symbol of camp life, to the remains. No one among the Dunne-za known to me had known a person who had gone so far, although the story of the cannibal Tsekute, who was said to have eaten the parents of people known to me, was still fresh on the people's lips.

The performance of the Wechuge role seems to have been required more often when people from different groups came together. It seldom occurred within a group of people who were working smoothly together. One would suspect, therefore, that the incidence of Wechuge performance would increase with any increase in the rate of movement of individuals from group to group. Any situation that brought together many people who were unknown to one another or unused to living together would probably encourage the Wechuge role to develop. It seems significant that the story of Tsekute, the only actual person said to have become Wechuge, occurred at a time of maximum social upheaval and was linked to the elaboration of the Plateau Prophet Dance as described by Spier (1935) among the Dunne-za. In every case of Wechuge performer brought back within the social realm, the precipitating challenge came from a person or persons in some sense outside the social circle. "Women from another reserve" brought meat with fly eggs in it. Hearing the jukebox in town precipitated the appearance of Giant Spider. A young man fascinated by guns but unable to hunt brought on the wolf with shiny teeth. In every case, Wechuge came as an outsider who threatened the group from within. Even the whiteperson with flash camera or radio brought a response from the Dunne-za which clearly indicated that the power must be respected.

In conclusion, I should like to return to the question of comparing the cannibal theme in Algonquian and Athapaskan cultures. I do not know from the available ethnography if the cannibal monster belief and behavior labeled "windigo psychosis" is symbolically linked to the vision quest, medicine power, and mythic man-eating monsters in Algonquian cultures as it is among the Dunne-za. The literature tells us only that cannibal monsters existed in myth and behavior in Algonquian societies that were also known to have the vision quest and medicine powers.

Perhaps the behavior described as "windigo psychosis" was not integrated into cannibal monster myth, the vision quest, and a belief in medicine power among the Algonquians in the way I have described for the Dunne-za. The Dunne-za themselves articulated differences they perceived between themselves and the Cree. Cree medicine could be bought and sold, for instance, but in the only case I knew of where a Dunne-za bought medicine from a Cree the purchaser (who was the very same Asah whose medicine was Frog) was thought to have been swindled.

Within the context of boreal forest cultural adaptations there must, of course, be considerable variation in the ways homologous elements of culture are integrated, but I would be very much sur-

prised to find an element of belief and practice as basic as the cannibal theme to be simply unintegrated into the mythical and metaphysical nexus of Algonquian culture. Supposing that it had at some
time been integrated into myth and medicine in a way somewhat
similar to that of Wechuge among Dunne-za, then one might look
to history to explain the apparent differences between windigo and
Wechuge. In general, the Algonquians have experienced a longer
period of disruptive influence from contact with Europeans than
the Dunne-za and have particularly undergone more pressures that
caused mixing of populations. Given an aboriginal system of meaning like that associated with Wechuge, one would expect an increase
in Wechugelike incidents and perhaps an ultimate transformation of
the concept from strength to weakness. In time, fear of the performance might become more compelling than the reintegration of
its cure.

I return to the questions posed at the beginning of this paper: Are
Athapaskan and Algonquian peoples of the boreal forest so different
from one another that the cannibal monster belief has opposite
meanings in the two contexts? If the meanings are different, why is
this so? Is the idea of windigo psychosis an interpretive projection
from our own categories of thought? In light of the preceding detailed description of Wechuge and its place within an integrated set
of symbols and meanings, I can offer the following suggestions.

First, Athapaskan and Algonquian behavioral adaptations to the
boreal forest are similar in general outline. Both cultures include a
concept of medicine power, the vision quest, and myths about giant
animals transformed by a culture hero. Descriptions of Athapaskan
and Algonquian social organization and personality indicate a general similarity. Differences with respect to ownership of hunting territories have been shown to be largely a product of different acculturative experience. In both areas, human patterns of life must be
integrated with the patterns of animal life. Observers have described
the cultural psychology of the two groups of people in similar terms.

It may be, however, that from similar natural and cultural environments the Algonquians and Athapaskans developed a common
image of the cannibal in two equally possible but different directions. Among the Dunne-za, Wechuge is truly feared and must be
killed if he cannot be cured, but a person's performance of the Wechuge role is a sign of his medicine's strength, not of his personal

weakness. It is the *role* that is feared rather than the person acting in it. It may be that the Algonquians fear windigo because, in it, the role of cannibal has consumed the person of the actor. Such a shift in emphasis could perhaps account for the apparently greater incidence of violent death among the Algonquians as an outcome of a windigo incident. It may also be that the Dunne-za pattern of behavioral taboo relating myths about giant animals, the vision quest, and the performance of a cannibal role is simply not part of the Algonquian complex. Perhaps the similarities between windigo and Wechuge result from an integration into Dunne-za conceptual terms of specific elements of the windigo complex (eating of the lips, ice in the gut, burning of the body). The comparison of Wechuge and windigo points out a lack of information on the symbolic integration of Algonquian myth, vision quest, and belief in supernatural power.

Second, I have suggested that if the meanings of Wechuge and windigo are different in the two contexts, the divergence could have come about either through a lengthy movement of the cannibal image in two equally possible but different directions within the two traditions or through a more rapid shift in the meaning of windigo due to recent acculturative influences. The latter hypothesis seems the most economical and may account for a large part of whatever real difference in meaning exists between the two cannibal images. Although windigo may never have been performed specifically upon the violation of a medicine taboo in the way I have described for Wechuge, it seems likely that it was at one time a role performance somehow connected to a concept of medicine power. Perhaps the flux of history changed it as it changed the aboriginal system of resource use. Perhaps an image of both power and fear came to be largely one of fear. It is well known from other parts of the world that the dislocation of stable social relationships, systems of meaning, and ecological adaptations is often accompanied by an increase in witchcraft activity and related breaches in confidence.

Finally, the literature on windigo starts from an assumption that it is a culturally patterned form of psychosis. It attempts to explain the relatively few instances of cannibal behavior, and the more common fear and anxiety about it, by reference to generalizations about underlying Indian personality characteristics. The assumption that windigo belief and behavior are psychotic has gained a kind of tacit acceptance because of our own culture's willingness to reify the labels we have become accustomed to using to describe a phenomenon we do not otherwise understand.

Windigo behavior may indeed prove to be a sign of personality disintegration among Algonquian peoples. There certainly is a commonsense reaction that tells us you have to be crazy to want to eat your friends and relatives. The element of compulsive desire and craving for human flesh that appears in many of the windigo cases may point to a "psychotic" breakdown of normal emotions, motivations, and satisfactions in people who kill or are killed as cannibal monsters. However, although it is contorted, even aberrant, windigo behavior differs from most psychotic behavior in our own culture in that it is believed to be genuine and real by the members of society as well as by the afflicted individual. People believed to be psychotic in our culture believe themselves to be actors in situations, the reality of which is not subscribed to by normal members of society. Normal people do not accept the psychotic's claim that he is Napoleon in our society, in contrast to the Algonquian situation, in which the person who acts like a cannibal monster is genuinely believed to be one. Our labeling system, when applied to the windigo phenomenon, breaks down on close examination. We label the behavior of the windigo actor as psychotic but not the beliefs of those who accept his role as real.

I conclude that any understanding of either belief or behavior must emerge from an understanding of its context, be that culture history or case history. We can only understand belief or behavior as a meaningful element in articulation with other elements of meaning. I think I know enough of the Dunne-za Wechuge performance in the context of its relation to vision quest experience, myth, and medicine to distinguish it from behavior I have seen labeled as psychotic in our culture and to question the labeling of Algonquian windigo as psychotic by the culture of anthropology. I trust there are those among us who will be in a position to respond to some of the questions raised by this comparative essay, and we should be fortunate to hear from them of their knowledge.[1]

NOTE

1. Robert Brightman has reviewed the windigo phenomenon in relation to linguistic and ethnohistorical information and written

about its possible relation to Wechuge. He points out that "no comparable concepts have been described for Athapaskans other than Beavers, and the wechuge complex is best explained through diffusion rather than convergent or independent development" (Brightman 1988: 360). Brightman concludes that windigo is meaningful in relation to Algonquian ideology rather than in relation to any material conditions. I would add that Wechuge is also meaningful in relation to Dunne-za ideology. Despite similarities between the formal features of windigo and Wechuge, the latter is probably as well ingrained in Dunne-za ideology as is windigo for the Algonquians.

Anthropologica, 1976

FOUR

THE PROBLEM OF DISCOURSE

Anachuan, 1968

The Dunne-za negotiate relations with one another and with the other sentient persons of their environment within the delicate discourse of stories and mutual understandings. This section describes some of the problems that arise when Native people come into contact with people whose experience is fundamentally different from their own.

In August 1988, I organized a conference within the International Summer Institute for Structural and Semiotic Studies (ISISSS) called "Cultures in Conflict: The Problem of Discourse." I took this title from the opening statement that lawyers Leslie Pinder and Arthur Pape identified as central to a lawsuit they argued for the Dunne-za and Cree of the former Fort St. John band. The case concerned the loss of reserve lands the Dunne-za call the "Place Where Happiness Dwells." The first paper in this section describes that trial in the words of Native participants, expert witnesses, and the judge, who denied the Indians' suit. The paper identifies differences between Dunne-za discourse and that of a Western judicial system. Although it describes legal issues, it is really about language and communication. I wrote it for a special issue of *Canadian Literature*.

"When Poison Gas Come down Like a Fog" describes problems of discourse in relation to an oil well that leaked poison gas near the Blueberry Reserve. "In Doig People's Ears" is a tribute to Howard Broomfield's soundscape and ethnographic recording with the Dunne-za. It describes Howard's documentation of discourse between the Dunne-za and their neighbors. The final paper in this section, "Documenting the Normal, Perverting the Real," contrasts a negotiated Indian style of discourse with one that is used to suppress the Indian voice and the authenticity of Indian experience. I presented it originally in a session on "Natives and the Media" organized by Stephen Riggins at the 1987 Society for Applied Anthropology meetings.

CULTURES IN CONFLICT

The Problem of Discourse

On January 12, 1987, Mr. Justice George Addy of the Federal Court of Canada began hearing a breach of trust suit against the federal government. The suit had been initiated by chiefs Joseph Apsassin and Gerry Attachie, representing the Blueberry River and Doig River bands of Cree and Dunne-za Indians, who live in the North Peace River area of British Columbia. The case is referred to as *Apsassin* v. *The Queen*. The Indians claimed that the Government of Canada had failed to honor its fiduciary responsibility, as required by the Indian Act, in negotiating the surrender of IR-172, land reserved to the bands under the terms of Treaty 8, signed in 1899. Lawyers for the two bands asked the judge to review evidence relating to a meeting called by the Indian agent which took place on September 22, 1945. Following that meeting, documents authorizing the land surrender were submitted to a justice of the peace in Rose Prairie, British Columbia, for authentication. The government then transferred title from the Department of Indian Affairs to the Veterans Land Administration and made land available to veterans through a "soldier's settlement" program. In the 1950s and 1960s, substantial quantities of oil were discovered beneath the former reserve lands.

The trial lasted forty days. As it opened, the plaintiffs' lawyers, Leslie Pinder and Arthur Pape, explained the issues upon which their clients sought judgment. Leslie Pinder summarized the central issue as follows:

> The lawsuit was based on the fact that the Federal Crown, having a fiduciary obligation to understand these People, breached

that obligation, and failed to obtain the consent to this transaction . . . failed to act as a proper fiduciary ought to have acted—
in fact, gave away the estate of these People (their inheritance),
to itself, sold the land to itself in a conflict of interest, and
robbed these People of an adequate future and a proper land base.

Arthur Pape pointed out that Mr. Justice Dixon of the Supreme
Court of Canada had ruled in a related case to the effect that "the
purpose of this Surrender requirement in the Indian Act is clearly to
interpose the Crown between the Indians and prospective purchasers
or leasees of their land so as to prevent the Indians from being ex-
ploited . . . The fiduciary obligation is the law's blunt tool for the
control of this discretion." Pape identified the issue of communication between cultures as being central to a decision about whether
the surrender was taken as a responsible exercise of the government's
trust responsibility.

> Did the fiduciary give prudent advice to the person owed the
> duty, and was the transaction, in fact, a prudent one in the best
> interest of the person to whom the duty was owed? . . . The
> Court must first understand who those People were and how
> they would have come to such a Surrender gathering, with what
> assumptions and knowledge, and then to look at what the
> Crown Agent did and ask whether that would have fulfilled the
> duty of explaining to these People what their rights and pos-
> sibilities are, and explaining to them whether such a thing might
> be a prudent thing for them to do . . . The Court has to find out
> in the Eighties who those People had been 40 years before, and
> that involves both the Elders giving evidence and experts like
> Hugh Brody giving evidence, trying to assist the Court to un-
> derstand that.

Pinder and Pape explained in their opening statement that "the
problem of discourse" was central to the case. They argued that, in
order to judge whether the surrender was valid under the terms of
the Indian Act, Mr. Justice Addy would have to understand the ways
in which hunting peoples of the Canadian subarctic make decisions
in matters of vital concern to them. He would have to understand
Dunne-za/Cree discourse and how it relates to the discourse of his

own legal tradition. The trial ended on March 27, 1987. On November 4, 1987, Mr. Justice Addy gave his decision. He dismissed the claim of the Indians. His decision is under appeal. In his judgment he wrote that the Dunne-za/Cree "had no organized system of government or real law makers. They also lacked to a great extent the ability to plan or manage, with any degree of success, activities or undertakings other than fishing, hunting and trapping. It seems that many of their decisions even regarding these activities, could better be described as spontaneous or instinctive rather than deliberately planned." Regarding his assessment of the testimony elders gave at the trial, he wrote:

> Due to the manner in which these witnesses testified and in the light of the evidence from witnesses from the defense and certain documentary evidence . . . I am forced to the conclusion that their testimony was founded (and, in most cases, perhaps unconsciously) on the fact that oil was discovered on the reserve some thirty years later, rather than on a true recollection and description of what actually took place at, and previous to, the surrender meeting in 1945. It is perhaps a case of the wish being father to the thought.
>
> They were certainly not what might be termed disinterested witnesses since some 324 million dollars was being claimed on behalf of the Band which now numbers about 300 members. It is of some significance also that none of these witnesses stated that they or anyone else had actually informed either Mr. Grew or Mr. Gallibois that they were not consenting nor did they state that they had publicly spoken out against the surrender in the presence of Mr. Grew or Mr. Gallibois.

The judge evaluated the testimony of anthropologist Hugh Brody about Dunne-za/Cree culture as follows: "[Brody] impressed me as an informed champion and an enthusiastic supporter of the native peoples' cause generally and of the Dunne-za Cree in particular but, by the same token, as a person who conspicuously lacked the objectivity required of an expert witness on the subject of whether informed consent was obtained in 1945 as well as on the actual importance to the plaintiff Band of IR-172 at that time."

In August 1988, I organized a conference within the International Summer Institute for Structural and Semiotic Studies (ISISSS) at the University of British Columbia entitled, "Cultures in Conflict: The Problem of Discourse." One session within that conference brought together people who had been involved in the Dunne-za/Cree case. I was particularly anxious to review this problem of discourse, because I have known the Indians who were plaintiffs in this case over a period of thirty years and was puzzled by the conclusions Mr. Justice Addy drew from the evidence presented to him. I have written extensively about the Dunne-za in the form of scholarly papers and most recently in a narrative ethnography, *Trail to Heaven*. I attended nearly every day of the court proceedings and took extensive fieldnotes.

It may seem odd for issues heard before a federal court judge to appear in an issue of *Canadian Literature*, but perhaps the judge thought it odd to be asked to consider the "problem of discourse" in his courtroom. A central issue of the trial was both anthropological and literary in that it focused critical attention on conflicting modes of discourse. The Indians asked us to listen to them. They asked us to understand the way they arrive at decisions. They asked us to accept their decisions regarding IR-172, a piece of land they call the "Place Where Happiness Dwells."

Discourse is a problem, but it is also and more fundamentally a powerful and enabling form of human communication. Human communication is more than the simple transfer of objective information between impartial and interchangeable intelligences. Humans do not just copy and transmit information in the way that one computer communicates with another. Human communication also creates a point of view or a context within which information becomes imbued with meaning. Human communication is a cultural accomplishment and a means of defining cultural identity. As Nuu-Chah-Nulth elder Simon Lucas said in a speech at a benefit for Meares Island, from which I quoted at the beginning of the conference: "It's important that we remain different. That way, you and I will get to know the meaning of understanding. What it means to understand another man's culture."

Through our discourse with one another we negotiate a world in which we can understand our differences. Discourse establishes the syntax we use to create meaning and comprehension. It uses meta-phors that layer one set of meanings on top of another for synergistic effect. Two speakers, or two cultures, are more than the sum of their parts. Discourse is only a problem when we talk past one another or worse use talk to suppress another person's ability to express him- or herself freely. Discourse is as old as language. It is as fundamental to human experience as is culture. It is also as new and as fragile as each new breath of life. We create our culture in the act of speech and in the intersubjectivity of discourse. We negotiate and perform our cultural reality in communication with one another. We create shared but separate realities through the discourse of our conversations with one another.

The original Latin meaning of discourse is "a running to and fro." We run to and fro with ideas and understandings in the ongoing discursive intersubjectivity that pervades normal everyday life. Discourse is essential to the typically human, dynamic interaction and feedback between culture and experience which first evolved within the cultures that hunting and gathering people negotiated with one another thousands of years ago. Discourse is the form that enables people to communicate freely while at the same time living responsibly within a nourishing and sustaining social order. Discourse connects people of different generations as well as those who are in face-to-face contact.

The oral traditions of people who are native to this land are a form of discourse that connects them to the land and to the generations that have gone before. Their discourse has given them a highly developed form of government that is different from our own. Their discourse honors individual intelligence rather than that of the state. Their discourse also demands a responsibility to past generations, to the land, and to generations as yet unborn. Their discourse honors and enables both individuality and social responsibility.

The discourse of Native people takes place within real time, but it is meaningful in relation to a time of mind, a mythic time. Performer and listener share both a common time frame and a complementary knowledge of that mythic world. They share a common responsibility to the names that are fabulous in their lands. Their relationship to the names and to one another is conversational. The "running to and fro" of their conversation takes place in the same time as their common experience, but it also takes place in the time of their ancestors. The names of these ancestors and their lands are parties to the conversation. The discourse of Native people is meaningful because they share a common and complementary point of view, a common time and place in the world, a common or complementary set of ideas about how to interpret experience, and a common responsibility to the land and its government.

Discourse is essential to the typically human, dynamic interaction and feedback between culture and experience that first evolved within the cultures that hunting and gathering people negotiated with one another thousands of years ago. The oral traditions of these people allowed them to be remarkably flexible, adaptable, and ready to take advantage of variations in the resource potential of their environments. We know from contemporary ethnography (see Ridington 1988a for a review of that literature) that knowledge necessary for informed decision making is widely distributed among adult members of small-scale hunting and gathering communities. The egalitarianism found in these communities functions successfully because individuals are expected to be in possession of essential information about their natural and cultural environment. Discourse within such oral cultures is highly contexted and based on complex, mutually understood (but often unstated) knowledge.

Hunting and gathering people typically live in kin-based communities where most social relations take place between people who know one another well. Because people share knowledge of one another's lives, they code information about their world differently from those of us whose discourse is conditioned by written documents. They know their world as a totality. They know it through the authority of experience. They live within a community of shared knowledge about the resource potential of a shared environment. They communicate knowledge through oral tradition. They organize information through the metaphors of a mythic language. They reference experience to mutually understood information. They communicate with considerable subtlety and economy.

Hunting and gathering people code information in a way that is analogous to the distribution of visual information in a holographic image. If you take a small scrap of a hologram and look at it carefully, you can reconstruct the entire image it represents. In contrast, if you take a small scrap of an ordinary photograph, all you have is that portion of the visual field represented by the scrap. A hologram codes information differently from a photograph. Its image gets grainier and grainier as the sample is reduced, but it remains an image of the totality.

People like the Dunne-za/Cree live storied lives. You are a character in every other person's story. You know the stories of every person's life. You retain an image or model of the entire system of which you are a part. Each person is responsible for acting autonomously and with intelligence in relation to that knowledge of the whole. Each person knows how to place his or her experience within the model's meaningful pattern. Each person knows the stories that connect a single life to every other life. People experience the stories of their lives as small wholes, not as small parts of the whole. The stories of lives are not meaningless components of a coded message analogous to phonemes; rather, they are metonyms, small examples of a meaningful totality.

Oral performance in a small-scale hunting and gathering culture plays creatively upon a mutually understood totality. Each performer's speech evokes and is meaningful in relation to everything that is known but, for the moment, unstated. Each story contains every other story. Each person's life is an example of the mythic stories that people know to exist in a time out of time. Experience within a closely contexted oral culture is meaningful in relation to a totality that is taken for granted. Storied speech is an example of that totality, not simply a part of it. Storied speech makes subtle and esoteric references to common history, common knowledge, common myth. Each person is, therefore, responsible for acting autonomously and with intelligence in relation to that knowledge of the whole. From within the familiarity of shared, culturally constructed metaphors and assumptions, the essentially creative and transactional quality of human communication may not be obvious. It is only when we attempt discourse with people who are unwilling to listen to our words, to understand our experiences, that we find ourselves talking at cross-purposes. Attempted discourse between different cultures may create conflict, ambiguity, even oppression. The "cultures in conflict" conference looked at examples of discourse between cultures and peoples who have found themselves in conflict with one another. It also looked at the possibility for communication that Simon Lucas articulated, the discovery of "what it means to understand another man's culture."

The following is an account of the trial as discussed at the "Cultures in Conflict" conference. Participants in the session in order of their appearance were as follows:

Robin Ridington, anthropologist and convener of session
Gerry Attachie, plaintiff and chief of the Doig River band
Hugh Brody, anthropologist and expert witness at the trial
Arthur Pape, counsel for the Dunne-za/Cree
Leslie Pinder, counsel for the Dunne-za/Cree

The following narrative combines excerpts from the 1988 conference, fieldnotes I took at the 1987 trial, and my own interpretations of the texts created in this discourse. Chief Gerry Attachie of the Doig River band described his understanding of issues raised by the case following my introduction to the session.

> Yeah, OK, I guess. What happened was, we, back in 1945 we lost a good land there. Just about eight miles north of Fort St. John. We, seven bands that signed a treaty—back in 1899. Seven bands in Fort St. John area. And, we, we had eighteen section of land there, just north of Fort St. John, about seven miles. And we live there all our lives, and up until 1945, we lost it and then, the government promise our people that time they could get lot of money, and then, so they give up the good land and then, later on, they been promise that they could get lot of money every year and then for a couple of years they receive, I believe, ten dollars apiece—each person.
>
> Later on money stop coming in so they kind of wonder why they don't get anymore, and then, I remember, ever since I remember back about in the late fifty, people were, they could get together lot of times, just amongst themselves our people, and then they said that, "I wonder what happen," they say. "We don't get any more money," and then, but just amongst themselves they discuss this problem, and then, off and on we could mention that they been promise that they could get a lot of

money every year—a long time. I don't know how long. Finally, uh, I got involved with the band way back in 1974 and I try to find out what happen to IR-172 and then, one day I pick up a, I borrow a book from the library and it's called *Peacemaker*, which was written in Peace River country there—in the Fort St. John area. And, I came across one, like, story about IR-172, Fort St. John. They call us Fort St. John Beaver band, about that time. They still call us today—Fort St. John Beaver band. And, I read— in that paper, in the book, it says that the land been sold 1945 and then later they discover that the mineral rights which up to that IR-172 were forgotten here.

Then, there's lot of oil over there, and gas. Then, I remember what people were complaining about—like, before. And, one day, I sat down with some elders, and then they told me exactly what happen, and then, about that time, my grandmother was still alive, and then every time I take her to town and then she said, this was, "We lost a good land," she said. And then, then she tell me a story about how people get together there every year. They celebrate and then people all have a good time to- gether there. And, but after 1945 when the land been sold and then people never get together again. Even relatives. They don't see each other again and then some of them died. Like, I just talk to some farmers around there, just recently. They said, one time there were about four or five hundred tepees, they say, and then they could hear drums about twenty miles away. People were having a powwow in there. Our people.

Anyway, I—after I found out what happen to IR-172, I set a meeting with Indian Affairs superintendent that work in Fort St. John. His name was Johnny Watson, and then I told him that, we set a date and then we sat down and we talk about IR-172 and then he said, "There's something wrong in here," he said. "Something happen in here." And, so, he brings out all the documents. About three feet high papers. And, oh boy [he laughs] then was how it's all started, and we got a lawyer and then we hire a local lawyer there. His name is Gary Collison and then he start doing some research and then, came to Vancouver, I believe—up in here. And, he done some work on that about a week, I guess. And then, later on, we got another lawyer, which is Art and Leslie and Rick—Rick Salter, too. And we start this case about back in about 1977, and '78, and then we finally went to court 1987, January, January—out here, and we bring our elders, too. We bring some people that were there that time when the surrender took place, and we, we learn a lot in court and then we went through pretty, pretty rough, rough, hard time and took us forty days, I believe.

We were in court for forty days, and after, we had some elders there and then later on they were pretty—they were disappointed because what happen was they believe that the judge and the justice lawyer didn't believe them, when they have their testimony. They, they think the elders were lying and then they, they felt bad about it. Like, our, our people you know, you ask them, if you ask them too many question and then they might— you know, sometime they get upset. One question over and over again and then—like John Davis. When we're, we're doing discovery and then, one of the elders, name of John Davis, that, we going to meet again I told him one morning and then he said, "How many meetings we have to go through," he said, and then, he's getting tired. When, like our people, you know, if they say something, you know, they don't want to repeat things over and over again, 'cause. Anyway, we done a lot of work in here and then hopefully we'll get something out of this—in the end. And, well—

Yeah, I just want to say another thing. We, we had people that were at the 1945 surrender. We had people that, still around. They were, they're still alive, and hopefully that they could settle this while they were, while they're still alive and we also, last few years, when we start working on this case, a lot of people were want to get involve. The people that were there. That time. And just, just recently there's some farmers, local people in Fort St. John that, when they heard about this case that we lost the first round and then they, they, they really feel, they were upset. They said that, you know, they told me that we were beat and then, they say that hopefully you people get something out of this 'cause, you know, they, they felt really bad, and we, we had some people that were involve that time. Some people from outside, like teachers and some priest, Catholic priest.

They, they had good testimony, and we tape some of them and
then we, what I believe is we should have these people before
the court case, and then would have been different too.

One of the people Gerry mentioned was an elder named John
Davis. The following are excerpts from his testimony as led by lawyer Arthur Pape.

A.P.: John Davis, I want you to tell the judge stories about when
   you were a little boy and no whitemen were in your country.
   Tell the judge where you and your family lived when you were a
   little boy, before the whitemen came.
J.D.: Long time ago, when there was no whitepeople, there were
   two stores. One of the storekeeper's name was Davis. What I can
   remember I will say. What I do not remember, I will not say. I
   cannot read and write. I only can remember. Before the whitemen came, we were bush people. When they came, where we
   live, they said, "This my land," and we have no more. We can't
   read or write. We only can remember it. Since not too long ago
   that my people started to go to school.
A.P.: Tell the judge when you saw the whitepeople come in big
   boats up the river.
Judge: When he's going into a long answer, ask him to stop so she
   [the translator] can repeat.
A.P: John Davis. Try and say your stories a little bit at a time so
   Lana [Lana Wolf, the translator] can tell us what you are saying.
   Please tell us again about the boats because we didn't understand
   it all.
J.D.: Big boat come. People started having things that they
   didn't have.
A.P.: What did the boat look like?
J.D.: White boat. In the back of it there was a wheel, like a wagon
   wheel.
A.P.: Did the boat have a pipe on it like a stovepipe?
J.D.: Yes, two. One is used for horn.
A.P.: What did it sound like when it made its noise?
J.D.: It make a sound like a cow.
A.P.: When whitepeople came, what did they do on the land?

J.D.: First time two men came and they started building cabins.

Judge: We should know how old you are.

A.P.: The judge wants to know how old you are. Can you tell him?

J.D.: I don't know my age.

Judge: For the record, let's say he looks old to me. He's not a teenager.

A.P.: When those whitepeople came, what was the place where your family lived in the summer?

J.D.: Place we call Indian Lands.

[break]

A.P.: John Davis. When Dr. Brown [former Indian agent] talked to [Chief] Succona, was there an interpreter to tell Succona what Dr. Brown was saying?

J.D.: A guy named Johnny Beatton.

A.P.: When Johnny Beatton talked for Dr. Brown, could the Indians understand what Dr. Brown was saying?

J.D.: Johnny Beatton could speak a little bit of Beaver.

A.P.: Did you sometimes hear Johnny Beatton speak for Dr. Brown?

J.D.: No, I can't understand English.

A.P.: Did you understand Johnny Beatton when he spoke Beaver?

J.D.: Yes.

A.P.: Can you tell some things that Johnny Beatton said in your language for Dr. Brown?

J.D.: About the land. People don't want to sell, but it was still sold.

A.P.: What did Johnny Beatton tell Succona for Dr. Brown when he talked to him about the land?

J.D.: Indian Boss wants to sell the land.

A.P.: What did Johnny Beatton say in your language would happen after you sold the land?

J.D.: Before he translate that for Dr. Brown, that person wasn't alive.

A.P.: I don't understand, John Davis. Could you say that again?

J.D.: Johnny Beatton was speaking for people. He was helping the Indian people for long time. The Small Indian Boss wasn't helping.

A.P.: Do you know the name of the Small Indian Boss?

J.D.: Gallibois. Yes, Gallibois.

Judge: Is Gallibois the Small Indian Boss?

J.D.: He was the Indian Boss but he never help Indians.

[break]

A.P.: John Davis. What did Johnny Beatton say to Succona about
selling the land?

J.D.: He told him not to sell it. The Indians are poor.

Judge: Did he hear Johnny Beatton say anything to Succona?

A.P.: The story you have just told about Johnny Beatton. Did you
hear him say that to Chief Succona?

J.D.: I was there. I hear.

A.P.: Did Johnny Beatton say those things in your language when
he talked to Succona?

J.D.: He speak a bit Beaver.

A.P.: Where was the place you were when you heard Johnny Beatton talk about that to Succona?

J.D.: Moose Creek, Moose River.

A.P.: What time of year? What season?

J.D.: Summertime.

A.P.: What did Succona want to do when he talked to Johnny
Beatton about the land?

J.D.: He told him not to move, that he should stay where he is and
build cabins.

Judge: Not sure. What did Succona say?

J.D.: Johnny Beatton told him but he didn't want to.

Judge: What did Succona say?

J.D.: He just want to go out hunting and he sold the land.

A.P.: Why did he want to sell the land?

J.D.: "Gonna be lots of money," the Indian Boss told him. They
just took it. They never saw nothing.

Following Gerry's description of his experience as plaintiff in the
case, anthropologist Hugh Brody told the story of being an "expert
witness."

Well, I'll begin. I think I'll just tell the story of the trial as I
experienced it, and a very awful experience it was, too. First of
all, I think it's really important to say that trials, that court procedures, public hearings, are very seductive for persons like me.
I've spent fifteen, twenty years having the extraordinary privilege

of living with, working with, Native peoples in northern Canada, and all the time, there is this growing sense of doubt about what on earth it is that really I'm up to, and whether really I should be doing it, and to what extent it's exploitative. The doubt, I'm sure as in all anthropologists, grew and grew in me, grows and grows in me, so when a court case comes along, it's seductive because it seems to allay the doubt. Here at last is something the people themselves have initiated. It was Gerry and his fellow chiefs and elders who wanted this action. Their lawyers and they themselves say there's something I can do to help with this action. So here at last is a place to put all this anthropology. A place where it might actually do something, where it might right a wrong—a wrong which in the course of my work I've heard a lot about. A chance to explain, in a place where it needs to be explained, some of what I've been lucky enough to learn about.

Leslie and Art came to me and said they wanted an opinion for the court case which touched on many things, including the nature of leadership and decision making in Dunne-za/Cree society, an opinion which touched also on the nature of the use to which IR-172 had been put over the years and the place it had in the Dunne-za/Cree economy in the 1940s. Here were subjects which the people themselves had wanted to get across to the outside world, and I think parenthetically it's terribly important to know that many Dunne-za and other northern Native peoples that I've met feel that if only the white world knew more, it would be a juster world. They equate knowledge with justice, and I've often been pressed by people I've worked with to make the information available as publicly as I can, to write accessible books, to make films, so as others will know, and if they know, they'll treat aboriginal people better.

So, the motivation for writing the opinion was very strong for me, and I was very optimistic about doing it. I wrote an opinion in which I try to describe the complicated nature of decision making in Dunne-za/Cree society, the complexity of the authority and lack of authority system; the richness and subtlety of an economy that required that reserve land in the 1940s as a summer gathering place; the spiritual dimensions to that summer gathering place; why those drums were heard twenty miles away (that Gerry was talking about); what those drums really meant—not just as music, but as metaphor, as stories, as knowledge, as economic reality, all intertwining in that very complex way that they do in northern hunting systems. And I wrote an opinion which also explained something about the use of the lands in the economy as a whole. It's a short opinion, about forty pages long.

Prior to giving evidence, I went to the court to sit in on some of the elders giving evidence. Elders like John Davis, whom Gerry mentioned, but others, and some of the young people giving evidence. And I was confronted by the extreme unpleasantness (for me, and I speak for myself), the extreme unpleasantness of the setup.

The judge represents that world to whom they have to tell it. Elders who are interrupted, not only by the judge's manner, but also by the lawyers for the Crown. Elders whom I'm sure have never been interrupted, as Robin was saying [in my introduction to the conference], when telling these stories—being interrupted every second sentence. The interpreter struggling to make sense of what's being said. An atmosphere in which nothing can stand as a fact, and yet the people speaking in the court believing in facts more, perhaps, than any other peoples in the world, peoples for whom truth is always the objective, constantly being accused of untruthfulness either directly or in implication.

You have a sense of the impossibility of it that's hard to communicate. And sometimes a sense of the hopelessness of it. And you can't—I found it almost impossible to stop wondering, "What really should be done in this court?" When I got on the stand, I was led by Art, very skillfully, through what it was I had to say about leadership and decision making, and as always, when talking about these things, I got excited about it. Enthusiastic. And I remember in particular two things that I think serve as illustrations of the whole problem of the procedure, at least from my point of view, and perhaps more generally than that.

First, I tried to convey to the judge what it was like to be at the receiving end of Dunne-za decision making. So, you come into a Dunne-za community, or you're living in a Dunne-za community, and you're trying to plan your life. And the people whom you're dependent upon don't make decisions in a way with which people like us are familiar. So I tried to take him, as it were, through a hunting trip. I tried to take him out hunting by telling him a typical hunting trip story, and as I remember it, I told it very fully, and at considerable length, and with a great deal of excitement.

The judge's reaction to all the stuff I, and of course others, had told him about decision making was to say, in effect, "Well, it seems to me that there isn't a society there. I mean, if they don't make decisions coherently, if there isn't someone responsible for making a decision, if there isn't a leader who says, 'Well we're going to do X' and others who follow, then there isn't a society. Sounds like chaos, and I find it very hard to believe." And in fact, at one point, as I understood it (though Art and Leslie can correct me if I'm wrong), what I said about decision making seemed to dispose him towards dismissing the whole action. I mean, if there isn't any society that's coherent and makes decisions the way ours does, then how can they be bringing an action to the courts?

So, far from managing to take the judge on a hunting trip, far from succeeding in bringing him into some sort of connection with Dunne-za culture and thinking, I managed to alienate him, I think very deeply. And when I read his judgment, that suspicion was somewhat confirmed. I mean, he dismissed my evidence, sort of out of hand.

The second example—that might attempt to explain the use to which IR-172 (the land that was stolen, or taken) had been put in the 1940s, it was, as I said earlier, as a summer gathering place. In these documents to which Gerry referred, it's many times noted that it was only used for the odd few weeks of the year, but, of course, hunter-gatherer culture requires places you use for an odd few weeks of the year as part of an annual system which exists as a whole, and if you pluck out one segment of the annual system, you can threaten the whole system. If you pluck out the summer gathering place, which is the one spot where all the various bands, and indeed other groups, meet, in order to exchange crucial information and goods, then you are really mounting a fairly direct assault against the system as a whole.

I tried to explain all this (led by Art) again quite fully and talked about the difference between summer uses and winter

uses, which, in relatively modern times, reduces to a difference
between summer hunting and winter trapping. This was done
very carefully and it's very concrete evidence which, you would
think, no one would have too much difficulty with. Under cross-
examination, the lawyer, one of the lawyers for the Crown, produced a map which had been made as part of a research project
which I had helped coordinate in the late seventies—a map
which showed all the trapping areas of all the Dunne-za/Cree
people—and he pointed out with some satisfaction that on this
map IR-172, the lands in question, didn't seem to figure, and
therefore appeared to show to the court that IR-172 wasn't an
important place, and somehow, and this is where we again come
to the problem of discourse, I didn't seem to be able to show
him that his map was of trapping, which is, of course, the au-
tumn-winter-and-early-spring part of the seasonal round and not
the summer part of the round, so that IR-172's absence from a
trapping map was exactly what we should have expected!

There's something about the legal procedure that is terribly at
odds with Dunne-za/Cree and other hunter-gatherer and probably all other Indian cultures, and it's the nature, let me say that
again—it's the extent to which the court procedure is a game.
We met earlier this morning, Gerry and Leslie and Art and I,
and someone was saying (I think that's Gerry) that John Davis,
one of the elders who gave evidence, didn't seem to be taken
seriously, or didn't seem to be trusted by the lawyer for the
Crown. And it struck me suddenly that lawyers for the Crown,
when cross-examining, or all lawyers when cross-examining, neither trust nor mistrust. It hasn't anything to do with believing
or not believing. It's simply a game that's being played with
facts—with arguments. The job of a cross-examining lawyer is
to discomfort, to unsettle, to confuse.

Elders from the Dunne-za/Cree bring their case to the court
because they believe there's some direct relationship between
knowledge and justice, but that cross-examining procedure, and
perhaps the whole court procedure, actually breaks any such
simple equation. As you experience it on the stand, you don't
feel a relationship between knowledge and justice. What you feel
is someone playing games with you. And elders (and I can just
about cope with that), but elders in the Dunne-za/Cree *can't*

cope with it. They sense that they're being played with in some way, and they might come to the conclusion that they're being mistrusted, disliked, doubted by the cross-examining lawyer. And that will, in fact, cause them to fall silent—and that happened several times in the case—that if somebody doesn't believe what you're saying, you shut up. That's the dignified thing to do. But of course that's failing to play the game completely. That's the thought I think I want to leave everyone with.

[applause from the audience].

Gerry had been listening attentively as Hugh Brody told his story. He asked to conclude with a few further thoughts:

Yeah. I just want to say one thing before we leave here. In the early, in the late 1800, in Peace River country (they call that Peace River 'cause Beaver Indians made peace with Cree Indians, so they call it Peace River), anyway, in the early 1800, late 1800, the Hudson's Bay Company had a trading post at Peace River. I guess by that time they were, they were starving, and our people were supporting them. Like, they hunt for them. Make drymeat for them. Grease. And I had a, this guy named Johnny? Johnny Beatton? [Question put to Robin Ridington, who responds, "Frank Beatton."] Frank Beatton, yeah, Frank Beatton. I had his diary here; I had it at Robin's place here. It's his diary from 1860 to 1923. He, he's running the Hudson's Bay, Hudson's Bay Company. He's working for Hudson's Bay Company. In the late 1800, our people were hunting for them. They—that's how they survive. But nothing been, you don't read it in the paper. I found a diary after that court—court case, and then, when I mention, when I was reading the diary to our elders, I took them back, way back and then, they, they remember, when our people were hunting for early traders.

And, I just want to say one thing. We, we—we had treaty rights. We had rights, but we have to fight for it all the time. Every time you turn around, you got to fight. And then I was in the AFN [Assembly of First Nations] meeting in Edmonton, early this spring and then I talk to some of the elders and they told me that, "We always going to be small," they told me, "'cause Government they have power in a piece of paper." That's how we lost first round in this case. They believe the papers more than the elders' testimony. It's, it's pretty sad, you know. Thank you.

Gerry made four important and related points in his concluding remarks. (1) The Dunne-za and Cree established peaceful relations with one another long ago. They did so as sovereign nations. (2) When the whitemen came, Indians provided for them from the store of their accumulated knowledge. "They were starving, and our people were supporting them . . . they hunt for them." (3) Although he did not say so explicitly, the indirect and intended implication of Gerry's discourse was to remind us all that Indians who feed one another and live in peace feel responsible to one another. When you feed someone you expect that person to feed you, if and when he or she is able. (4) Gerry's experience in court confirmed what he and the elders had learned when they lost their land in the first place. Whitemen believe paper over the testimony of people who speak from experience. "Government they have power in a piece of paper. That's how we lost first round in this case. They believe the papers more than the elders' testimony. It's, it's pretty sad, you know. Thank you."

It is pretty sad, you know. John Davis said:

> What I can remember, I will say.
> What I do not remember, I will not say.
> I cannot read and write.
> I can only remember.
> Before the whitemen came, we were bush people.
> When they came, where we live they said,
> "This my land."
> And we have no more.
> We can't read and write.
> We only can remember it.
> Since not too long ago
> that my people started to go to school.

John Davis's words were quoted in a journal called *Canadian Literature.* You can read and write. It is quite some time ago that our people started to go to school. You can read and write, but you can also remember. You can remember that John Davis is a man of knowledge. He is a man who gained knowledge through his experience of life in the bush. You can remember that his people helped the early fur traders. He and the Dunne-za who went before him took care of the whitepeople when they were new to the country. They fed the strangers from their knowledge of the land. They fed them as people with whom discourse was possible. They expect a return of that consideration. Reading his words brings you into his world. Reading his words begins a return of the discourse. John Davis understands his life in relation to the world as a whole. Gerry Attachie understands what his grandmother told him about the Place Where Happiness Dwells. He does not understand why the government should hold power over him from a piece of paper. He does not accept something that is unintelligible to him or his people.

Canadian literature begins in the discourse that Native people have with one another and with the sentient persons of their environment. It begins in the highly contexted language of their myth. It begins in the discourse of oral tradition. Literary critics need not be as literal-minded as judges. We can understand that people like John Davis make decisions on the basis of knowledge, not instinct. We understand that paper can carry lies as well as truth. We need not be constrained by our culture's privileging of paper so as to "believe the papers more than the elders' testimony." The problem of discourse is more general than any problematic of literary criticism. It is a human problem. It is also a human glory.

You have read what I have written from my knowledge of Dunne-za/Cree life. You have attended to the words of Gerry Attachie, John Davis, and Hugh Brody. I will leave you with a question. How can we know what happened on September 22, 1945? How can we know what it meant to the people who were there? Did the Dunne-za/Cree knowingly surrender the Place Where Happiness Dwells? Did the trial resolve the problem of discourse or merely reproduce it? You be the judge.

Canadian Literature, 1989

WHEN POISON GAS COME DOWN LIKE A FOG

A Native Community's Response to Cultural Disaster

> Just like you blowing something, sounds like that.
> And they knew it right away, something happened down
> there.
> And pretty soon, just like a fog come down.
> Come down the hill.
> —Angus Davis, Blueberry band, interviewed by Howard
> Broomfield in Fort St. John, British Columbia,
> August 11, 1979

The Blueberry Reserve is a community of Cree and Beaver Indians about 72 kilometers north of Fort St. John, British Columbia. The Dunne-za are Athapaskan-speaking people who lived in the upper Peace River country as bands of nomadic hunters at the time of first contact in the late eighteenth century. The Cree at Blueberry are Algonquian speakers whose ancestors first came to the Fort St. John area as hunters, trappers, traders, and employees of the Hudson's Bay Company.

From 1800 until 1942, when the Alaska Highway opened up their territory to a massive influx of settlers, the Dunne-za continued to subsist largely from hunting and trapping. Throughout the nineteenth century, they traded furs for guns, snare wire, traps, beads, knives, fabric, tobacco, and alcohol. During the twentieth century there was a gradual increase in trade for foods such as flour, sugar, tea, rice, and potatoes. Several bands continued to make their camps in and around the area which is now occupied by the postwar boom town of Fort St. John until they were forced to move farther into the bush.

Following the signing of Treaty 8, lands near the present town of Montney, British Columbia, just north of Fort St. John, were set aside as a reserve for the Indians who traded into Fort St. John. With the agricultural development of the north Peace River area following World War II, the federal government wished to make these lands available to returning war veterans. In 1945, the government obtained a surrender of IR-172 from Indian Affairs to the Veterans Land Administration. In 1950, the present Doig and Blueberry reserves were established. These reserves were supposed to provide the Indians with a base from which they could continue their traditional hunting and trapping way of life. At the time this land exchange was taking place, the government agents did not tell the Indians about the possibility of major oil exploration in the hunting and trapping areas surrounding the Doig and Blueberry reserves. Such exploration did begin in the 1950s and resulted in a massive development of wells, pipelines, pumping stations, storage facilities, and accompanying supply and support systems. In addition to the disturbance of game habitat caused by the oil development itself, increased access to the lands used by the Blueberry and Doig people for trapping and hunting brought in a new influx of white hunters and farmers. Larger tracts of land, previously thought uneconomic for agricultural development because of the lack of access roads, were bought up by developers and cleared with heavy equipment. Hunting and trapping became increasingly difficult for the people of Blueberry as these large-scale industrial and agricultural developments went on around them.

While they retained a strong commitment to the values and perceptions of their past way of life, the Blueberry people, recognizing their greater need for cash income as their hunting lands diminished, also sought jobs as guides, slashers for pipeline and oil exploration projects, and agricultural workers. However, they did not gain any direct benefit from the development itself. Instead of being close to a source of food and cash income from the bush, they found themselves isolated in a remote area where supplies could only be brought in from town at considerable expense. They found themselves in a culture based on the possession of motor vehicles but without the skills or high income required to maintain them. Compared to the surrounding white community, the Blueberry people had become poor and unable to control or benefit directly from the economic development of their former lands. Under the new conditions, their skills as hunters and trappers responsible for managing their own resources became less relevant as these resources diminished or came under the control of settlers, government agencies, and large corporations.

The economic and social position of the Blueberry people was not good when, in 1976, a Calgary-based oil company brought in an oil well just outside the reserve boundary and on the only road giving access to the reserve. The well was of a type known as a sour gas well, meaning that the oil deposits are overlaid by a dome of hydrogen sulfide gas. A chain link fence surrounded the immediate well site and prominent signs warned "Danger, Poison Gas." As soon as the operation of the well commenced, the people of Blueberry began to complain of its negative effects. A person walking past the well was unable to avoid an unpleasant exposure to the gas under normal operating conditions. Furthermore, the gas could be routinely detected in the village, which was less than 700 meters from the well site.

As soon as the well had been brought into production and the Indians realized the problem they were being asked to live with, they began to investigate possible solutions. For three years they complained of headaches and a general lack of well-being, which they attributed to long-term low levels of exposure to hydrogen sulfide gas. They brought these complaints first to the Department of Indian Affairs, then to the Medical Services Administration (the federal agency responsible for looking after Native health), and finally to the provincial Pollution Control Board. Each agency claimed that the problem was out of its jurisdiction and passed the matter on to another agency. As of the summer of 1979, the Pollution Control Board had set up ambient air monitors on the reserve to measure monthly average levels of gas, but none of the agencies indicated that it would be within its power to take any concrete action to eliminate the problem. The most that they seemed willing to do was to validate with quantitative data the information the Indians had from their own direct experience.

Then on July 16, 1979, the well developed a major leak, resulting in a cloud of the poison gas rolling down into the village.[1] The gas came "down like a fog" from the well site located on a hill above the village, at approximately 8:00 P.M. The band chief was among those who heard the sound of gas escaping and saw the cloud begin to move toward the houses. There was sufficient time for him to alert every household to the danger. As a result, all were able to evacuate the village safely. Although some people experienced adverse effects from acute exposure to the gas during their escape, no lives were lost. In an interview later in town, the chief described his actions: "I told them to get out of here. It's poison gas, eh. It was covering Blueberry. You can't see across the reserve. It was covered with a cloud of smoke." [Did everybody leave then?] "Yes, everybody left."

The evacuation, although difficult, was accomplished without serious injury. Had the incident happened at night in the dead of winter, it is very likely that many lives would have been lost. Although the company did manage to shut down the well so that people could begin to return home after about a week, the Indians petitioned, through a lawyer retained by the Union of British Columbia Indian Chiefs, for an injunction from the Supreme Court of British Columbia against resumption of operation until some solution to the problem could be worked out. This petition for an injunction was accepted as a temporary measure by the company, but in June 1980 it petitioned the court to lift the injunction and allow it to resume production after the installation of what are claimed to be advanced fail-safe devices. After initially reserving judgment on the matter, on July 1, 1980, the judge finally agreed with the company that the injunction should be lifted.

In its petition to the court asking that the injunction be continued, the band stated that under no circumstances were they willing to live close to such a known hazard. Therefore, they were negotiating with the federal government to secure funds to remove the entire village to a safer location. Their plea was simply that the injunction remain in effect until their move could be completed. At the time of writing, the court's decision is under appeal by the band.[2]

This paper is an examination of issues raised by the conflict between the oil company and the Blueberry band. In particular, I will point out the contrast between values and perceptions of hunting and gathering people and those of people in industrial society. My own work has been with the oral traditions of the Dunne-za. My closest informant from 1964 through 1969 was the Dreamer or prophet Charlie Yahey, a member of the Blueberry band. He is no longer living, but two of his grandchildren are currently band chief and councillor. Although they have developed skills in dealing with representatives of industrial society, they retain many of the values of their heritage as nomadic hunting people. In presenting information obtained from Charlie Yahey and others of his generation, I am presenting some of the cultural and intellectual milieus in which present band leaders were raised. Their way of dealing with industrial society reflects this hunting and gathering heritage. My information relates only to Dunne-za culture, but many of the generalizations about the quality of life in a traditional boreal forest hunting society also apply to the Cree tradition. The events relating to the Blueberry case were documented by myself, Jillian Ridington, and Howard Broomfield in 1979 and 1980.

TRADITIONAL DUNNE-ZA VALUES AND PERCEPTIONS

As with many hunting and gathering people living in band-level societies (Leacock 1978), the Dunne-za have always valued personal autonomy and its concomitants, individual competence and responsibility. Boys and girls were trained to find their way in the bush alone and to be able to take care of themselves. This training focused on the child's vision quest encounters with supernatural animals or powers from mythic times. In the vision quest experience and the training that led up to it, children learned how to use information from this cultural tradition in making their own decisions about the situations in which they found themselves. This training encouraged children particularly to sharpen their powers of observation. They learned to see the intelligence of their world through their own informed intelligence as individuals. Traditional myths were a way of coding their culture's intelligence in a way that complemented the child's own individual intelligent observation. One myth that was a charter for the vision quest, for instance, described the empowerment of Saya, the culture hero (Ridington 1978a). He is associated with the daily and seasonal movements of the sun and moon. Dunne-za children learned a cycle of stories about Saya's transformations as they learned to take their own direction by reference to the sun's daily and seasonal bearing relative to their own position and destination. They were expected to make their own intelligent and responsible decisions based upon personal observation and cultural tradition. The intelligence of this tradition was received as a tool for autonomous, individual decision making rather than as a prescription for any particular course of action.

The Dunne-za believe strongly in the authority of personal experience. They were adept at describing their experiences with eloquence and accuracy. To "know something" was to have experienced it personally. They said that a person who gained supernatural power from his or her vision quest experiences "knew something." This same reliance on the authority of personal experience underlay Dunne-za shamanism. Dreamers like Charlie Yahey were people who traveled the "trail to heaven" and returned to tell the story of their dream journey. As Charlie Yahey put it, "The Dreamer dreams ahead for everybody." In times past, Dreamers were probably hunt chiefs who visualized the pattern of a communal hunt and directed the deployment of band members in the hunt. In this case, the Dreamer's vision was accepted, much as the information brought back by a scout who traveled the trail ahead would be given credence. If the hunts were too often unsuccessful, people would conclude that his perception of the patterning of events was faulty and cease to follow his direction. The Dreamer was believed largely on the strength of his personal experience of a range of vision beyond that of ordinary people, not because of the authority of his position. One old person succinctly pointed out this distinction in a contrast he made between priests and Dreamers. "Both," he said, "tell people about heaven, but the priest only speaks from what he has read in books, while the Dreamer tells what he has experienced because he has been there."

Dunne-za traditions allow for leadership without the need for social hierarchy as we know it. They emphasize reliance on individual observation as it was informed by the tools of tradition and communicated between individuals for the benefit of all. At the personal level, these values were developed through the vision quest and the training leading up to it. At the level of social life, they may be seen in the extraordinary sensitivity of traditional bands to the opportunities and constraints of the local ecology. This sensitivity was clearly evidenced in their response to ecological hardship requiring larger concentrations of people to split into smaller bands. A key to their adaptation as nomads was their ability to move from one resource area to another before a failure of supply had actually been experienced.

Many of the stories I collected dealt with the problem of group fission in response to ecological stress. A decision to split into smaller bands was made by individual "camps" rather than collectively. When a large group of people camped together for too long, straining the resources of a given area, generalized reciprocity would break down as hunters gave what meat they had only to their nearest relatives. This situation inevitably caused bad feelings between those who received meat and those excluded from the distribution. This bad feeling neatly defined the lines along which fission would take place. Many of the stories referred to conflicting guidance from different Dreamers during these times of scarcity. In these cases each smaller group would follow the vision of its own Dreamer. In these ecologically sensitive situations, social conflict may have been an important mechanism for distributing people intelligently throughout an overall resource area. At the heart of the fission process was the culturally and experientially informed judgment of individuals.

Other stories told how certain powers derived from individual vision quest experiences were important in warning people of threats that others could not see until it was too late. One of these powers was Wolverine. The stories recount how a person with Wolverine medicine had a particular intelligence about traps because of the way Wolverine is said to escape from a snare by lifting it over his head (Ridington 1980c). Wolverine medicine represented both a person's ability at trapping animals and the ability to detect dangerous situations that might trap people. The heightened ability to detect a threatening situation as symbolized by Wolverine reflects the more general sensitivity to danger of individuals in Dunne-za culture. The normal characteristic response of these nomadic hunters when confronted with harm or the threat of harm was to move to a safer location. Often these moves also entailed the fission of larger groups into smaller bands along the lines of fracture already evidenced by social conflict within the larger group.

VALUES AND PERCEPTIONS OF INDUSTRIAL SOCIETY

Because the general values and perceptions of people in industrial society should be well known to us, I will simply point out some of the more obvious contrasts to the generalizations I have made about hunting and gathering society and the Dunne-za in particular. Perhaps the most striking contrast is the reliance we place on the power and authority of social hierarchy. Although in our day-to-day lives we attempt to keep ourselves out of danger by the application of simple, informed intelligence, in more complex or ambiguous situations we refer to the judgment of higher authorities. Our institutionalized form of education strongly conditions us to believe there are right and wrong answers that are known to those superior to us. Even in situations where the "right" answer conflicts with our individual judgment and observation, we are socialized to submerge our true feelings and produce the correct response. Although this conditioning is not absolute and, indeed, the entire scientific method rests on an informed skepticism, there are few of us who have not experienced some negative sanction for making an observation contrary to the opinion of established authority.

In order to develop the contrast between the values and perceptions of hunter-gatherers and people in industrial society, I propose to distinguish between two uses of the word *intelligence*. One of these I will call human intelligence, the other cultural intelligence. Human intelligence is the ability with which we are endowed as members of our common species. At its simplest, it enables us to figure out how things in our perceptual field fit together into a coherent pattern. The dog who winds its leash around a tree and must wait for one of us to unwind it lacks simple human intelligence. The person who carries a container to a source of food and returns to where it may be shared with others is certainly showing human intelligence. However, even such a basic act as I have described, undoubtedly going back to the times of early Homo sapiens, introduces an element of complexity beyond that of being able to unsnarl oneself from a leash wrapped around a tree. This added element is what I have called cultural intelligence. Cultural intelligence, unlike individual human intelligence, is a system of information. It is intelligence in the sense now largely taken over by the so-called intelligence community. The carrying bag is more than an object, an artifact. It is a system of information that has become available to the individual user through the social mechanism of tradition. Throughout the millennia during which people have lived as hunters and gatherers, the intelligence of our biological endowment has been informed by a growing body of cultural intelligence. As long as we remained within the bounds of the hunting and gathering adaptation, cultural intelligence continued to provide information on a scale relevant to the requirements of individual intelligence.

The conflict between the oil company and the Blueberry band sharply contrasts the cultural intelligence of hunting and gathering people with that of people in modern industrial society. In order to illustrate this contrast, I will summarize the arguments brought by both sides. I will also refer to interviews with a Blueberry band councillor and lawyers acting for the oil company and the band recorded immediately after the hearing ended.

THE CONFLICT

Counsel for the Blueberry band argued that the oil well has been a health hazard even during normal operation. She presented testimony of band members complaining of headaches and general malaise that they attributed to the continuous presence of hydrogen sulfide gas in the village as well as expert medical opinion validating these personal claims. She reminded the court that the band's wish was to move from a site they considered no longer habitable and that they wished the injunction to remain in effect only until the move could be carried out. Counsel for the oil company argued that although normal operation of the well might be polluting and constitute an annoyance, hydrogen sulfide levels were within acceptable limits and not a demonstrable health hazard. He pointed out that life in industrial society inevitably involves annoyance and risk. In an interview which was recorded after the hearing, he explained this argument.

> The court's jurisdiction in a matter like this is to act as between citizen and citizen, if one party has committed a common wrong towards the other. In this case, the pleadings allege that the company was negligent and committed a nuisance in allowing the escape of hydrogen sulfide gas. On that basis, the threat of further escape, the consent injunction was made. The court's role or jurisdiction to continue that injunction depends upon some evidence that there's a threat of a further nuisance or further escape, and we've attempted in our evidence to show that there is no risk inherent in this facility. We've made it as safe as human inge-

nuity can make it. Now having said that, it's recognized by everyone in our society that we live with risks every day. We saw Mississauga evacuated. We have nuclear power plants and we saw the Three Mile Island incident. There are risks inherent in living in modern-day society that the society learns to accept. Now the regulation of those types of risk is made on a different level than the juridical level. That's basically a technical decision made by politicians and duly appointed experts. So, for instance, in the oil and gas industry, there's technical boards who set down standards that facilities must meet and buffer zones around which populations will not be allowed to encroach. And we've in this case tried to show that the buffer zone between our facility and the Indian reservation is adequate to protect the Indians even in the event of a catastrophe. (Interview with council for the company by Jillian Ridington, Robin Ridington, and Howard Broomfield, June 19, 1980)

During the hearing, the company's lawyer presented evidence about the effects of various levels of hydrogen sulfide. Workers in the petrochemical industry are permitted to work eight-hour shifts in an atmosphere containing up to 10 parts per million (ppm); 100 ppm is considered a health hazard, 500 ppm is fatal to weak individuals, and 1,000 ppm is fatal to all. He then argued that the 500 ppm isopleth (the radius of a given level of contamination) in the worst-case scenario should the well blow out again after resuming operation would be only 200 meters, while the 100 ppm isopleth would be 700 meters. The village is approximately 700 meters from the well but below it in a valley subject to temperature inversion under certain atmospheric conditions. Council for the band reiterated the band's position that they considered the site uninhabitable, while the company council countered with his argument that the risk is no different from risks faced by millions of people in industrial society. After reserving his decision for several weeks, the judge apparently concurred with the company's argument that life in industrial society entails inevitable risk. The injunction was lifted. The band subsequently lost an appeal of the decision.

We also interviewed a councillor for the band and talked to him at some length in a less formal setting. The following are excerpts from the taped interview.

Q.: What do you think people will do if they start up the well again before you move out?

A.: The people say they just gonna move out; go camp somewhere like what they done last summer.

Q.: If the well had blown in the middle of the night in winter what would have happened?

A.: I don't know; probably kill all the people, 'cause it's powerful, that thing. Hydrogen sulfide gas, hydrogen sulfide poison gas.

Q.: Are the people really afraid of it?

A.: Oh yeah, after what had happened last summer they should be afraid.

Q.: You were talking about a case that happened up there when some people got killed.

A.: Oh yeah, there's one guy tell me about happened same thing. Sixty people got killed. Forgot which guy tell me.

Q.: Have you noticed that people are sicker since this happened?

A.: Some people get headache. Like me, I get headache just about all summer now. My eyes are really bother me. It's just like suffering me very slowly, kind of getting worse and worse.

Q.: How do the people feel about moving?

A.: They want to move out of that place and are really happy to move out of there. That's why we want to get that study. Try to get least twelve houses before freeze-up. But what I figure we gonna do is get these foundations built up before freeze-up and start on the houses. Probably finish before February, twelve houses. Next year we can finish the rest.

Q.: What you want now is to keep the well shut down until you can finish those houses?

A.: That's right, give us time to study.

Q.: What was it like when people first came back?

A.: When the well blew out . . . when they came back to get some stuff and they open the door, it's pretty stink inside. Have to open up both side door and let the air out. They throw out most of our groceries. Blankets, they have to wash it.

Q.: When they got the injunction and people came back to live at Blueberry, was everyone scared?

A.: Oh yeah, don't trust that well no more.

Q.: Did many people not come back?

A.: Yeah.

Q.: How long has the band been there?

A.: Quite a while. Since, I don't remember, probably around '49, 1949.

Q.: All your life almost. You grew up there. The thing that I found listening to the hearing was that the judge and the lawyers for the company, the owner of the company, none of them seem to really understand the problems up there. They don't know what it's like to live there.

A.: They don't understand because they don't live there. They only there once. Even that boss, he's there once, come back. They don't know what's going on 'cause . . . us, we know what's going on 'cause we live there. From that same well, one guy got paralyzed. There's a tank, that big tank. Going up, trying to open up to get that crude oil or something and he got dizzy and fall down and got paralyzed. Tom Carcier, about a couple of years ago. There's one guy too, almost same kind of thing. Want get a crude oil. He was going, he park there and get off. Stand there for a while. Start to get dizzy. So he ran to the main road. He go back and then try it again. Start to get dizzy again. So he stayed in the road. So I guess one of the boys from Blueberry came and gave him a ride to the guy who look after the well. Carcier. So he went go tell him so they shut that thing down.

Q.: What's your feeling about the whole hearing?

A.: Bad! Sometime the way they talk, I don't understand them. Like they say about Alberta, what Alberta law is. Alberta got their own law. It's not B.C.

Q.: I was really amazed at the judge saying it's really OK to have risks like this, that there's nothing wrong with it; but he doesn't have the same risk.

A.: Seems to me the judge helping those other guys, that company. If he live down there he'll find out. He'll said, "Oh, I better move back." He'll be scared.

(Excerpts from interview with band councillor Gerry Davis by Jillian Ridington, Robin Ridington, and Howard Broomfield, June 19, 1980)

Hunting and gathering people generally focus considerable attention on the potential of their environment for benefit or harm. The speed with which these people have been observed to adopt useful artifacts of industrial technology indicates their responsiveness to their perception of potential benefit. Their sensitivity to seasonal variation and the flexibility of their band sizes are well documented. Local variations in the distribution of resources are generally reflected in variations of adaptive strategy. Geographical mobility and flexible band size and structure are important means of avoiding dangers that might result from a discontinuity between resource distribution and the deployment of people. Particular environmental hazards are quickly noted and acted upon where possible. The nature of such hazards is validated by the authority of personal experience.

Both the band councillor and the company lawyer presented evidence about the hazards of exposure to hydrogen sulfide gas in various concentrations. The Indian's account was based on his own experience or the experience of people who told him their personal observations. The lawyer's account was based on the reports of "duly appointed experts." The Indian's information related to three different levels of exposure. First is the chronic level experienced by everyone in the village during normal operation of the well. This he described as "suffering me slowly." Next were the cases of temporary paralysis experienced by company employees who were overcome by emissions from the well on the border of the reserve. Finally, he had been told of fatalities from hydrogen sulfide at other installations in the Peace River area. He and everyone else at Blueberry are convinced that the blowout experienced on July 16, 1979, when the gas rolled down on the village "like a fog," would have resulted in fatalities had they not evacuated immediately. The three levels of exposure to the gas correspond respectively to the effects reported by "duly appointed experts" for levels of 100, 500, and 1,000 parts per million as described by the company lawyer. Despite the company's assurance that "we've made it as safe as human ingenuity can make it," members of the Blueberry band are unanimous in their unwillingness to live that close to a source of lethal poison gas. They know on the basis of firsthand experience that human ingenuity could prevent neither chronic nor catastrophic emissions in the past, and they have little reason to believe that the fundamental hazard of living so close to a poison gas well can be truly overcome, no matter how much ingenuity the company claims to possess. They are not impressed by the claim that all people in industrial society pay the price of similar risks for the benefits they derive from the industrial adaptive strategy. They have experienced few of these benefits themselves. They are willing to move the village away from the source of danger, just as in the past a band would have responded to an environmental hazard by moving to another location. The well exists, and they do not trust it. Therefore, the intelligent response is to move to a safer location. They only want the well to remain shut down until the move can be completed.

Before the well blew out, the band attempted to get "expert" validation of their experience of a hydrogen sulfide hazard. They made their complaints known to both the Department of Indian Affairs and the Medical Services Administration. As a result of repeated requests for action, Medical Services requested that the provincial Pollution Control Board set up ambient air monitors around the reserve. In an interview we conducted with a doctor of the Medical Services Administration on June 26, 1979, three weeks before the well blew out, we were told that the experts did not consider the well to be a significant health hazard. Yet the doctor knew the deadly possibilities of hydrogen sulfide. The following are excerpts from that interview.

Q.: And you're from Medical Services?
A.: That's right. We have . . . we have six, there, at least there are six monitoring stations around the reserve. Now, I have just received the results. They started monitoring, they must have been monitoring, oh, Pollution Control Board's been monitoring 'em and I've received, I myself have received the results two or three weeks ago. From these results, basic, these results . . . We got the Department of Environment to have a look at them and basically they feel that there's not . . . no problem. But, however, these are sort of block, monthly across the board every month, and I would like to know highs and lows. I'd like it metered continuously. So that this where we are.
Q.: Also, that doesn't give you anything on long-term effects really, does it?
A.: Well, doesn't. I'm not worried about long-term effects. I mean we know what gas this is and we know this that and the other. What I would like to know maybe, for instance, oh, for now it

might be very, very high and it might be low for the rest of the
month and therefore you get a low sample, so that's really what
I like to . . .

Q.: What are the principal gases? Is it hydrogen sulfide?

A.: Yeah, hydrogen sulfide.

Q.: Do you know if there's any information on long-term effects of
various levels of hydrogen sulfide? How what you're monitoring
here compares with, say, urban areas where that gas is present
and that kind of thing?

A.: No, I don't know actually, I'm not a, I don't think there's any
long-term effects of hydrogen sulfide. There sure are some short-
term effects.

Q.: Such as what?

A.: Well, such as death. That's if you . . .

Q.: That sounds like a long-term effect to me.

A.: Ah, no, I'd disagree with you. At any rate, but what I'm sort of
saying is that if you, if you got hydrogen sulfide in a small room,
yeah, and you're taking deep breaths, ah, you'll die. Now here
with this wind blowing I would personally, would be, wouldn't
but, I'd like to know, I'd like to know, I'd like to have information so that I can advise these people.

Q.: Right now the wind is blowing away from the well.

A.: Yeah, I'm talking about, I'm talking about if it was in an enclosed room.

Q.: What about things like headaches, dizziness, nausea, that kind
of thing?

A.: No, I'd, no, I would say this is, this would be more of a carbon
dioxide type of picture you've been getting.

Q.: What about variations of temperature. This is a place with great
extremes. You know it goes from 90 degrees in the summer to
65 below in the winter, Fahrenheit.

A.: Personally, all I'd like to sort of say is, really, this isn't, in my
mind, a great health problem. Just from the one monitoring
we've got, and the other things is that certainly, I'd like to, I'd
just like to have . . . Well, I'm just going to repeat myself, I'd like
to have it monitored more closely. Just once a month isn't
enough.

Q.: What kind of levels do you have, though, compared to other
standards. Is there a minimum standard that's been set?

A.: Yeah, the proposed regulations these meet. Over a month period, yeah, these are within the limits.
Q.: What about breaking down into particles and that kind of thing. Does the equipment you have now do that?
A.: I don't have any equipment at all. The equipment there's Pollution Control Branch's. All I'm, I mean I haven't put the equipment up here. Pollution Control Branch is doing this. I'm sort of saying, OK, I want the results from you, Pollution Control Branch. And the results are sort of coming in a form where I've asked the experts to interpret it for me and this is what they've interpreted. And they're also, I think, the federal government has sort of said, well we might be able to get a regular analyzer up, maybe, what do you want? So I said, yeah, I said this . . . a monthly block ain't all this swift for me. I mean, I'm prepared to take your things that on a monthly average, there's no problem.
Q.: What action would you be able to take if you did find the readings indicated that they were above an acceptable level?
A.: Well, Pollution Control Board have sort of assured me that they were, I mean they're the responsible agency. And certainly ours, I mean I would, in my position, I would like to sort of say, hey, look, we've monitored this and got this.
Q.: If you found that it was over an acceptable level, what kind of things could you do to it? Is there ways that this present well can be filled, fixed up so that it is less, emitting less poisons, or would it have to be capped or what could be done?
A.: I really wouldn't know what powers the Pollution Control Branch have got. But well, I sort of do. I mean, they are under control. I mean, really without any doubt, if there is noxious, if this is noxious, the people here. I mean . . . I'd be looking for something to happen. I mean, I wouldn't just, yeah.
(Interview with Medical Services doctor by Jillian Ridington and Robin Ridington, Blueberry Reserve, June 26, 1979)

Until the well actually blew, requiring an evacuation of the Blueberry Reserve, the band's attempt to validate their own common-sense observation of a hazard met with the kind of frustrating interagency buck passing reflected in this interview. It was a classic case of conflict between the testimony of personal experience and the authority of experts with vested interests in the overall industrial sys-

222 THE PROBLEM OF DISCOURSE

tem that was responsible for the hazard in the first place. Nobody in Blueberry doubted that the well was a health hazard and a potential killer. Their call for the validation of experts was not to satisfy their own minds but merely to satisfy the intelligence of a culture that gave credence only to the authority of duly constituted "experts." Their own knowledge had to become official before it would be accepted by the society responsible for creating the hazard. Now that the well has blown and nearly killed them all, they still find themselves in a conflict between their own informed intelligence, which concludes the village site is no longer habitable, and the intelligence of "experts" hired by the oil company, who claim that the risk is negligible and that life in industrial society is inherently risky anyway. Neither of these arguments is particularly convincing to the people of Blueberry, given their past experience with expert opinion. In keeping with the intelligence of their hunting and gathering tradition, they choose to move away from the danger.

The company has alleged that the band's desire to move is in part the result of "social problems" experienced under present conditions. They argue that the danger from the well is being used as an excuse to make a move that might have been desirable had there been no well close to the village. It is true that the village was laid out by Indian Affairs Branch "experts." Their primary considerations were cost and bureaucratic rationality rather than the complex problems of creating a community made up of members of several Dunne-za bands and Cree families living in the same general area. The proposed new accommodation is being planned by the Blueberry people themselves. They have opted for a dispersed settlement more in keeping with the social realities of their community than an arbitrary concentrated grid system. In their minds, the desire to rectify errors made by government experts at the time the present village was laid out in no way diminishes the very real need to move from the present site because of its proximity to a source of poison gas that could kill them all. They hope that the new settlement laid out according to their own understanding of social reality will make it easier to correct the "social problems" experienced during the years they have been forced to live in an environment designed to conform to the cultural intelligence of industrial society rather than to the intelligence of their own hunting and gathering tradition. Unfortunately, the move can only be accomplished with the assistance of various government agencies. It remains to be seen whether the people of Blueberry will be successful in translating their own intelligence into a language capable of penetrating the intelligence of the alien culture surrounding them.

CONCLUSION

For many thousands of years, human culture has been on a scale relevant to the values and perceptions of individual human beings. For the most part, the culture of hunting and gathering people has informed them and furthered their understanding of the environmental conditions to which they have been closely adapted. Hunting and gathering cultures have particularly valued personal autonomy and the authority of individual experience. Traditional knowledge has generally furthered the human capacity for intelligent observation. Human culture may be seen as a system of information or intelligence. Under hunting and gathering conditions, this intelligence informed the intelligence of individual human beings. With the rise of more complex social systems and particularly of those social systems dependent on an industrial adaptation to the resource potential of the planet, cultural intelligence has often come to work against the intelligence of individuals. Although the work of specialists is essential for developing the specialized knowledge on which such an adaptive system is dependent, it very often relates more to the requirements of the system itself than to the basic needs of individual human beings. Indeed, our cultural intelligence has resulted in the obviously unintelligent capacity to destroy the entire species.

The simple desire of a band of former nomadic hunters to remove themselves from a source of poison gas they have experienced as hazardous brings into focus the more general hazard we all face as we struggle to continue our lives as individuals and as a species in the face of an inhuman intelligence that has taken on a life of its own. The people of Blueberry still think in terms of moving to a safer location, despite the limits imposed by industrial development on their former hunting and trapping lands, but those of us who were not raised in a hunting and gathering tradition realize that the group to which we belong is the entire species. The move we must make is not physical but evolutionary. Unless we are able to bring our culture's intelligence back to its traditional role of informing individual intelligence, all forms of intelligence may vanish from this world as if they had never been.

NOTES

1. Jillian Ridington and Howard Broomfield documented the events surrounding the accident in a thirty-minute radio documentary, "Suffering Me Slowly." It was aired by the Canadian Broadcasting Corporation on "The Hornby Collection" in January 1981.

2. The band's appeal was denied, but the move to a new village site was eventually carried out.

Human Organization, 1982

IN DOIG PEOPLE'S EARS

*Portrait of a Changing Community
in Sound*

Culture is revealed as much through the ordinary taken-for-granted sights and sounds of everyday life as it is through peak experiences that happen only infrequently. When I first began audio recording among the Beaver Indian people in the mid-1960s, I neglected ordinary sounds in favor of what seemed to me extraordinary. My choice of what seemed important and worth recording reflected a preference for high-profile ceremonial events and performances over periods of informality when, in my view, "nothing was happening." My choice of what to record was also constrained by having a very limited supply of reel-to-reel tape. Recordings from that period contain invaluable documentation of prophetic songs, oratory, and narrative but document very little in the way of conversations, environmental sounds, or the punctuation created by moments of silence.

After an absence from the Peace River country in the mid-1970s, during which time the shaman or Dreamer with whom I had worked passed away, Jillian Ridington and I returned in 1979 with audio documentarian Howard Broomfield. Broomfield had recorded with composer R. Murray Schafer on the World Soundscape Project and wished to collect material for an audio portrait of a particular community undergoing rapid cultural change. Thanks to an Urgent Ethnology Contract with the Canadian Ethnology Service, we were well supplied with tape. During the course of this and subsequent fieldwork supported by the Canadian Ethnology Service, we accumulated an archive containing hundreds of hours of recorded material. From this archive we have produced a series of audio documentary programs on various aspects of Beaver Indian life. These have been aired on Vancouver community radio CFRO, Canadian Broadcasting Corporation's "Our Native Land" and "The Hornby Collection," and in classrooms and academic conferences. They have also been presented to the Native communities in which they were made.

FROM DOCUMENT TO DOCUMENTARY

The Beaver audio archive is a collection of documents. The presence of particular sounds and settings in it reflects a complex and often opportunistic pattern of contact between ourselves and the people whose lives we wished to document. Sometimes our recording sessions became formal occasions during which people told us stories, recorded songs, or granted interviews on particular topics of interest. Sometimes our presence as documentarians had little or no effect on the pace or content of events. Because we recorded extensively, we were able to document many conversations and ordinary interactions with a minimum of interference.

Our overall objective was to record a wide range of soundscapes, settings, events, and interactions. These recordings are primary documents. They record what in the language of radio production are called "actualities." At the time they were recorded, these sounds were embedded in the context of ordinary life at a particular time and place. They were taken for granted by the people living and experiencing them. They were important pieces in the ongoing flow of experience that defined cultural reality for those people at that particular moment.

Echoes of the traditional soundscape were still present during the time of our fieldwork, and we recorded them whenever possible. The piece we produced for "Our Native Land," for instance, begins with the dawn chorus of birds on an early summer solstice morning, punctuated by the conversations of camp dogs calling back and forth to one another against the steady background of a river's water moving. The sounds are subtle and blend to create the unmistakable signature of a particular time, place, and season. These ordinary sounds of an early summer morning in a northern Indian village seemed quite extraordinary to Howard, for whom they were a new and different world.

Rather than impose our own judgment that some actualities were more important than others, we attempted to include in the archive a representative sample of sounds that were recognized as being in the public domain by people in the community. For ethical reasons, we did not attempt to record events that were clearly private and privileged. We did not record anything in secret and we always responded to requests that particular events not be recorded. Within the bounds of these constraints, however, we were able to document the significant sounds that made up the aural dimension of Beaver Indian culture during the time of our fieldwork.

By its very nature, the process of recording culturally significant sounds removes them from a context that is taken for granted. The recording of culture's aural dimension creates documents that must be recontextualized in order to be meaningful once again. The anthropologist's job is to create such a context. If the documents are to be presented in an aural medium rather than a written one, the new context must be created through the juxtaposition of sounds themselves. This new context transforms the documents of ethnographic field recording into a documentary that uses them as actualities of the culture.

IN DOIG PEOPLE'S EARS

The piece entitled "In Doig People's Ears" was produced by Howard Broomfield to illustrate the range of material in the audio archive. Doig River is the name of a reserve community northeast of Fort St. John. The piece is a documentary produced entirely from actualities taken from the archive of primary documents. It is like an aural catalog or sampler designed to accompany the written catalog created for the National Museum of Man, but it is organized according to categories significant to Beaver Indian culture rather than according to the usual reference categories used by a museum. It was particularly designed to give the people at Doig a feeling for the archive and its possible uses.

Unlike a conventional catalog that presents information piece by piece in a set order, "In Doig People's Ears" is a montage of sounds. It is a documentary piece rather than a collection of documents. It is a story, not a list. As such, it speaks to the sensibilities of people whose lives span preliterate and postliterate oral traditions. The piece may be experienced at an intuitive level of consciousness. It may be received in the way that dreams are received, to be analyzed later and by different techniques.

The piece is a documentary created as much for people of the culture it describes as for anthropologists or the general public. In traditional Beaver Indian culture, songs were "brought down from heaven" by shamans known as Dreamers. The piece begins by creating a sense of the context in which life took place when the Beaver people were hunters and trappers. It juxtaposes soundscape actualities and recordings of cultural events in a way that facilitates and reflects deeply entrenched Beaver Indian ways of listening and communicating. It presents soundscape information that formed the traditional basis of mutual understandings.

During their large summer dances, singers sang the Dreamers' songs and played hand drums. The chorus of voices and drums extended the community's soundspace far beyond the normal range of camp life. The sound reverberated deep into the bush. Dreamers presided over these gatherings. They told of the journeys they took in their dreams to the place beyond the sky. They spoke of the future. They sang new songs they had learned during the course of their journeys. They joined in the singing of songs brought down by Dreamers before them.

Beaver Indians visited whitepeople at stores and trading posts. They worked with them and sometimes socialized with them, but they did not live with them on a day-to-day basis. Until the 1950s, most Beaver people lived in isolated bush communities that were inaccessible to the whitemen and their machines. "In Doig People's Ears" tells the story of that time in both their own words and those of white old-timers who looked in on their world from the outside. These recollections of the past by whitepeople serve as a bridge to the introduction of actualities from the world in which the two cultures are in constant contact.

Strangers sometimes listened at the edge of the soundscape defined by the Dreamers' songs. One of these men was a young horse wrangler named Slim Byrns who told of his first meeting with the Indian people in 1929. One of the people at Doig took us around to visit him and record his story. The scene he described was strange and different to a young whiteman who was then new to the Peace River country. To the Beaver people it was as ordinary as the taste of moose meat or the sound of footsteps squeaking on snow when it is very cold. The sound of people singing and drumming and dancing together was as predictable as the turn of the seasons. They did not suspect then that their life in the bush would be threatened by machines and social forces beyond imagination. Slim Byrns described what he heard and saw:

> That whole valley down there below Clark's was filled full of tepees, and there must have been about a hundred head of horses, and it was in midsummer and it had been a very productive summer, and the horses were fat and shiny. And after they built their campfires down there and started playing their drums, in 1929 which is fifty years ago, it done somethin' to me that I shall never forget . . . with kinda mixed feelings. And we stayed up there at the top of the hill and grazed our horses and looked down into the valley and watched the campfires and seen them dancing around the fires. And that was my first really big experience with the Indians. They called it a tea dance.

The sounds of day-to-day life are taken for granted only as long as they are ordinary. In a community undergoing rapid change, ordinary sounds heard at one stage in a person's life may become exotic at a later stage. Beaver Indian people alive today grew up within a soundscape dominated by the sounds of wind, running water, squeaking snow, rustling leaves, and the soft fall of feet clad in moccasins on the trails of their country. Against this background of natural sounds, they listened carefully to the voices and movements of animals. They also listened carefully to the voices of people they knew and referred to by terms of relationship.

Voices rose and fell in song and blended with the complex sounds of drums to become a single instrument of many textures. Dreamers' songs were a metaphor for the soul's journey from this world's ordinary reality to the spirit world of dreaming. Singers held their drums close to their mouths and sang strongly toward the snares that were stretched across the inside of the drum's head. The soundspace where these two patterns of vibration met was highly charged. It was the center of a sacred circle of sound. Singers held their drums close so that others could not see inside their mouths. From this highly concentrated point where complementary waves of sound came together, the dreamspace of the Dreamers' songs spread in a circle out from where people were camped to the surrounding and sustaining bush.

Dreamers' songs were known as signs of the "trail to heaven." The drumbeat's regular rhythm was like the fall of feet on a trail. The song's "turns," its melodic contours, were described as being like the turns of a trail on earth. The Dreamers were people who had gone through the experience of dying and following a trail of song to heaven. They were able to tell people about the trail because they knew it from personal experience. In traditional Beaver philosophy, the soundscape created by singing and drumming represented a conceptual landscape that connected heaven and earth. The song trails followed by Dreamers were trails of the mind. Dreamers were people adept at following these spirit trails and returning to the body's earthly sanctuary. Their songs were trails of connection between mind and body, spirit and substance. When bands of related people who had been dispersed for the long winter came together to sing and dance during the easy days of midsummer, they created a soundscape that was large enough to surround and sustain the entire community.

Slim Byrns, standing at the edge of such an acoustically defined cultural space in 1929, was moved to say, "It done somethin' to me that I shall never forget." When I first danced close within the center of the soundscape created by people drumming and singing and dancing together around a common fire in 1965, it "done somethin'" to me that will be with me always. In a recording made in 1969, I began at the edge of the village. This was perhaps a tenth of the distance between the acoustic center of crackling fire, voices, snared drum heads, and the outermost extremity of the soundscape out in the dark surrounding bush. The recording documented a soundwalk toward the center of the sacred space. It appears in the audio documentary as an evocation of the scene Slim Byrns described. The circle of sound I captured on tape is now a treasured document from which a new context can be constructed in the form of an audio documentary.

As I walked slowly toward the center, the higher frequencies began to emerge from the low booming carrier wave of drumbeat vibrations. The powerful wailing chant of a remarkable lead singer,

Billy Makadahay, took up the center of attention. Then, other voices began to emerge from the chorus and, finally, the sound of people talking and laughing and the hot explosive staccato of the flaring fire emerged to complete the acoustic portrait of this ceremonial event. The recording documents a communal focus and intensity that I did not experience again among the Beaver people until the late 1980s. An entire community came together at the center of a soundscape of Dreamers' songs. In so doing, they evoked the spirits of those who had gone before. The recording documents a social setting that almost disappeared from the experience of Beaver people.

The sounds of voices rising and falling together in song were still ordinary when I first began recording. The dances I recorded in the 1960s were presided over by Charlie Yahey, the last Dreamer of the hunting and trapping way of life. My recordings of these events were from a different perspective than the one described by Slim Byrns in that I made my observations from the center of the soundspace. The recordings I made of Dreamers' dances document moments of an ancient tradition. Even the very act of making them had an effect on the order of that tradition. During the hot afternoons when people were resting between all-night dancing and singing, they asked me to play back recordings of the previous night. The Beaver people were and are quick to recontextualize innovations. In this case, the innovation was a document already abstracted from the context in which it was originally produced.

"In Doig People's Ears" opens with the voice of a very old man named Jumbie, whom I knew well when he was still an active hunter. He is singing feebly but with the intensity of someone recalling the empowering dreams of his childhood. The sound of his voice recalls a time when Beaver Indians trained their children to listen carefully for the sounds of animals in the bush. His song signifies a power he gained from the animals when he was a child living far away in time and space from the whitemen's town in which he now spends his last days. What was ordinary in his childhood had become an extraordinary sound when we recorded it. He is among the last of the Beaver Indians to have lived most of a long life in the bush. When I took him out of the Peace Lutheran Care Home and back to one of the reserves for a visit, he remembered the place as it had been when he was young. He said it "looked like a whiteman's town now." Then, he cupped his hands to his mouth and called out to his long-dead relatives. He called them by kin terms. He called to them and to the world he once held in common with them. He called out the proper terms of relationship to reconnect himself to that place. Although he did not recognize the place by sight, Jumbie trusted an evocation of its soundspace to connect him to his relatives in heaven. Howard was able to record that very special moment on tape and I captured it on film.

SOUNDS OF THE INDUSTRIAL AGE

The soundscape that Beaver children find familiar in the 1980s reverberates with vehicle engines, the buzz of fluorescent lights and teachers' instructions in the schoolroom, canned laughter and saturated sound tracks from television sets at home, chainsaws in the bush, and country and western music that is a presence as constant and pervasive as drumming and singing were to their elders in a previous generation. We recorded these sounds as well as the echoes of a previous ordinary reality that now seems like a distant dreaming of the old people. The old people were once children who took the world of bush and animals for granted, just as today's children accept their world without question. In years to come their reality will seem like a dream to other children as yet unborn.

We recorded conversations, interviews with band officials, and informal narratives. We accompanied Doig people to collect stories by old-timers like Slim Byrns from the white community. We recorded children talking, playing, and singing songs taught by missionaries. We even recorded silences. The archive is a stratified series of documents reflecting the sounds, language, and styles of people from different generations and a wide range of knowledge and experience. Some of the sounds in Doig people's ears are delicate and subtle. Others take up the entire acoustic field. Some evoke the world of the bush and its animals. Others place the listener in the midst of an industrial civilization.

The ordinary world that the archive documents will be extraordinary to the ears of people in other times and places. In years to come, Doig people may turn to the archive and hear themselves as they were at a particular moment in time. They may turn to recordings of today's ordinary sounds with the nostalgia and curiosity they now feel for recordings I made of Charlie Yahey in the 1960s. Unlike the recordings from that period, however, those in the present archive document the full range of familiar acoustic environments. "In Doig People's Ears" is a documentary montage of sounds familiar to Beaver Indian people. It is a sampler of history as they have experienced it. It is also a history of how the Doig people were experienced by the settlers who took over much of their land.

The generations at Doig are sharply divided in their use of language. The oldest people on record in the archive speak little or no English. The youngest speak English in preference to Beaver. People of the middle generations are most comfortable in Beaver and speak a distinctive form of "reservation English." The speech patterns that seem so ordinary at a particular moment in time are, in fact, the transient artifacts of a rapidly changing culture. The documentary piece blends these voices and their different ways of speaking into a portrait of culture change. Even the white old-timers speak a language of horses, trails, and the fur trade that is far removed from the contemporary scene.

The Peace River country supported the Beaver people and their ancestors for thousands of years before the whitepeople came. Even in today's world the Beaver retain a sense of belonging to the country. Its sounds and rhythms still provide them with security and identity. They are still hunters. The land is large enough to swallow up the sounds of machines. Snow still squeaks underfoot when it is very cold. Brash young men still whistle to dare the spirits that are the northern lights to dance down toward them. A style of speaking and singing has survived even the change of language.

The sounds of drumming and singing were muted for a time but are now being renewed. It is not unusual to hear the old-time music coming from a home or summer arbor. Upon approaching closer, one discovers that the music is being produced by a tape recorder and the recording is one I made of Charlie Yahey in the 1960s. In part because of my presence in the life of the Beaver people, what once seemed to me an extraordinary sound has now become part of their ordinary acoustic environment. Cassette copies of my original tapes are in constant demand. With true northern Athapaskan adaptability, people use the newly available technology to preserve a tradition that remains important to them. They have even found a useful purpose for the resident anthropologist who would otherwise be quite useless in the bush.

DOCUMENTARY TECHNIQUE AND ANTHROPOLOGY

The audio documentary pieces we have produced from the archive of primary documents tell the story of an Indian community's changing ways of listening to the world around them. The pieces speak both to members of the community and to outsiders. They use a medium that respects the sensibilities of people still operating within an oral tradition. They also attempt to communicate a feeling for that tradition to people in our own culture who are conditioned to learning through the sequential ordering and authority of the printed word.

Ordinary life is synesthetic. It blends experiences from different senses, different times, different places, and even different cultures into a coherent, meaningful whole. The mind blends and mixes information stored in personal memory and cultural codes. Past experience takes on different meanings as it becomes integrated into successive contexts. Audio documentary pieces can blend sounds from a particular cultural field as the mind blends experiences from a particular personal field. We make sense of our present experience by reference to the past, and we modify our interpretation of past events by reference to the present.

An audio documentary medium allows the anthropologist to present a montage of actualities that tell a story about a culture's past and present. These actualities modify one another's meanings within the context of the documentary. They can evoke the past to modify experience of the present. They can suggest alternative perspectives on the past. The montage has a synergistic effect. It creates a momentary singular experience that gives the listener an opportunity to form a mental image of the events and settings being represented. The anthropologist must be responsible for using the medium to convey understandings that derive from informed anthropological thinking. It must not be used merely for dramatic effect; rather, dramatic effect must be brought to the service of anthropology. Audio documentary techniques are particularly effective for communicating a sense of how a moment in the life of a person or culture is part of an ongoing process of culture change.

An old cowboy tells about how the Indians came together to sing and dance in the 1920s. His story rings true because of his recollection of their fat and shiny horses. A young Indian boy talks about wanting to become a lawyer. He knows the world he grew up in will not exist when he is mature. He says, "There isn't going to be a Doig here forever," but the sound of singing and drumming continues to be part of the land and its people. An old man calls to his relatives in heaven and listens for a reply in the sounds of wind and water. Together, these separate documents create a documentary reality.

Old and new blend into the experience of the moment. In times gone by, Beaver people consolidated their personal powers through dreams. They have not given up that way of organizing their experience. Dreams allow a person to integrate personal experience with cultural form. Dreams permit a reinterpretation of past experience and a prefiguring of what may be experienced in the future. Culture is an important template in the structuring of both processes. The child in his or her vision quest encounters giant animals known already through the many stories told of them. The Dreamer negotiates the trail to heaven because he is able to "grab hold of" a trail of song with his mind.

In the past, individual experience could be interpreted as the personal manifestation of a truth that is timeless and enduring. Individual children came into contact with the powers of mythic time and space through their vision quest experiences. They came to know the stories of their culture as stories of their own lives. Myths relevant to the particular powers they encountered in the bush served to guide them throughout the rest of their lives. During the course of a lifetime, a person could expect to grow into full realization of the medicine powers encountered as a child. The meaning of that childhood time out of time came into focus through dreams in later life.

The meaning of any particular experience changes as it becomes recontextualized throughout the various stages of a person's life. When the Beaver people were living in isolated bush communities, they could understand individual experiences by reference to a common culture and the mutual understandings that come from knowing a common world of nature. Their dreams brought them together as people of a common mind, just as their Dreamers brought them together as people of a common ceremonial order. They shared a mutually understood everyday reality of taken-for-granted sights and sounds. Jumbie was seeking that reality when he called out toward the sky to locate himself by reference to his departed relatives.

Beaver people today continue to share the mutually understood everyday realities of taken-for-granted sights and sounds. Our documentary representations of their world blend actualities from everyday life to create the distinctive sound signature of a reserve community as it exists in the 1980s. Part of that sound signature is an echo of the past. The Beaver language is still spoken by people of all ages. Various forms of "reservation English" are spoken by older people according to age, sex, and particular life experiences. People still sing the Dreamers' songs upon occasion, and every household listens to them regularly on tape. People still hunt and trap. They scrape moosehide and make moccasins.

Another part of their everyday reality is the machine world of today. Young people know cars and trucks as their parents knew horses and wagons. Nearly every household has a radio and tape deck. Many have television. The sounds and sights of the world beyond Doig have become signatures of their day-to-day lives. The reserve is surrounded by installations of the oil and gas industry. Pipeline pumping stations and wells send their sounds out into the stillness of the bush. We recorded machines and the electronic media as part of the soundscape.

Although the Beaver people now communicate with whitepeople on a regular basis, their world is still distinctive and very different from that of the surrounding white communities. They retain a style that outsiders seldom encounter. Our recordings document people of this community as they are to one another. The documentary form of presentation assembles actualities from these documents to create an aural portrait of the community.

CONCLUSION

It is normal for human beings to experience the present as authentic and real. Sensation is more immediate than recollection. Although we know and even remember times when various details of life were different from the way we experience them in the present, we are usually persuaded to accept the way things are, no matter how we choose to compare them with the past. As members of the human species, we are biogenetically programmed to accept the developmental changes of an individual life cycle. Hunting and gathering cultures have traditionally reinforced this programming through symbol systems that integrate a person's experiences at various stages of life. These cultures also facilitate communication between people of different generations. We are probably less well programmed to accept continual changes in the cultural instructions by which we attempt to make sense of our lives.

Traditional Beaver culture was rich in symbols for integrating a person's experiences at various stages in his or her life cycle. Vision quests, traditional myths, and dreaming were the principal channels through which people made contact with their own past and future selves. Because the developmental cycle could be expected to repeat itself from generation to generation, Beaver culture had time to develop subtle symbolic pathways to connect the experiences of children with those of mature adults and elders. Beaver names, particularly the names of Dreamers, were sometimes composites meaning something like "old person–young person." Old people looked to their childhood vision quest experiences as a source of empowerment. Children experienced these same vision quests as a directing force in their lives.

Culture change is a way of life for people in the modern industrialized world. Our institutions and symbol systems emphasize changes in culture rather than the cyclical developmental changes of individual life cycles. The Beaver people are experiencing the transition from being relatively autonomous hunting nomads to being a settled minority within an industrial state. They are moving from living conditions of relative stability to ones in which unthinkable changes are the norm. The rate of their culture's change is enormous. The generations now experiencing this change are unique. The transition from hunting and gathering to food producing and industry is a highly transient phenomenon. It is taking place in only a few parts of the world today. The present process almost completes a global transformation that began shortly after the end of the last major glaciation.

The Beaver archive of aural actualities documents a very special and distinctive process in human culture history. The information it contains may be of theoretical significance in ways beyond those that are obvious to us at the moment. The changes on record here happen only once in a culture's history. They are unique to these generations, and they are irreversible. The Beaver people are as aware of their situation as we are, but they are reacting to it in ways that are distinctively their own. Even in the midst of the modern world they retain a flexibility, pragmatism, and sense of their own individual and communal worth that is a legacy from the nomadic hunting past.

The documentary tapeworks we have created describe a poignant moment in human history. These pieces speak to the dream-thinker within each of us. The techniques of audio editing and mixing allow the material to suggest patterns and connections in the listener's mind. Beaver people have accepted much of our work as ordinary. They experience it as they experience their everyday lives. We have become a part of their taken-for-granted reality. We have become a resource base from which they draw documentary information about their own past. We also give them certain insights into the intricacies of the modern world.

People from other cultures may perceive the world of our documentary productions as extraordinary. The productions attempt to create a synesthetic blend of ideas and experiences from the actualities we have recorded among the Beaver people. We are like Slim Byrns in 1929, grazing our horses at the edge of an alien soundscape that has already "done somethin'" to us. Perhaps the original documents in the archive and our documentary productions may contribute to an understanding of the cultural changes that now threaten the very survival of our species in the nuclear age. We are all the aboriginal people of this planet. We and the Beaver people are members of a common species facing a common peril. In times gone by, intelligent human beings moved away from situations they knew to be life threatening. Today our species is at risk, but we cannot move away because we are people of the entire biosphere rather than a particular territory within it.

If we survive the present crisis, soundscape documents of a people undergoing the transition from hunting and gathering to an industrial way of life may be of value in planning for the future through an understanding of the past. Upon maturity, Beaver Indians dreamed back to their childhood vision quest experiences for guidance. If our species achieves maturity, it may look back to its hunting and gathering heritage as a source of enlightenment. The electronic media make it possible to preserve actualities from other times and places, but without the intelligence of human understanding these sounds lose all meaning and value. Human intelligence and understanding evolved with the hunting and gathering way of life. As hunting and gathering pass from actuality into memory, members of the species must adapt human intelligence to vastly different cultural conditions. In the nuclear age, failure to make this adaptation will probably terminate the entire species. The intelligence of our hunting and gathering ancestors is a resource we cannot afford to ignore.

Anthropologica, 1983

DOCUMENTING THE NORMAL, PERVERTING THE REAL

Contrasting Images of Native Indian Experience

Oral performance in a small-scale hunting and gathering culture plays creatively upon the understanding that each person has of a shared totality. Each performer's speech evokes and is meaningful in relation to everything that is known but, for the moment, unstated. Each story contains every other story. Each person's life is an example of the mythic stories that people know to exist in a time out of time. Experience within a closely contexted oral culture is meaningful in relation to a totality that is taken for granted. Storied speech is an *example* of that totality, not simply a part of it.

From within the familiarity of a shared repertoire of culturally constructed metaphors and assumptions, the essentially creative and transactional quality of human communication may not be obvious. It is only when we attempt discourse with people whose assumptive worlds are different from our own that we find ourselves talking at cross-purposes and discover that our different metaphors have been supporting different realities. Attempted discourse between the worlds of different cultures may create conflict, ambiguity, even xenophobia. Discourse may also be used as an instrument of exploitation. To illustrate this possibility, I will describe an instance of the coercive discourse available within the medium of an "open-line" broadcast and contrast it with the consensual style of communication used by communities of northern Canadian Native people. The contrast is particularly stark in that, while the broadcast in question was about Indian self-government, it used its authority to suppress callers who attempted to initiate the shared and negotiated style of discourse that typifies Indian government.

240

DISCOURSE IN A NORTHERN HUNTING SOCIETY

According to Woodburn (1982), hunting and gathering people with "immediate return" systems of production and exchange are "profoundly egalitarian." Most hunting societies of the Canadian subarctic fit Woodburn's profile. The egalitarianism of these societies is integral to their adaptive strategy (Ridington 1982a, 1988a). Individuals are expected to use their knowledge and experience to establish a personal relationship to the world of nature, a world they view as inhabited by animate beings or "persons" with whom they can make direct contact. A dominant characteristic of this adaptive individualism is a principle of noninterference with the autonomy of other people. Christian and Gardner point out an "unwritten cultural rule" among the Athapaskan Slavey Indians with whom they have done fieldwork. The Slavey don't "interfere with someone engaged in a line of thought, a task or other endeavor, but allow him to finish out his intention." They will not "stop someone in work or travel without good cause," nor will they "interrupt a speaker or interrupt a deliberate silence" (1977: 25). Respect for individual autonomy is fundamental to northern Native discourse.

Although northern Native people respect individual autonomy, their individualism is not anarchic or antisocial; rather, it is based on a deeply rooted understanding that each person must be responsible to all sentient beings of the world in which he or she lives. A basic metaphor of these cultures is that animals and natural phenomena are themselves sentient individuals. They are "people." They are part of an ongoing discourse. Subarctic Indians feel responsible to the sentient animals and natural forces, just as they feel responsible to one another. They negotiate relations with these "people" in the same way that they negotiate relations with one another. In both cases, a person is autonomous in these negotiations but is also considered responsible for any consequences that may result. Subarctic Indian people know the stories of one another's lives, just as they know the stories that explain the features of an environment they share. They reference individual experience to commonly held information. This information is coded in a metaphoric language and brought to mind through commonly held oral traditions. Leaders in such an egalitarian society are people who articulate what is commonly known rather than people who tell others what to do.

Outside observers who come into contact with subarctic people have been astonished at their lack of formal authority. They have mistaken this lack of social hierarchy for a lack of leadership. Such misunderstandings may have disturbing consequences when communication results in legally binding decisions that influence the lives and well-being of Indian people within the modern world. Misunderstandings may also be deliberately initiated by members of the mass media. They may use the authority of their control over a medium that is hierarchical rather than discursive to "interfere with someone engaged in a line of thought" for the purpose of controlling that person's ability to participate in political discourse within the modern world.

The discourse of northern hunting people takes place within real time, but it is meaningful in relation to a time of mind, a mythic time. Performer and listener share both a common time frame and a common knowledge of the world. Their relationship is conversational, a "running to and fro." Conversation takes place in the same time as their common experience. Their discourse is meaningful because they share a common or complementary point of view, a common time and place in the world, and a common or complementary set of ideas about how to interpret experience. Just as the act of speech is itself an individual's creative realization of the potential made possible by his or her culture's lexicon and grammar, the act of narrative performance is also an act of creation. The act of performance is an act of authorship. An oral performance is the realization of a cultural potential. It brings a cultural possibility into actuality. In an egalitarian northern hunting culture it is also a product of negotiated discourse.

MEDIA DISTORTION OF INDIAN REALITY: A WORST-CASE SCENARIO

The mass media of modern society perform very different kinds of transactions from the shared discourse of egalitarian hunting and gathering people. They have the potential for being a powerful instrument for social control. The structures through which the media create assumptions about reality are more likely to be hierarchical than consensual. Statements made by journalists in the print and electronic media become documents that both contribute to and validate the general public's world view. Like the discourse of egalitarian society, these documents establish compelling metaphors and assumptions about the nature of reality, but unlike egalitarian discourse, the metaphors of the mass media are not the product of consensual negotiation. They structure the very terms through which we receive and interpret information.

The unstated assumptions of our mass media tell people what is "normal." The language of their discourse with us conveys messages about "reality" as well as objective information. The media are largely supported by commercial or state interests, dedicated to influencing audience attitude and action. This bias is commonly accepted without question. People raised within such a system of communication do not readily recognize or comprehend systems of communication structured on different principles. Similarly, people raised within a system of consensual discourse may be profoundly shocked at how the mass media distort their reality. They are simply not accustomed to being interrupted in their thoughts and endeavors.

The following describes one such instance. In April 1986, the premiers of Canada's provinces met with the prime minister and leaders of the national Native organizations in a "First Minister's Conference" to discuss the possibility of entrenching Native self-government in the new Canadian constitution. Section 37 of the 1982 Constitution Act specifically mandates that a series of such conferences be held. In Vancouver, radio station CKNW devoted an edition of its popular open-line show, hosted by Gary Bannerman, to the issue of Indian self-government. The station has stated that it viewed the program as an opportunity "to identify matters of public interest and to provide a forum for debate of those issues." It claimed that its open-line format is merely an expanded version of the normal discourse through which people negotiate issues and ideas on a face-to-face basis. It did admit, though, that the host of this particular show had considerable control over the shape of that discourse. "We are," the station wrote in response to a Canadian Radio and Telecommunication Commission (CRTC) inquiry into the broadcast, "mindful that on-air personnel have privileged access to an opinion-making medium, and their performance, therefore, is of critical importance to the maintenance of CKNW's journalistic integrity, principles, and policies" (CRTC Documents, letter from CKNW president and general manager to CRTC secretary-general, July 22, 1986).

Despite the station's claim that Bannerman maintained "journalistic integrity" in his role of open-line host, a transcript of the broadcast clearly indicates that Bannerman did, in fact, take advantage of his "privileged access to an opinion-making medium" when he introduced the topic of Indian self-government with a ten-minute invective against Indian people. I would argue that his performance was, in fact, a classic example of how the mass media can be used to impose a set of assumptions about the world, in this case the world of Native Indian leadership and decision making. Bannerman's opening statement appears to have been thought out in advance and, if not fully scripted, was probably spoken from notes. His tone of voice was full of innuendo. There could be no doubt that Bannerman held a negative view of Indians. A caller whose experience differed from Bannerman's fundamental assumptions could expect to be viewed in the same negative light. The content of his remarks indicated an ignorance of Indian reality as well as of the constitutional process under which the First Minister's Conference was being held. Bannerman began with a statement that could be taken for a jingoistic but nonetheless legitimate journalistic opinion. He described the conference as a "Disneyland." He then said that any agreement in principle about self-government with "details to be negotiated later" meant that "The Chief gets all the money and then the Chief can self-govern. The Indian Band can self-govern. Now, if he wants to fly off to the Bahamas and deposit it in a bank account, I guess he's free to do that. That's what I mean, details to be negotiated later."

Still at the edge of stating a journalistic opinion, Bannerman went on to disclaim any historical responsibility on the part of non-Indians for the present disadvantages Native people are experiencing. Quickly, though, he crossed the border from opinion, misinformed and one-sided as it may have been, to making serious and unfounded racist allegations about Indian people. What he said seemed to follow from his previous disclaimer that non-Indians cannot be held responsible for problems Indians are facing. It seemed to flow logically from what he said, that if non-Indians were not to blame, then the Indians must be themselves responsible for their problems. Going one step further in what appeared to be a logical chain of argument, Bannerman asserted that Indian social problems are entirely their own fault because of what he intimated is their inherently incestuous nature. At this point he had moved far beyond fair journalistic comment. He said:

Every Native Indian alive today has got everything to do with the tragedy of Native peoples, the fact that they have got the highest rates of incest in Canada, the highest rates of alcoholism in Canada, the highest rates of crime, and misery and poverty and failure, you name it. Where is their responsibility for themselves? It's far too easy, so easy, to say—that's because we were screwed by history. Absolute nonsense. They have privileges that the average Canadian doesn't have. Endless privileges, whether it comes to fisheries, handouts, meetings, grants. And what do they do with them? The brother has a child with his sister, is what they do with them.

On the subject of government responsibility for social problems among Native people, Bannerman asserted:

Sure, the Canadian Government's to blame. The tragedy that we perpetuate on the Native peoples is that nobody gives them a kick on the backside and says, "Go do something for yourself." They're patronized to oblivion . . . It's patronization. It's the problem. Giving them too much constantly, saying we're sorry for what happened 200 years ago. That's the problem. But self-government? Where every month you send a cheque for $300,000 to the Chief and say, "Do with it whatever you want." That kind of self-government? That kind of self-government will lead to the worst kind of crime and irresponsibility imaginable. Even the honest Chief will buy $300,000 worth of beer. The crooked one will deposit it in the Bahamas. And Brian Mulroney says we'll look after the details later. Unbelievable, these people. Unbelievable.

And yes, I can share some guilt, and I think all of us share some guilt. But the guilt's not stealing anything from them. The guilt's giving them too much. And governments that just simply bend over backwards to patronize them more. What do you think about it? It's 685-0491.

The open-line show can be one of modern culture's most compelling forms of information control, precisely because it creates an illusion of democratic participation that masks the host's almost absolute power to manipulate the appearance of reality created by his medium. The remainder of the program was set in an electronic version of a classic call and response format. Call and response is a form of reality management in which the radio host (or columnist) "calls" his audience in a language that establishes his assumptive world. The call and response form establishes a positive feedback between the host's initial statement and responses that support him. The respondents (telephone callers on the air; letter writers in a newspaper) are encouraged to speak within the language of the caller's assumptive world. Those who do not share the caller's assumptive world are at a considerable disadvantage. In this form of communication there is no real "running to and fro," no genuine discourse.

As the caller continues to speak within the language of his assumptive world, respondents who disagree with him are made to look like deviants. Supportive responses are contextually defined as "normal" and correct. The call and response form feeds back negatively upon the communicative power of an outsider. It reinforces the language of those it defines as insiders. The host's call to his respondents has the authority of an authorized text upon which they are empowered, by the medium, to make variations. His call encourages respondents to speak in the language they have heard on the air in the same way that neophytes to a CB network gain entry to it through their use of its argot.

Bannerman set the tone and language of "correct" response with his unfounded allegations of incest "They have privileges . . . And what do they do with them? The brother has a child with his sister, is what they do with them." He invited responses by saying, "685-0491. Your calls to the program. Most interested in your views on the so-called Native rights issue and the Prime Minister meeting with the Premiers this week."

As Bannerman completed his invective, the telephone responses began to come in. Of the fourteen responses aired, eleven were passionately in support of Bannerman and three disagreed with him. The first respondent said, "Yes, Good morning, Gary, how are you? You know, Gary, I would like to say Amen, Amen a thousand times to what you just said there. You know, actually if these Indians get on the road, you know so help me God, I bet 35 years from now, they'll be like these Ethiopians over there. That's what will happen."

The caller's response echoed Bannerman's initial invective. It echoed the invective but it rephrased it in a more charismatic and evangelical form of expression, "Amen, Amen . . . so help me God," seasoned with a xenophobic reference to something vaguely bad happening to "these Ethiopians over there." The speaker responded to Bannerman's call by generalizing his reference from Native Indian to "foreigner." Indians become equated with "these Ethiopians," thus redefining the category of "Native" into its opposite, that of "foreigner."

Bannerman spoke in a less careful and less grammatical style during the phone-in segment of the program. His syntax began to fail and his speech became an impressionistic montage of images. He replied to the first caller's xenophobic reference to "these Ethiopians" with an additional stereotype, that Indians are like naughty children who deserve to be punished: "Well, I don't necessarily believe that to be true. Is that what—but what I am absolutely certain, I have no doubt in my mind whatsoever, is that they have been killed with kindness over the years and no matter how kind you are to them, they want more. Is that, in fact, what they really need is that they have to be shaken by the shoulder, just like a little kid that's misbehaving."

The second caller attempted to disagree with Bannerman's assumptions and was treated very differently from the first. He began:

Yes, Gary. I have just a few comments to make. First, number one, the Natives were given a raw deal from the start.
Bannerman:
That may be true.
Caller:
For hundreds of years they ruled themselves and they ruled themselves well, and . . .

Bannerman interrupts with an assertion that Indian history is unknowable. His assertion reinforces a distinction between "us" and "them":

I'm not sure about that. None of us were there.
Caller:
   If you check the American historians, those that were there, they know. And on top of this, you are starting to sound like Bill Bennett [a former premier of British Columbia]. Hit everybody and give nobody credit. And I just disagree with that completely.
Bannerman:
   Been on any reserves lately?
Caller:
   Yes, I have.
Bannerman:
   What do you think about the incest? What do you think about the levels of intoxication? What do you think about murder rates? What do you think about, well, let's talk about the obvious. About 16 abandoned cars rotting in everybody's front lawn. I mean. What do you think about that? Do you think they are noble people?
Caller:
   The Natives are as noble as the blacks. I'm black. I know. And, uh, I'll tell you something. I don't know which reserves you've been on, but a lot of them are not like that.
Bannerman:
   You're absolutely right. The minority are not like that. The majority are like that. That's the problem.

This segment of the broadcast reveals how Bannerman manages and discredits his respondent's personal experiences of Indian life. When the respondent answered that he had "been on reserves lately," Bannerman launched an invective that asserted an association between "abandoned cars" and incest on Indian reserves. In his assumptive world, one is taken as evidence for the other. The effect of this association is to implant an altogether unsubstantiated and damaging racist stereotype in the minds of people who already accept the stereotype that Indians have abandoned cars in front of their houses. It is also a key element in his use of racist assumptions to discredit the political objectives of Native people. If Natives can be stigmatized as incestuous, it then follows that they may be genetically (racially) inferior. If they are racially inferior, it may seem reasonable to deny their political aspirations on the grounds that they are mentally and physically incapable of governing themselves. On a more subliminal level, Bannerman's assertions of incest suggest that people who cannot "govern their animal instincts" would be incapable of governing themselves politically. These racist associations are congruent with his statement that "what they really need is that they have to be shaken by the shoulder, just like a little kid that's misbehaving."

After the black respondent had been repeatedly cut off and insulted, the following nine calls were adulatory. Bannerman handled them in the classic call and response form:

Caller:

I have to agree with you 100 per cent. I'm glad to hear someone on the radio and someone say what you've said. I used to work for Indians Affairs. I'm retired now. I worked for 10 years in Indian Affairs in Vancouver, and what you have said this morning is really music to my ears, because I believe with you at 100 per cent. I have a saying about this, I say the Indians who lost and fought war, it's just a crime, you can't do anything about it, but I do appreciate the fact how you tell the people how much land they didn't own. They couldn't possibly have owned all of the Canada like this.

Bannerman:

Not even close. They didn't occupy much more than they occupy today.

Caller:

No.

Bannerman:

If you study the history as to where the bands were, where their tribal fishing areas, their tribal hunting areas were, even the most nomadic Indian from the village . . .

Caller:

Absolutely.

Bannerman:

Didn't go much beyond the reserve. That's the reserve today.

Bannerman's allegations are entirely without reference and are, in fact, contradicted by abundant ethnohistorical and ethnographic documentation.

Another caller responded: "Gary, I don't always agree with you. But today I have to agree with you 100 per cent, 101 per cent. Gary, what I would like to suggest is that you take a copy of the tape that you certainly have, and I'm sure that you could enlist a few hundred thousand names to be added to your comments to send it to Ottawa before these people make decisions."

When a Native elder who turned out to have been awarded the Order of Canada called in to dispute the allegations that were passing between Bannerman and his previous nine callers, he treated her in a brusque and patronizing way. As she tried to tell him that her own experience of being an Indian does not correspond to his allegations, Bannerman countered that she is an exception that proves the rule. Thus, his ungrounded assertions were held to be more valid than her lifetime of experience. The exchange, in part, is as follows:

Caller:
  Hello Mr. Bannerman. I'm rather upset with some of the things that you have said. I'm a Native Indian woman from the prairies and I know a lot different things than you do, but I don't want to sound like I know more than you do, which I don't know how to speak like you can. And I know a lot of the things that you were saying are the first time I've ever heard them about incest and stuff like that. Maybe I'm with the wrong crowd. I don't hear these things so freely. I have raised a big family and I have children that are working in real estate, and they are, my family has not been in those kind of troubles.
Bannerman:
  I'm delighted to hear that, Ma'am.
Caller:
  I would like to say that we have Indians that are in real estate and we have doctors and nurses and lawyers and clergy and we have our own Indian religious leaders and they are very, very good. And I don't hear the wrong things that you're talking about. I hear more of the good things. I hear them over the radio, on TV, that's the only place I see them and I hear about them. So it's really a big, you know, make my heart miss a beat

when I heard these things. I think it's terrible. 'Cause I work for
my people for nothing.

Bannerman:

You don't believe that what I said exists?

Caller:

Not, maybe.

Bannerman:

You don't believe in the preponderance of life on most
reserves?

Caller:

You know, there's as much on the whitepeople's side.

Bannerman:

Well, there's some, there certainly is, I'm not denying that.

Caller:

And.

Bannerman:

But.

Caller:

I think you should bear that in mind and I think you're going
to make a lot of enemies for yourself and/or the public. Bennett
has a lot of enemies among the people and I don't think that's a
good way to bring about good feelings for people to get along
in this world, to bring all kinds of dirt into the, in front of them,
there's enough of it around that we don't have to just talk about
it and not do anything. And there's a lot of whitepeople that are
living that way and they're glad to voice their opinions, and I
don't think they know anything about Indians. They have to . . .

Bannerman:

Madam, what I'm suggesting is, why all of the special privileges?
Why the special concessions?

Caller:

I have no . . .

Bannerman:

Why federal provincial conferences? And I think that with all the
proper opportunities, Native people are capable of anything in
our society, as you've proven, as your family has proven.

Caller:

I think that they have and my family was raised on a reserve. I
was born on a reserve and I didn't know English when I was

seven and I went to school, to a boarding school. We were
trained and learned to live a different life from what other people
have learned to do. And I'm seventy two-three years old and I
know a lot. I got my Order of Canada for trying to help my
people. Not with salary, big wages or anything, but just because
of what I've done. So I'm . . .

Bannerman:

Well, Ma'am, I think you, your family are to be commended, but
I think you're a little unrealistic if you think that you and your
family are the norm. You're not the norm at all. The norm is a
very tragic situation. And the majority. The jails are full of Native people. And they're a human tragedy. It's not that they're
inferior people. Is that the fact of the matter is—that the Native
leaders and our Canadian political leaders have lived a history of
dishonesty, is the truth is not being told to anybody. And the
truth is the very success story you've related, of your family. And
I wish you the very best. But as long as we are engaged in political deception, that is what is going on in Ottawa these days,
they'll be no solutions. Thank you.

Bannerman then terminated the conversation.

Bannerman's assumptions about the reality of Indian people were
not idiosyncratic. In fact, he articulated a form of racism that can be
traced back to the early days of British Columbian history. What
Bannerman said was hauntingly similar to statements written more
than a century before by Joseph Trutch, a principal architect of British Columbia's Indian land policy. Trutch is on record as having said,
among other things, that

the Indians really have no right to the lands they claim, nor are
they of any actual value or utility to them . . . It seems to me,
therefore, both just and politic that they should be confirmed in
the possession of such extents of land only as are sufficient for
their probable requirements for purposes of cultivation and pas-
turage, and that the remainder of the land now shut up in these
reserves should be thrown open to pre-emption. I think they are
the ugliest & laziest creatures I ever saw, & we shod. as soon
think of being afraid of our dogs as of them . . . We have in B.C.

a population of Indians numbering from 40,000 to 50,000, by far the larger portion of whom are utter savages living along the coast, frequently committing murder and robbery among themselves, one tribe upon another, and on the white people who go amongst them for purposes of trade, and only restrained from more outrageous crime by being always treated with firmness, and by the consistent enforcement of the law amongst them to which end we have often to call in aid the services of H.M. ships on the station. (Joseph Trutch, "Report on the Lower Fraser Indian Reserves, 28 August, 1867" and Joseph Trutch, June 23, 1850, cited in Fisher [1971: 3, 5]; Joseph Trutch to Sir John A. MacDonald, October 14, 1872, cited in Cail [1974: 297–298])

DOCUMENTING INDIAN REALITY: A VIEW
FROM PERSONAL EXPERIENCE

I first met Indian people in 1959, when I was nineteen years old. The people I met were Athapaskan Beaver Indians. Ironically, I met them near a place called Trutch on the Alaska Highway in British Columbia. I had come to Trutch to join friends who were building a wilderness cabin in the Prophet River valley. Trees along the trail leading down into the valley were marked with blazes. I had seen trees blazed by Italian boy scouts in the forests of northern New Jersey. The name "Chipesia" was written in pencil on some of the blazes. I thought the name sounded Italian and jumped to the conclusion that Italian boy scouts had vandalized the forest. It is normal to interpret what we see in terms of what we know and expect to find. My assumptive world included Italian boy scouts. It did not then include Indians.

Not long after I came to the valley, a group of Indians arrived at our cabin site on horseback. It was my first encounter with what I thought of then as "real-live Indians." One of them was Johnny Chipesia. He was not an Italian boy scout vandal. My assumptions about the world were beginning to change. As my friends and I talked with him, some of the boys rode across the river. Soon we heard the ping of a .22-caliber rifle shot. The boys returned in less than an hour with a deer, neatly skinned and quartered. This was not the way people hunted deer in Maryland and New Jersey, where each fall I saw cars returning from the woods with whole deer lashed to their fenders. These Indians knew something about deer and about the northern forest that I had not imagined possible.

This was my first encounter with the delicate discourse of an egalitarian hunter-gatherer communication system that depends on establishing and maintaining mutual understandings based on shared experience. It was my first lesson in learning within that system. Johnny Chipesia, I understood later, wanted us to know that this valley, although perhaps formally listed as Crown land in a land registry office somewhere, was Indian land because of the intimate knowledge he and his people had of it. Johnny's way of telling us we were on his land was to feed us from it. The deer meat we shared established a basis for continuing communication.

I began documenting Dunne-za culture as an anthropologist in 1964. I experienced the events of that summer as an anthropological rite of passage known as fieldwork. I had been socialized to think of people, particularly Indian people, as the proper and inevitable subjects of an objective and imperial social science. I expected to learn *about* them rather than *from* them. I assumed that what I experienced as a person and what I reported as a social scientist would be related only in that one was instrumental to the other. The people with whom I was living, however, had no such notion. They did not know or care about the world of professors, graduate students, comprehensive examinations, and anthropological theory. They knew and cared about the world of camp and bush they held in common. They knew and cared about the animals. They knew and cared about one another. They did not explain their world to me directly nor, I quickly learned, did they respond to direct interrogation. Rather, they communicated with me in a way that allowed me to share in at least some of their understandings. They watched to see what I was learning. When I showed signs of communicating intelligently within their system of knowledge, they would recognize my accomplishment by expanding the depth of their discourse. They shared the authority of what they knew without imposing themselves upon my autonomy. They assumed that, as a human being, I was capable of learning from experience.

I expected the experience of fieldwork to be entirely different and separate from its results. I tried valiantly to gather information as if my interactions with the Dunne-za were external to the process. As time went on and I came to share more completely in the life of a small hunting band, I began to realize that this instrumental separation of experience from accomplishment made no sense at all to the people with whom I was living. If I were to understand their world, I would have to discover a language of translation between their experience and my own. I found myself in a culture where knowledge and power flow directly from experience. I could not afford to ignore my own experience as valid and central to my task as ethnographer. I could not afford to ignore that I was learning *from* the Dunne-za, not simply *about* them.

FROM DOCUMENT TO DOCUMENTARY

From the beginning of my work as an anthropologist with the Dunne-za, I used a tape recorder to document what I thought were important sounds and events. Initially, I used the tape recorder only when I thought that "something was happening." My criteria for judging when to turn on the machine were not significantly advanced from the criteria I used to interpret Johnny Chipesia's blazes as the work of Italian boy scout vandals. I recorded during what I considered artistic or oratorical performances. I stopped recording during conversations and the silences with which they were punctuated.

In 1979, I was introduced to the potential of doing audio ethnography at a different level of sophistication when Jillian Ridington and I began to collaborate with audio documentarian Howard Broomfield. Howard taught us how to be listeners. During the next six years, we collected an archive amounting to several hundred hours of audio tape. These recordings are primary documents of the sounds and settings we encountered during our visits to Dunne-za communities in northeastern British Columbia between 1979 and 1985. They reflect what seemed normal to us and to the Dunne-za at the time they were happening. They reflect the stories through which northern hunting people negotiate relations with one another and with their environment. They reflect our own involvement with the people and events of a northern Native community.

The recordings we made document a world the Dunne-za took for granted. Every normal human being experiences the world through the categories of his or her culture. Much of what we hear and see seems so ordinary and "natural" that we do not recognize that these sights and sounds present us with highly cultural information. When we experience another culture we are struck at first by a different and unfamiliar set of sights and sounds. Audio recordings and photographs of foreign sights and sounds may appear exotic and extraordinary to an outsider. They may not make sense to us initially, or we may interpret them incorrectly. Sights and sounds recorded in the same culture at different times may also seem strange. What was ordinary and "normal" when it was documented may seem different and extraordinary in the context of a different time.

Audio documents are called "actualities" in the language of radio and television production. Actualities from a past or foreign culture are primary documents of that culture's everyday appearance. They are documents of its soundscape. Soundscape, as defined by composer and historian R. Murray Schafer, is "any acoustic field of study . . . a musical composition . . . a radio program . . . an acoustic environment." According to Schafer, "the general acoustic environment of a society can be read as an indicator of social conditions which produce it and may tell us much about the trending and evolution of that society . . . A soundscape consists of events *heard*, not objects *seen*" (1977: 7–8). Actualities documenting changes in a soundscape over time provide primary evidence about the "trending and evolution" of that culture's change. Actualities document the information and understandings that underlie a culture's discourse. When used by the modern mass media, actualities may also be used to control and manipulate that discourse.

CONCLUSION

Electronic media may be used either to suppress the genuine experience and discourse of people in an oral culture or to document and share it. The contrast between these two purposes brings to mind Sapir's distinction between what he called "genuine" and "spurious" cultures. Sapir described genuine culture as "the expression of a richly varied and yet somehow unified and consistent attitude toward life, an attitude which sees the significance of any one element of civilization in its relation to all others." In such a culture "nothing is spiritually meaningless" and "no important part of the general functioning brings with it a sense of frustration, of misdirected or unsympathetic effort." The genuine culture is particularly distinguished by its attitude toward individual autonomy of thought and action. Sapir said that "a genuine culture refuses to consider the individual as a mere cog, as an entity whose sole raison d'être lies in his subservience to a collective purpose that he is not conscious of or that has only a remote relevancy to his interests and strivings . . . the major activities of the individual must directly satisfy his own creative and emotional impulses" (Sapir 1924, cited in Mandelbaum 1963: 314–315). Sapir's "genuine culture" is one that defines itself through the stories of people's lives. In such a culture, discourse continues to run to and fro freely.

The CKNW open-line program described above exemplifies the worst of what Sapir had in mind in imagining a spurious culture that suppresses discourse based on experience. Sapir describes the spurious culture as one "that does not build itself out of the central interests and desires of its bearers" but "works from general ends to the individual, as an external culture" (Sapir 1963: 316). The Bannerman show clearly functioned as an instrument to suppress the authentic experience of Native people and those who know them firsthand. It also powerfully built up cultural stereotypes that are external, in Sapir's terms, to actual informed experience. Such a reliance on external authority is antithetical to the individualism and egalitarianism on which communication in small-scale hunting and gathering societies is based. In contrast to the communication of northern hunting people who will not "stop someone in work or travel without good cause" or "interrupt a speaker or interrupt a deliberate silence," Gary Bannerman's program both encouraged people to respond to the call of his assumptive world and cut off the few who attempted to challenge it. His program cut off the stories of their lives. It cut off the running to and fro of their discourse.

The storytelling traditions of northern hunting people represent a genuine form of cultural communication in Sapir's terms, in that they "work from the individual to ends." Northern hunting people negotiate a mutually understood and accepted view of the world by consensus and agreement. Their style of communication is egalitarian. Their lives are storied in the running to and fro of their discourse. A narrative style using actualities from Indian discourse is an appropriate means of translating their cultural reality. The open-line radio show is an effective instrument for suppressing it. The mass media are not, however, the only possible instruments of a spurious and authoritarian suppression of Indian reality. Anthropology can itself be spurious and hierarchical if it imposes its own assumptive world on the people it studies. Anthropologists must be willing to learn from the people they study as well as about them. The distinction between learning from and about a people corresponds to Sapir's contrast between genuine and spurious approaches to knowledge. Learning from the people we study is internal to individual experience. Learning about them may be external to it.

An audio documentary style using actualities from everyday life is one way to approach an internal or "genuine" language of anthropological communication. A narrative style of writing is another. Both can reflect the anthropologist's own experience of learning from the people of a culture. Documentary and narrative ethnographic forms are particularly well suited to communicating the culture and experience of egalitarian northern hunting people. Both are ways of telling stories. They connect to the stories northern Native people tell of their own lives. The language of anthropology is itself a transaction. It can either tell the story of Indian reality or suppress it. Such a language must use the metaphors and media of our own culture, but it must also be genuine in its reflection of a genuine culture's style of communication. Storytelling through the written word and through audio actualities is one way of documenting the normal discourse of a culture that is genuine in Sapir's terms.

EPILOGUE

Books package words, not experiences. These stories in a language of anthropology are words that take the reader through my experiences and through those of the Dunne-za as I have come to understand them. They describe experiences but they do not materialize them. Only the reader can make that connection. They do not give you the smell of poplar smoke, the taste of moose meat, the sound of Dunne-za voices laughing. Words do not give you the squeak of very cold snow underfoot. They do not give you the sound of a distant river on a summer solstice night.

Words are like dreams. They reflect experience and they also inform it. Like words, dreams do not materialize experience. Only the dreamer is capable of that transformation. You are the reader. You are the dreamer. You have the power of materialization, the power of understanding. Take these words and dream into them. They will take you to a place that is real. You cannot go there and you cannot go away from there.

APPENDIX

Material Relevant to the Beaver Indian Audio Archive Which Is on File with the Canadian Museum of Civilization, Hull, Quebec

A. Original audio documents
  1. Reel-to-reel tapes recorded on a Uher 4000 Report L between 1964 and 1971 (30 hours)
  2. Reel-to-reel tapes recorded on Uher 4000 series mono and stereo tape recorders in 1979 (95 hours)
  3. Cassette tapes recorded on a JVC KD2, Sony TCD-5M, and Superscope CD-330 between 1980 and 1983 (130 hours)
B. Completed audio documentaries
  1. "Soundwalk to Heaven" (50 min.), Howard Broomfield and Robin Ridington, CFRO Vancouver 1979
  2. "Trails of the Dunne-za: A Suite of Four Radio Pieces" (four 5-min. pieces), Howard Broomfield, Jillian Ridington, Robin Ridington, CBC "Our Native Land" 1980
  3. "Suffering Me Slowly" (60 min.), Howard Broomfield, Jillian Ridington, CBC "The Hornby Collection" 1981
  4. "Nextdoor Neighbors" (30 min.), Howard Broomfield, Robin Ridington, CFRO Vancouver 1981
  5. "Old Time Religion" (60 min.), Howard Broomfield, Robin Ridington, 1982, presented as a slide-tape docudrama at the 1982 Canadian Ethnology Society meetings
  6. "In Doig People's Ears" (42 min.), Howard Broomfield, Robin Ridington, consultant, 1983, composed for a conference on the "Sociology of Music: An Exploration of Issues," Trent University, August 1983
C. Completed video documentary
  1. "In Doig People's Ears: Portrait of a Changing Native Community" (30 min.)

D. Catalogs
   1. Catalog of Dunne-za archive cassette collection, June 1981–July 1982, Howard Broomfield
   2. Catalog of Beaver Indian slides, 1984, Robin Ridington and Myrna Cobb
   3. Directory of audio tapes in the Dunne-za archive, 1984, Myrna Cobb and Robin Ridington
   4. Catalog of Beaver Indian negatives, 1984, Robin Ridington and Myrna Cobb
E. Final reports on research contracts with the Canadian Ethnology Service
   1. Beaver Indian Aural History: Final Report on Contract No. 1630-1-053
   2. Beaver Indian Aural and Musical Traditions: Final Report on Contract No. 1630-1-481

REFERENCES

Armitage, Peter
    1987   Tshekuan issishueu Mitshikapeu?: The Fart Man in Innu Religious Ideology. Paper presented at 1987 CESCE Conference, Quebec City.

Benedict, Ruth
    1934   *Patterns of Culture*. Boston: Houghton Mifflin.

Bernstein, Basil
    1971   *Class, Codes and Control*. London: Routledge and Kegan Paul.

Bierstedt, Robert
    1950   An Analysis of Social Power. *American Sociological Review* 15: 730–738.

Black, Mary
    1977a   Ojibwa Power Belief Systems. In *The Anthropology of Power*, ed. Raymond D. Fogelson and Richard N. Adams. New York: Academic Press, pp. 141–152.
    1977b   Ojibwa Taxonomy and Percept Ambiguity. *Ethos* 5(1): 90–118.

Brightman, Robert
    1988   The Windigo in the Material World. *Ethnohistory* 35(4): 337–379.

Brody, Hugh
    1981   *Maps and Dreams*. Vancouver: Douglas and McIntyre.

Brown, Jennifer
    1986   Northern Algonquians from Lake Superior and Hudson Bay to Manitoba in the Historic Period. In *Native Peoples: The Canadian Experience*, ed. R. Bruce Morrison and C. Roderick Wilson. Toronto: McClelland and Stewart, pp. 208–243.

Cail, Robert E.
    1974   *Land, Man and the Law: The Disposal of Crown Lands in British Columbia, 1871–1913*. Vancouver: University of British Columbia Press.

Canadian Radio-Television and Telecommunications Commission (CRTC)
    1985   Transcript of Radio Broadcast—Gary Bannerman Open-line
            Program on CKNW-AM, April 3, 1985, New Westminster,
            B.C. Documents relating to a complaint by the Nishga Tribal
            Council and the Musqueam Tribal Band.
Chomsky, N.
    1957   *Syntactic Structures*. The Hague: Mouton.
Christian, Jane, and Peter M. Gardner
    1977   *The Individual in Northern Dene Thought and Communication:
            A Study in Sharing and Diversity*. National Museum of Man
            Mercury Series No. 35. Ottawa: National Museums of Canada.
Cooper, J. M.
    1933   Cree Witiko Psychosis. *Primitive Man* 6: 20–24.
De Laguna, Frederica, and Catharine McClellan
    1981   Ahtna. In *Handbook of North American Indians*, vol. 6, ed. June
            Helm. Washington, D.C: Smithsonian Institution, pp.
            641–663.
Eliade, Mircea
    1964   *Shamanism: Archaic Techniques of Ecstasy*, trans. Willard R. Trask.
            Bollingen Series 76. Princeton: Princeton University Press.
Faraud, H. J.
    1866   Dix-huit ans chez les sauvages: Voyages et missions de Mgr.
            Henry Faraud. Paris: R. Ruffet.
Feit, Harvey
    1986a   Hunting and the Quest for Power: The James Bay Cree and
            Whitemen in the Twentieth Century. In *Native Peoples: The Ca-
            nadian Experience*, ed. R. Bruce Morrison and C. Roderick Wil-
            son. Toronto: McClelland and Stewart, pp. 171–207.
    1986b   James Bay Cree Self-Government and the State: Conflicting
            Interpretations and Analyses. Paper presented at the 4th Inter-
            national Conference on Hunting and Gathering Societies, Lon-
            don, September 8–13, 1986.
Fenton, William
    1974   The Advancement of Material Culture Studies in Modern An-
            thropological Research. In *The Human Mirror: Material and
            Spatial Images of Man*, ed. Miles Richardson. Charlotte, N.C.:
            Louisiana State University Press.
Fisher, Robin
    1971   Joseph Trutch and Indian Land Policy. *BC Studies* 12: 3–33.
    1977   *Contact and Conflict: Indian-European Relations in British Colum-
            bia, 1774–1890*. Vancouver: University of British Columbia
            Press.

Fortes, Meyer, and E. E. Evans-Pritchard, eds.

1940 *African Political Systems*. London: Oxford University Press.

Geertz, Clifford

1973 *The Interpretation of Cultures*. New York: Basic Books.

Godelier, Maurice

1975 Modes of Production, Kinship and Demographic Structure. In *Marxist Analysis and Social Anthropology*, ed. M. Bloch. London: Malaby Press.

1977 *Perspectives in Marxist Anthropology*. Cambridge Studies in Social Anthropology No. 18, ed. Jack Goody. Cambridge: Cambridge University Press.

Goulet, Jean-Guy

1987 Ways of Knowing with the Mind: An Ethnography of Aboriginal Beliefs. Paper presented at 1987 CESCE Conference, Quebec City.

Gumperz, John J.

1977 Lecture to Language Planning Colloquium. Summer Institute of the Linguistic Society of America, University of Hawaii. (Cited in Scollon and Scollon 1979: 185.)

Hall, Edward T.

1983 *The Dance of Life: The Other Dimension of Time*. Garden City: Anchor/Doubleday.

Hallowell, A. Irving

1942 *The Role of Conjuring in Salteaux Society*. Philadelphia: Publications of the Anthropological Society 2.

1955 *Culture and Experience*. Philadelphia: University of Pennsylvania Press.

1960 Ojibwa Ontology, Behavior, and World View. In *Culture and History: Essays in Honor of Paul Radin*, ed. Stanley Diamond. New York: Columbia University Press, pp. 19–52.

Hay, T.

1971 The Windigo Psychosis: Psychodynamic, Cultural and Social Factors in Aberrant Behaviour. *American Anthropologist* 73: 1–19.

Helm, June

1965 Bilaterality in the Socio-territorial Organization of the Arctic Drainage Dene. *Ethnology* 4(4): 361–385.

1981a Introduction. In *Handbook of North American Indians*, vol. 6, ed. June Helm. Washington, D.C.: Smithsonian Institution, pp. 1–4.

———, ed.

1981b *Subarctic.* Vol. 6, *Handbook of North American Indians.* Washington, D.C.: Smithsonian Institution.

Helm, June, et al.
1975   The Contact History of the Subarctic Athapaskans: An Overview. In *Proceedings: Northern Athapaskan Conference, 1979,* vol. 1, Service Paper No. 27, ed. A. McFadyen Clark. Ottawa: National Museums of Canada.

Henriksen, Georg
1973   *Hunters in the Barrens: The Naskapi on the Edge of the White Man's World.* Newfoundland Social and Economic Studies No. 12.

Honigmann, John J.
1949   *Culture and Ethos of Kaska Society.* Yale University Publications in Anthropology No. 40. New Haven: Yale University Press.
1981   Expressive Aspects of Subarctic Indian Culture. In *Handbook of North American Indians,* vol. 6, ed. June Helm. Washington D.C.: Smithsonian Institution, pp. 718–738.

Ives, Jack Watson
1985   Northern Athapaskan Social and Economic Variability. Ph.D. dissertation, Department of Anthropology, University of Michigan, Ann Arbor.

Jarvenpa, Robert
1982a Intergroup Behavior and Imagery: The Case of Chipewyan and Cree. *Ethnology* 21(4): 283–299.
1982b Symbolism and Inter-Ethnic Relations among Hunter-Gatherers: Chipewyan Conflict Lore. *Anthropologica* 24: 43–76.

Jenness, Diamond
1937   *The Sekani Indians of British Columbia.* National Museum of Canada Bulletin 84. Anthropological Series No. 20 (Ottawa).

Keesing, Roger
1987   Anthropology as Interpretive Quest. *Current Anthropology* 27(2): 161–176.

Krech, Shepard III
1980   Northern Athapaskan Ethnology in the 1970s. *Annual Reviews in Anthropology* 9: 83–100. Palo Alto: Annual Reviews.
1986   *Native Canadian Anthropology and History: A Selected Bibliography.* Winnipeg: Rupert's Land Research Center, University of Winnipeg.

Landes, R.
1938   *The Ojibwa Woman.* New York: Columbia University Press.
Laughlin, Charles, and Eugene D'Aquili
1974   *Biogenetic Structuralism.* New York: Columbia University Press.

Leacock, Eleanor
1954   *The Montagnais Hunting Territory and the Fur Trade.* American Anthropologist Memoir No. 78, vol. 56(2).
1978   Women's Status in Egalitarian Society: Implications for Social Evolution. *Current Anthropology* 19(2): 247–276.
1981   Seventeenth-Century Montagnais Social Relations and Values. In *Handbook of North American Indians*, vol. 6, ed. June Helm. Washington, D.C.: Smithsonian Institution, pp. 190–195.
Lechtman, Heather
1977   Style in Technology—Some Early Thoughts. In *Material Culture: Styles, Organization, and Dynamics of Technology. 1975 Proceedings of the American Ethnological Society*, ed. Heather Lechtman and Robert Merrill. New York: West Publishing, pp. 12–13.
Lee, Richard B.
1979   *The Kung San: Men, Women and Work in a Foraging Society.* Cambridge: Cambridge University Press.
Lenneberg, Eric
1967   *The Biological Foundations of Language.* New York: John Wiley.
Lévi-Strauss, Claude
1966   *The Savage Mind.* Chicago: University of Chicago Press.
Marano, Lou
1982   Windigo Psychosis: The Anatomy of an Emic-Etic Confusion. *Current Anthropology* 23(4): 385–412.
Marcus, George, and Michael Fisher
1986   Anthropology as Cultural Critique. Chicago: University of Chicago Press.
Martin, Calvin, ed.
1987   *The American Indian and the Problem of History.* New York: Oxford University Press.
Mason, Otis T.
1895 (1966)   *The Origins of Invention.* Cambridge, Mass.: MIT Press.
McClellan, Catharine
1975   *My Old People Say: An Ethnographic Survey of Southern Yukon Territory.* National Museums of Canada Publications in Ethnology 6(1). Ottawa: National Museums of Canada.
McClellan, Catharine, and Glenda Denniston
1981   Environment and Culture in the Cordillera. In *Handbook of North American Indians*, vol. 6, ed. June Helm. Washington, D.C.: Smithsonian Institution, pp. 372–386.
Miller, G. A., E. H. Galanter, and K. H. Pribram
1960   *Plans and the Structure of Behaviour.* New York: Holt, Rinehart and Winston.

Miller, Walter B.
  1955   Two Concepts of Authority. *American Anthropologist* 57(2): 271–279.
Morris, Brian
  1985   The Rise and Fall of the Human Subject. *Man* 20(4): 722–742.
O'Neil, Marion
  1928   The Peace River Journal, 1799–1800. *Washington Historical Quarterly* 19(4): 250–270.
Oswalt, Wendell H.
  1973   *Habitat and Technology: The Evolution of Hunting.* New York: Holt, Rinehart and Winston.
  1976   *An Anthropological Analysis of Food-Getting Technology.* New York: John Wiley and Sons.
Parker, S.
  1960   The Windigo Psychosis in the Context of Ojibwa Personality and Culture. *American Anthropologist* 60: 603–623.
Preston, Richard J.
  1975   *Cree Narrative: Expressing the Personal Meaning of Events.* National Museum of Man Mercury Series No. 30. Ottawa: National Museums of Canada.
  1980   The Witiko: Algonkian Knowledge and Whiteman Knowledge. In *Manlike Monsters on Trial,* ed. M. Halpin and M. Ames. Vancouver: University of British Columbia Press, pp. 111–131.
Richardson, Miles
  1974   *The Human Mirror: Material and Spatial Images of Man.* Charlotte, N.C.: Louisiana State University Press.
Riches, David
  1982   *Northern Nomadic Hunter-Gatherers: A Humanistic Approach.* London: Academic Press.
Ridington, Robin
  1968   The Medicine Fight: An Instrument of Political Process among the Beaver Indians. *American Anthropologist* 70(6): 1152–1160.
  1969   Kin Categories versus Kin Groups: A Two-Section System without Sections. *Ethnology* 8(4): 460–467.
  1971   Beaver Indian Dreaming and Singing. In *Pilot Not Commander: Essays in Memory of Diamond Jenness,* ed. Pat and Jim Lotz. *Anthropologica* 13(1–2): 115–128.
  1976a Wechuge and Windigo: A Comparison of Cannibal Belief among Boreal Forest Athapaskans and Algonquians. *Anthropologica* 18(2): 107–129.
  1976b Eye on the Wheel. *Io* 22: 68–81.

1978a *Swan People: A Study of the Dunne-za Prophet Dance*. National
Museum of Man Mercury Series, Canadian Ethnology Service
Paper No. 38. Ottawa: National Museums of Man.

1978b Metaphor and Meaning: Healing in Dunne-za Music and
Dance. *Western Canadian Journal of Anthropology* 8(2–4).

1979 Sequence and Hierarchy in Cultural Experience: Phases and the
Moment of Transformation. *Anthropology and Humanism Quarterly* 4(4): 2–10.

1980a Trails of Meaning. In *The World Is as Sharp as a Knife: An An-
thology in Honour of Wilson Duff*, ed. Donald Abbott. Victoria:
British Columbia Provincial Museum, pp. 265–268.

1980b A True Story. *Anthropology and Humanism Quarterly* 5(4):
11–14. Published by the Society for Humanistic Anthropology.

1980c Monsters and the Anthropologist's Reality. In *Manlike Monsters
on Trial: Early Records and Modern Evidence*, ed. M. Halpin and
M. Ames. Vancouver: University of British Columbia Press,
pp. 172–186.

1981 Beaver. In *Handbook of North American Indians*, vol. 6, ed.
June Helm. Washington, D.C.: Smithsonian Institution,
pp. 350–360.

1982a Technology, World View and Adaptive Strategy in a Northern
Hunting Society. *Canadian Review of Sociology and Anthropology*
19(4): 469–481.

1982b When Poison Gas Come down Like a Fog: A Native Community's Response to Cultural Disaster. *Human Organization* 41(1):
36–42.

1982c Telling Secrets: Stories of the Vision Quest. *Canadian Journal of
Native Studies* 2: 213–219.

1983a Stories of the Vision Quest among Dunne-za Women. *Atlantis*
9(1): 68–78.

1983b From Artifice to Artifact: Stages in the Industrialization of a
Northern Native Community. *Journal of Canadian Studies*
18(3): 55–66.

1983c In Doig People's Ears: Portrait of a Changing Community in
Sound. *Anthropologica* 25(1): 9–21.

1986d Texts that Harm: Racist Journalism in B.C. *Currents: Readings
in Race Relations* 3(4): 6–11.

1987a Models of the Universe: The Poetic Paradigm of Benjamin Lee
Whorf. *Anthropology and Humanism Quarterly* 12(1): 16–24.

1987b From Hunt Chief to Prophet: Beaver Indian Dreamers and
Christianity. *Arctic Anthropology* 24(1): 8–18. University of
Wisconsin Press.

1987c   Fox and Chickadee. In *The American Indian and the Problem of History*, ed. Calvin Martin. New York: Oxford University Press, pp. 128–135.

1988a   Knowledge, Power and the Individual in Subarctic Hunting Societies. *American Anthropologist* 90(1): 98–110.

1988b   *Trail to Heaven: Knowledge and Narrative in a Northern Native Community*. Iowa City: University of Iowa Press. (In Canada, Vancouver: Douglas and McIntyre.)

1989   Cultures in Conflict: The Problem of Discourse. *Canadian Literature* (in press).

Ridington, Robin, and Tonia Ridington
1970   The Inner Eye of Shamanism and Totemism. *History of Religions* 10(1): 49–61. Reprinted in *Teachings from the American Earth: Religion and Philosophy of the Indian and Eskimo*, ed. Dennis and Barbara Tedlock. New York: Liveright.

Rogers, Edward S.
1981   History of Ethnological Research in the Subarctic Shield and Mackenzie Borderlands. In *Handbook of North American Indians*, vol. 6, ed. June Helm. Washington, D.C.: Smithsonian Institution, pp. 19–29.

Rushforth, Scott
1981   Speaking to "Relatives-through-Marriage": Aspects of Communication among the Bear Lake Athapaskans. *Journal of Anthropological Research* 39(1): 28–45.

1986   The Bear Lake Indians. In *Native Peoples: The Canadian Experience*, ed. R. Bruce Morrison and C. Roderick Wilson. Toronto: McClelland and Stewart, pp. 243–270.

Sahlins, Marshall
1965   On the Sociology of Primitive Exchange. In *The Relevance of Models for Social Anthropology*, ed. M. Banton. ASA Monographs No. 1.

Sapir, Edward
1924   Culture, Genuine and Spurious. *American Journal of Sociology* 29: 401–429. Reprinted in Mandelbaum, 1963, *Selected Writings of Edward Sapir in Language, Culture and Personality*. Berkeley: University of California Press.

Savishinsky, Joel S.
1974   *On the Trail of the Hare*. New York: Gordon and Breach.

Schafer, R. Murray
1977   *The Tuning of the World*. Toronto: McClelland and Stewart.

Scollon, Ronald, and Suzanne B. K. Scollon
  1979   *Linguistic Convergence: An Ethnography of Speaking at Fort Chipe-wyan, Alberta*. London: Academic Press.
Sharp, Henry S.
  1986   Shared Experience and Magical Death: Chipewyan Explana-tions of a Prophet's Decline. *Ethnology* 24(4): 257–270.
  1987   Giant Fish, Giant Otters, and Dinosaurs: "Apparently Irrational Beliefs" in a Chipewyan Community. *American Ethnologist* 14(2): 226–235.
  1988   *The Transformation of Bigfoot: Maleness, Power and Belief among the Chipewyan*. Washington, D.C.: Smithsonian Institution Press.
Shearer, John, Charles Laughlin, and John McManus
  n.d.   A Biogenetic Structural Model of Phenomenological Phases.
Smith, David
  1973   *Inkonze: Magico-religious Beliefs of Contact-traditional Chipewyan Trading at Fort Resolution, NWT, Canada*. National Museum of Man Mercury Series No. 6. Ottawa: National Museums of Canada.
  1982   *Moose-Deer Island House People: A History of the Native People of Fort Resolution*. National Museum of Man Mercury Series Paper No. 6. Ottawa: National Museums of Canada.
  1985   Big Stone Foundations: Manifest Meaning in Chipewyan Myths. *Journal of American Culture* 18: 73–77.
Speck, Frank
  1935   *Naskapi: Savage Hunters of the Labrador Peninsula*. Norman: University of Oklahoma Press.
Spencer, Robert F., and Jesse Jennings
  1977   The Native Americans. New York: Harper and Row.
Spier, Leslie
  1935   The Prophet Dance of the Northwest and Its Derivatives: The Source of the Ghost Dance. *American Anthropologist*, General Series in Anthropology 1.
Spier, Robert
  1970   *From the Hand of Man: Primitive and Preindustrial Technologies*. Boston: Houghton Mifflin.
Steward, Julian
  1955   *Theory of Culture Change*. Urbana: University of Illinois Press.
Swartz, Marc, Victor Turner, and Arthur Tuden
  1966   *Political Anthropology*. Chicago: Aldine.
Tanner, Adrian
  1979   *Bringing Home Animals: Religious Ideology and Mode of Produc-tion of the Mistassini Cree Hunters*. Social and Economic Studies

No. 23. St. John's: Memorial University Institute of Social and Economic Research.

Teicher, M. I.
1960   Windigo Psychosis: A Study of a Relationship between Belief and Behaviour among the Indians of Northeastern Canada. In *Proceedings of the 1960 Annual Spring Meeting of the American Ethnological Society*. Seattle: American Ethnological Society.

VanStone, James W.
1974   *Athapaskan Adaptations: Hunters and Fishermen of the Subarctic Forests*. Arlington Heights: AHM Publishing.

Whorf, Benjamin Lee
1936   An American Indian Model of the Universe. In *Language, Thought, and Reality*, ed. John B. Carroll. New York: John Wiley and Sons, pp. 57–64.

Wilson, Colin
1969   *The Philosopher's Stone*. New York: Crown Publishers.

Witherspoon, Gary
1977   *Language and Art in the Navajo Universe*. Ann Arbor: University of Michigan Press.

Woodburn, James
1982   Egalitarian Societies. *Man* 17(3): 431–445.

INDEX

Cree Indians, 24, 81, 98–99, 106–
108, 177, 185–187, 203, 206,
210, 222. *See also* Dunne-za/
Cree court action; James Bay
Cree Indians; Mistassini Cree
Indians
*Cree Narrative: Expressing the Per-
sonal Meanings of Events*, 107
Crown Agent, 5, 187, 200,
202, 254
cultural core, 64
cultural intelligence, xiv, 12, 15, 68,
70–71, 116, 118, 143, 162,
202, 210, 213–214, 222–224
cultural psychology, 6, 178
*Culture and Ethos of Kaska So-
ciety*, 108
Culture and History, 104
culture and personality, 100, 107
culture hero. *See* Jesus; Saya;
Usakindji
"Cultures in Conflict: The Problem of Discourse," 185, 189,
192–193
Cygne, 74, 76

Davis, Angus, 206
Davis, Anno, x
Davis, Gerry, 217
Davis, John, x, 195–198, 200,
202, 204–205
Davis, Mary, xi
Davis, Pat, xi
Davis, Tar, xi
Dawson Creek, British Colum-
bia, 23
Decutla, 80–82
Deda. *See* Davis, Mary
De Laguna, Frederica, and Cather-
ine McClellan, 65–66
Dene Indians, 109–110

Department of Environment, 219
Department of Indian Affairs, 186,
193, 207–208, 219, 222, 249
Dishinni. *See* Cree Indians
divination, 100–118. *See also*
scapulimancy
Dixon, Justice, 187
Doig River, Doig River Indian Re-
serve, Doig River Indian band,
British Columbia, x, 22–24,
185–186, 193, 207, 227–228,
232–233, 235
Dominic, Charlie, x
Dominic, Tommy, xi
Dunne-za/Cree court action (*Apsas-
sin* v. *The Queen*), x, 185–205
Durkheim, Emile, 144

Eagle, 30–47. *See also* Giant Eagle;
Thunderbird
Earth diver motif. *See* Muskrat
Edmonton, Alberta, 203
Eliade, Mircea, 30, 68
"Environment and Culture in the
Cordillera," 116
Eskama, x
Eskimo. *See* Inuit

Faraud, H. J., 83
Father Clement, 46
Federal Court of Canada, 186
Federal Crown, 186–187
Federal Government. *See* Govern-
ment of Canada
Feit, Harvey, 100–101, 103, 106
Fenton, William, 84
fiduciary obligation, 186–187
Field, Zolie, x
First Minister's Conference, Ot-
tawa, 243–244, 246, 251
Fisher, Robin, 253

Ridington, Edie, xi
Ridington, Jillian, xi, 210, 215, 217, 221, 224–225, 255, 261–262
Ridington, Juniper, xi
Ridington, Robin, 17, 20, 26, 32, 60, 64–70, 72–73, 76–80, 82, 87–89, 101, 106, 112, 114, 116–117, 131, 135, 137, 191, 193, 200, 203, 210–212, 215, 217, 221, 224–225, 241, 261–262
Ridington, Tonia. See Mills, Antonia
Ridington, William, Sr., xi
Riggins, Stephen, 185
Rocky Mountain Fort, 74
Rocky Mountains, 74, 87
Rogers, Edward S., 101
"Role of Conjuring in Saulteaux Society," 107
Rose Prairie, British Columbia, 169, 186
Rushforth, Scott, 100–101, 108–109, 112

Sahlins, Marshall, 88, 147
Salter, Rick, 195
sapient intelligence, 68, 70
Sapir, Edward, 107, 256–258
Savage Mind, 86
Savishinsky, Joel S., 110
Saweh. See Jumbie, Granny
Saya, xv, 17, 19, 22, 31, 69–74, 76, 78–79, 92–95, 130, 133–138, 141–142, 210
scapulimancy, 66, 99, 103. See also divination
Schafer, R. Murray, 225, 256
Scollon, Ronald, and Suzanne B. K. Scollon, 101, 108, 110–111, 114–115

Scott, David R., 40
Secret Teachings of the Ages, 46
Sekani Indians, 52, 63, 74, 81
self-government. See Native Indian self-government
shaking tent performance, 107
Sharp, Henry S., 111
Shearer, John, Charles Laughlin, and John McManus, 124–125, 140
Sikanni Chief, 74, 76
Sikanni Chief River, British Columbia, 74, 76
Sitama. See Chipesia, Julie
Slavey Indians, 81, 110, 112, 241
Small Indian Boss. See Gallibois, Mr.
Smith, David, 67–68, 111
Snake, 174
Society for Applied Anthropology, 185
Society for Humanistic Anthropology, 3
"Sociology of Music: An Exploration of Issues," 261
"Some Aspects of Communication in a Northern Dene Community," 112
Soundman. See Broomfield, Howard
soundscape, 226, 228–232, 238, 256
sound signature, 226, 236
soundwalk, 230
"Soundwalk to Heaven," 261
Speck, Frank, 65–66, 68, 101–103, 105–108
Spencer, Robert F., and Jesse Jennings, 66
Spider Man (Spider Person), 18, 162, 168
Spier, Leslie, 177

Wolf, Lana, 196
Wolf, Louis, x
Wolf, Pete, x
Wolverine, ix, x, 4, 34–38, 45,
   212. *See also* Nowe Nachi
Wolverine Man (Wolverine Person),
   36, 162
Woodburn, James, 113, 241
Woodland Indians, 67, 68
World Soundscape Project, 225
World War II, 207
Wuscide. *See* Chipesia, Johnny

Yagatunne, 9, 72–73, 76, 79–80,
   94, 114, 129, 211, 230, 235
Yahey, Charlie, x, 72–73, 79, 82,
   113–114, 168, 209–211,
   231, 233
Yeklezi, 23, 26–28

Zimmer, Heinrich, 30
Zogo, 39
Zuni Indians, 145